CRITICAL
INSIGHTS
Charles Dickens

CRITICAL
INSIGHTS

Charles Dickens

Editor
Eugene Goodheart
Brandeis University

Salem Press
Pasadena, California   Hackensack, New Jersey

Cover photo: The Granger Collection, New York

Published by Salem Press

© 2011 by EBSCO Publishing
Editor's text © 2011 by Eugene Goodheart
"The *Paris Review* Perspective" © 2011 by Elizabeth Gumport for *The Paris Review*

∞ The paper used in these volumes conforms to the American National
Standard for Permanence of Paper for Printed Library Materials, Z39.48-1992
(R1997).

Library of Congress Cataloging-in-Publication Data
Charles Dickens / editor, Eugene Goodheart.
    p. cm. — (Critical insights)
Includes bibliographical references and index.
ISBN 978-1-58765-691-0 (vol. 1 : alk. paper)
1. Dickens, Charles, 1812-1870—Criticism and interpretation. I.
Goodheart, Eugene.
    PR4588.C3586 2011
    823'.8—dc22
2010030136

PRINTED IN CANADA

Contents

About This Volume, Eugene Goodheart   vii

Career, Life, and Influence

On Charles Dickens, Eugene Goodheart   3
Biography of Charles Dickens, Patricia Marks   8
The *Paris Review* Perspective, Elizabeth Gumport for *The Paris Review*   15

Critical Contexts

Charles Dickens in His Times, Shanyn Fiske   21
Charles Dickens's Critical Reputation, Laurence W. Mazzeno   41
Order in Disorder: Surrealism and *Oliver Twist*, Nancy M. West   59

Critical Readings

Another Version of Pastoral: *Oliver Twist*, Joseph M. Duffy, Jr.   83
Mourning Becomes David: Loss and the Victorian
    Restoration of Young Copperfield, Alan P. Barr   105
Eccentricity as Englishness in *David Copperfield*,
    Julia F. Saville   125
Expectations Well Lost: Dickens' Fable for His Time,
    G. Robert Stange   145
The Sense of Self, Monroe Engel   159
Structure and Idea in *Bleak House*, Robert A. Donovan   178
"True Legitimacy": The Myth of the Foundling
    in *Bleak House*, Michele S. Ware   208
Hard Times and the Structure of Industrialism:
    The Novel as Factory, Patricia E. Johnson   221
Little Dorrit, Lionel Trilling   234
Charles Dickens, James Joyce, and the Origins
    of Modernism, Matthew J. Bolton   248

Resources

Chronology of Charles Dickens's Life   267
Works by Charles Dickens   271
Bibliography   273

About the Editor   281
About *The Paris Review*   281
Contributors   283
Acknowledgments   285
Index   286

About This Volume

Eugene Goodheart

This volume begins with a biographical sketch of Charles Dickens by Patricia Marks, followed by a brief evocative account of Dickens's capacity to see the world through the eyes of a child, provided by Elizabeth Gumport for *The Paris Review*. In the "Critical Contexts" section, Shanyn Fiske addresses the historical context in which Dickens wrote, and Laurence W. Mazzeno discusses the vicissitudes of the author's reputation from the beginning of his career to the present. According to Nancy M. West, Dickens's realism encompasses the dream life and hallucinatory states of his characters. Focusing on *Oliver Twist*, but alluding as well to other novels, she explores the ways in which Dickens blends fantasy and reality in a manner that anticipates surrealism.

Given Dickens's prolific achievement as a novelist, the essays that follow in the "Critical Readings" section necessarily cover only a selection of his novels. Joseph M. Duffy, Jr., describes the vulnerable passivity of the orphaned Oliver Twist, manipulated, exploited and brutalized by the social reality of city life, which is "so much larger and more powerful than human feeling." Oliver is one of many abused children in Dickens's work. The novel imagines a pastoral alternative to London in the countryside. Oliver is rescued from the clutches of Fagin, so personal good triumphs over personal evil, but "society remains unvanquished." Alan P. Barr addresses what is only tangentially noted by most critical readings of *David Copperfield*, the price paid by the maturing of the eponymous hero, the mourning over his loss of innocence. Julia F. Saville takes up the question of the eccentricity of the Dickensian character in her treatment of *David Copperfield*. Following John Stuart Mill in his essay "On Liberty," she sees eccentricity as a positive quality, reflecting the nonconformist virtue of English character. In my introduction to the volume, I present a less flattering account of the obsessive-compulsiveness of Dickens's characters. The question of the value of eccentricity is a lively topic for discussion and debate.

G. Robert Stange views *Great Expectations* as a moral fable in which a young man develops "from the moment of his first self-awareness, to that of his mature acceptance of the human condition." As the title of his essay "Expectations Well Lost" suggests, the novel is a story of disillusionment and guilt.

Monroe Engel discusses *David Copperfield* and *Great Expectations* as autobiographical novels that have in common the ambitions of their protagonists, David and Pip, respectively, to rise in the world from lowly origins. The outcomes, however, differ. *David Copperfield* "is a success story," whereas *Great Expectations* "describes a movement away from success." Engel views the later novel as "a correction to the conventional optimism" of the earlier novel and the more mature work in form and content. Robert A. Donovan's wide-ranging essay on *Bleak House* focuses on the plot of the novel, a detective story that discovers the responsibility that members of society have for one another. Dickens's imaginative career is informed by a passion for social justice. As he shows in *Bleak House*, the enemy of justice, paradoxically, is the law as embodied in the Chancery. Michele S. Ware addresses "the mythic impulse" at work in *Bleak House*, namely, the myth of the foundling who in discovering her parentage apparently confirms "a stable, systematic, and predictable society." She argues that Dickens develops, in the narrative of Esther Summerson, an alternative myth in which what matters is not one's parentage but rather one's innate qualities of goodness and nobility. This alternative myth fails, according to Ware, because Esther's nobility and the reward she finds in her marriage to Allan Woodcourt and life in Bleak House "pales in comparison" to the dark and incorrigibly corrupt world Dickens depicts.

Patricia E. Johnson shows how the very structure of *Hard Times* represents the entrapment of the inhabitants of Coketown in a dehumanizing industrial system from which they cannot escape. Fancy, as figured in the circus, strikes a note of hope, but it does "little more than decorate" the factory walls that enclose both the characters of the novel and its readers. In his essay on *Little Dorrit,* Lionel Trilling reminds us of what is true of other Dickens novels as well: "It is about society in relation to the individual human will." Dickens was "at the time of *Little Dorrit* . . . at a crisis of the [aggressive social] will." In Trilling's reading of the novel, the guilty will, most immediately represented by Arthur Clennam, seeks its own negation. Peace comes from the retreat from society. In its spiritual aspiration, *Little Dorrit* belongs with *The Divine Comedy* (little Dorrit is the Beatrice figure, the paraclete) and *Pilgrim's Progress*. Matthew J. Bolton challenges the conventional view, fostered by modernist writers, that the modern novel represents a radical break with the Victorian novel. He finds in Dickens's novels anticipation of the stream of consciousness and of the merging of narrative voice and a character's individual consciousness that mark modernist novels such as those of James Joyce. Dickens may be the most influential of all English novelists, having influenced Fyodor Dostoevski, Henry James, Joseph Conrad, and many others.

CAREER, LIFE, AND INFLUENCE

On Charles Dickens_____

Eugene Goodheart

A novelist of incomparable imaginative vitality, Charles Dickens is the greatest English dramatic writer since William Shakespeare. The reader of his novels has little difficulty imagining them enacted in the theater; it is no wonder that so many of them have found their way onto stage, film, and television. Like Shakespeare, Dickens was an actor as well as a writer, who read from his novels and stories to large audiences and performed in his own plays and in those of others. There is hardly a page in a Dickens novel that does not contain single sentences that within themselves create whole scenes, for example, this sentence from *Martin Chuzzlewit*: Martin, the young protagonist of the novel, sits

> in gloomy rumination by the stove, unmindful of the boarders who dropped in one by one from their stores and counting houses, or the neighboring bar-rooms, and after taking long pulls from a great white water-jug upon the side-board, and lingering with a kind of fascination near the brass spittoon, lounged heavily to bed; until at length Mark Tapley [Martin's devoted valet] came and shook him by the arm, supposing him asleep.

In this winding sentence paragraph, Dickens creates an entire scene, foreground and background, evoking the life of a society: the work, the recreations, and the habits of its members. (A section of the novel takes place in America, where on visits Dickens performed on stage. In the odd detail about the brass spittoon, he satirizes what he observed with a mixture of fascination and disgust, the American habit of spitting in public.)

There is also his gift for bringing to life a character at the very moment that he appears on the page. Again from *Martin Chuzzlewit*:

Then there was George Chuzzlewit, a gay bachelor cousin who claimed to be young, but had been younger, and was inclined to corpulency, and rather overfed himself: to that extent, that his eyes were strained in their sockets, as if with constant surprise; and he had such an obvious disposition to pimples, that the bright spots on his cravat, the rich pattern on his waistcoat, and even his glittering trinket, seemed to have broken out upon him, and not come into existence comfortably.

We are given a perfect visualization of someone uncomfortable in his own skin.

Dickens's characters have been variously characterized, sometimes disparagingly, as caricatures or eccentrics. (Eccentricity, as Julia F. Saville argues in her essay in this collection, may also be a mark of an admirable individuality.) Vivid and unforgettable as they are—think of Uriah Heep, Pecksniff, Mr. Micawber, Mr. Smallweed, Pumblechook, Wemmick, among many others in a huge gallery—they lack the roundedness and inwardness of people in real life. Characters such as Arthur Clennam in *Little Dorrit* and Eugene Wrayburn in *Our Mutual Friend*, endowed with complexity, an inner life, and a capacity for change, are not what we have come to call Dickensian. They resemble the recognizable people we find in the work of other novelists but are pallid in comparison to the Dickensian characters, who are comic or pathetic in their single-minded rigidity, their obsessive-compulsive behavior, and their repetitive rituals of speech and gesture. Is such a condition remote from the human condition in what we call real life? We like to think of ourselves as well-rounded, complex with inner lives and capable of growth and development; if, however, we honestly confronted ourselves, wouldn't we admit that we often remain stuck in one place, compulsively repeating ourselves in what we say and do? The psychology of a Dickensian character is comically externalized, the inner life projected outward in speech and action. The essence of the character lies in what we see and hear, and it is a character perfectly at home on the stage.

The Dickens theater, the site for comic entertainment and the pathos of melodrama, is also a powerful vehicle for social criticism. Dickens gives us scathing indictments of Victorian social and economic institutions: the orphanage in *Oliver Twist*, the dehumanizing judicial system in *Bleak House*, the industrial factory in *Hard Times*, and the debtor's prison in *David Copperfield* and *Little Dorrit*. Poverty and oppression are endemic in Victorian England, children—Oliver, David Copperfield, the young Pip, among others—being its most vulnerable victims. Dickens knew the suffering of children from the experiences of his own childhood. His father wound up in debtor's prison, and as a child he was sent to work in a shoe blacking shop. Blame, however, does not lie exclusively with institutions in Dickens's vision of society. The villainy of Fagin in *Oliver Twist* and Orlick in *Great Expectations* is personal, not institutional. Characters have a moral responsibility for their lives. Mr. Micawber in *David Copperfield* enters debtor's prison because of his financial fecklessness. The character of Pip, the protagonist of *Great Expectations*, is disfigured by social ambition and snobbery. Richard Carstone in *Bleak House* destroys himself in his futile pursuit (evident from the outset) of justice in Chancery. Dickens is not a social determinist who believes that all persons lack the power to determine their own destinies and are simply victims of forces greater than themselves. Institutions may encourage and exacerbate vices, characters are victimized and may be unable to overcome oppressive circumstances, but Dickens, the moralist, conceives of society as the scene of struggle between good and evil in which some individuals have the capacity to overcome adversity, resist oppression, and act with love and generosity toward other human beings. It is nevertheless the case that Dickens's exposure of institutional corruption, for instance of the legal system in *Bleak House*, did contribute to legislative reform.

He is a fierce critic of the Industrial Revolution. In *Hard Times,* he phantasmagorically visualizes the Coketown factories as monsters:

The Fairy palaces burst into illumination, before pale morning showed the monstrous serpents of spoke trailing themselves over Coketown. A clattering of clogs upon the pavement; a rapid ringing of bells; and all the melancholy-mad elephants, polished and oiled up for the day's monotony, were at their heavy exercise again.

The factory dehumanizes the factory operative and turns him into a "hand." As John Ruskin, the great art and social critic, pointed out, the division of labor inaugurated by the Industrial Revolution was really a division of the factory operative, reducing him to an industrial function. If Karl Marx, Dickens's contemporary, had written the novel, he would have turned Coketown into a scene of class struggle with the aim of radically transforming the economic and political system. But Dickens, fearful of violent revolution, has his working-class hero Stephen Blackpool resist the demagogic appeal of the trade union leader Slackbridge to join a strike against the factory owner. Instead, he appeals—in vain, as it turns out—to the conscience of his social superior, the factory owner Bounderby (whose name perfectly captures the essence of his character, an "ill-bred, social climber," as the dictionary defines the "bounder"), to make the necessary changes in the system. Like Ruskin and Thomas Carlyle before him, Dickens believed that all change begins with the moral and spiritual reformation of the individual person and with the need to "cultivate the fancy" and the affections. The circus in *Hard Times* is a trope of a humane imagination.

For all of Dickens's passion for moral transformation, the author's great gift was in the creation of characters of rigid will, incorrigibly fixed in their vices and obsessions. Pious frauds such as Pecksniff (*Martin Chuzzlewit*) and Uriah Heep (*David Coppperfield*), murderous villains such as Bill Sikes (*Oliver Twist*) and Blandois (*Little Dorrit*) are not only incorrigible in their vices but also symbolic of what appears to be the immoral and possibly irredeemable condition of contemporary society. At times Dickens forces change in a character, as in Gradgrind's sudden conversion in *Hard Times* when he realizes the price his daughter Louisa has paid for growing up in his fact-obsessed and mechanical environment, or as in Miss Havisham's contrition in *Great Expectations* for making Estella an instrument of revenge on the male of the species. When Dickens's imagination strains to redeem characters and the world against the oppressive and self-imprisoning realities of character and social institutions, sentimentality is often the result.

A main scene of the novels is the city of London. Dickens's London (most impressively represented in *Bleak House*) must be considered one of the great achievements in all of literature; its only rival is Honoré de Balzac's Paris. Dickens penetrates the encompassing fog of London to give us its labyrinth of streets and byways, and the people who walk them, the houses and decrepit flats and shops and the characters who inhabit them. The elaborate plots and subplots seem to provide a sort of moral map of the city in which we are made to see how characters from places and classes that appear to have nothing in common are ineluctably bound together. The realities depicted are grim—poverty, selfishness, greed, brutality, murder—but the narrative voice has a Christian inflection of hope that redemption is possible. The protagonists—Esther Summerson of *Bleak House*, Pip of *Great Expectations*, and Arthur Clennam of *Little Dorrit* (all guilt ridden, whether deserved or not)—are endowed with the capacity to achieve selflessness in love, in benefaction, and in the responsibility they take for others. Hope springs eternal in the novels, sustained by one of the most vital and powerful imaginations in all of literature.

Biography of Charles Dickens _____

Patricia Marks

Born on February 7, 1812, in Portsmouth, on Portsea Island, England, Charles Dickens was the son of John Dickens, a Naval Pay Office employee, and Elizabeth Barrow, the daughter of the Naval Conductor of Moneys. John Dickens's largely unsuccessful struggle to gain middle-class respectability was hampered not only by his parents' career in domestic service but also by the disgrace of his father-in-law, who left the country to avoid the consequences of a petty embezzlement. John Dickens's life in Portsmouth left a lasting impression on his son, who partially documented it in *Our Mutual Friend* with Rogue Riderhood's river activities, and who drew on it in *Dombey and Son*, in which the running of the river into the ocean represents the passage of life into immortality. John Dickens's improvidence and inevitable bankruptcy also deeply affected his son. His character is reflected in the impecunious but absurdly hopeful Mr. Micawber and, more abstractly, in Dickens's ambiguous attitude toward wealth, which he viewed as a highly desirable tool but worthless as a gauge of human value. In *Our Mutual Friend*, for instance, the novelist equates money with an excremental dust heap, but an inordinate number of his deserving characters also acquire wealth fortuitously: Oliver Twist, the parish boy, finds his near relatives; Nicholas Nickleby becomes clerk to the generous Cheerybles; and Esther Summerson comes under the protection of the well-to-do Jarndyce.

Dickens incorporated childhood associations into his stories as well. His nurse, Mary Weller, by her own dogmatic adherence, inculcated in Dickens a distaste for Chapel Christianity; his childhood love for theatricals blossomed into a lifelong fascination. (In fact, in 1832, only illness prevented him from auditioning at Covent Garden.)

Still, the most significant event of Dickens's youth was his father's imprisonment in the Marshalsea debtor's prison for bankruptcy. Dickens drew on this period of his life in many of his novels, especially *Da-*

vid Copperfield and *Oliver Twist*. John Forster, Dickens's friend and biographer, records the author's bitterness at being put to work at Warren's Blacking Warehouse in order to help pay his father's debts. Even worse than the degradation of the job for the young Dickens was the feeling that he had been abandoned. His family moved to Marshalsea to be near his father while he lived in a boarding house. While his period of employment in the warehouse could be measured in months, the psychological scars lasted for the rest of Dickens's life, as can be seen in his novelistic preoccupation with orphans and adopted families. Oliver Twist, Amy Dorrit, Pip, and Little Nell are all abandoned children in some sense, and they are forced into an early adulthood, oftentimes reversing roles with their parents or guardians to become their protectors.

At the age of fifteen, Dickens was apprenticed as a law clerk in Doctor's Commons, a civil law society. It was certainly the source of his profound dislike of pettifoggery, which is exhibited in the Jarndyce case of *Bleak House*. He then became a reporter in Parliament, and, at the age of seventeen, fell in love with Maria Beadnell, the daughter of a banking family who discouraged the attentions of the impoverished young man. This experience, as well as his unsuccessful marriage to Catherine Hogarth, daughter of the editor of the *Morning Chronicle*, likely contributed to Dickens's alternate idealization of women (such as Dora in *David Copperfield*) and mockery of their foibles.

At the time of his marriage, Dickens was writing text for a serial of sporting drawings by the popular illustrator Robert Seymour—a work that became *Pickwick Papers* upon Seymour's suicide. With its publication, Dickens's success came quickly. He became editor of *Bentley's Miscellany* (1836), and in February 1837, *Oliver Twist* began to appear, one month after the birth of the first of Dickens's ten children. Before *Oliver Twist* had finished its serial run, Dickens had begun *Nicholas Nickleby*, in which he drew on his dramatic interests to create the Crummles provincial acting company. Then, in 1840, Dickens arranged to edit *Master Humphrey's Clock*, which became a vehicle for both *The Old Curiosity Shop* and *Barnaby Rudge* (the story of the 1780 Gordon riots). Some of his immense creative energy came from the early happiness of his marriage, but some also from an effort to forget the death of his beloved sister-in-law Mary, who died in his arms when she was seventeen.

This period of activity ended in 1842 with a six-month visit to the United States. In letters, in *American Notes*, and in *Martin Chuzzlewit*, Dickens reveals his double vision of the country. Welcomed in Boston by such literati as Henry Wadsworth Longfellow, Dickens moved from the cultivated bluestocking milieu into a furious newspaper war over the lack of an international copyright agreement. Dickens came to believe that while democracy did exist in such model factory towns as Lowell, Massachusetts, America's much-vaunted freedom was an excuse for vulgarity on one hand and hypocrisy on the other. He was appalled at the conditions of slavery in St. Louis and dismayed by the flat stretches of the Great Plains and by the ever-present concern for partisan politics, money, and power. All of these he satirized bitterly in the American section of *Martin Chuzzlewit*.

At home again, he installed his sister-in-law Georgina in her lifelong role as his housekeeper to counter what he judged to be Catherine's growing indolence, which was surely symptomatic of their growing disillusionment with each other. Two years later, he began publication of *Dombey and Son*, his first planned novel. His next, the autobiographical *David Copperfield*, contains advice by the novel's heroine, Agnes, that he applied to his own life: "Your growing power and success enlarge your power of doing good." In March 1850, Dickens founded *Household Words*, a periodical that featured short stories, serialized novels, poetry, and essays. Here, Dickens published exposés of hospitals, sanitary conditions, political affairs, education, law, and religion, all written in a characteristically fanciful style. In these years, Dickens was engaged in amateur theatricals, partly to raise money to endow an impoverished actors' home. Between 1852 and 1857, he wrote three novels: *Bleak House*, his experiment in first-person narration; *Hard Times*, an attack on utilitarianism; and *Little Dorrit*, a semiautobiographical work. Becoming more and more estranged from his wife, he engaged in a strenuous and highly popular series of readings from his works, again bringing his dramatic talent into play. In June 1858, he published a much-criticized apologia for his marital separation; then, chafing at the restrictions imposed on *Household Words* by the publishers, Edward Chapman and William Hall, Dickens severed the connection and began *All the Year Round*, a new periodical of the same type.

His liaison with the actress Ellen Ternan,whom he met in 1857 when he was cast opposite her in a Wilkie Collins play, continued throughout the remainder of his life, during which he wrote *A Tale of Two Cities*, *Great Expectations*, and *Our Mutual Friend*, his last completed novel. He undertook another exhausting series of public readings, his reenactment of Nancy's murder in *Oliver Twist* proving the most demanding. In 1867, he left for a successful tour of the United States. He continued public readings until the end of his life.

Dickens died at Gad's Hill, near Rochester, on June 9, 1870, and is buried in Westminster Abbey. His last, unfinished novel, *The Mystery of Edwin Drood*, appeared posthumously.

From *Magill's Choice: Notable British Novelists* (Pasadena, CA: Salem Press). Copyright © 2001 by Salem Press, Inc.

Bibliography

Ackroyd, Peter. *Dickens*. London: Sinclair-Stevenson, 1990. The author, a major English novelist, writes a biography of Dickens that warrants the characterization of being Dickensian both in its length and in the quality of its portrayal of the nineteenth-century writer and his times. In re-creating that past, Ackroyd has produced a brilliant work of historical imagination.

Baker, William, and Kenneth Womack, eds. *A Companion to the Victorian Novel*. Westport, Conn.: Greenwood Press, 2002. Includes chapters on Victorian detective fiction and Charles Dickens. Bibliographic references and index.

Butterword, R. D. "A Christmas Carol and the Masque." *Studies in Short Fiction* 30

(Winter, 1993): 63-69. Discusses how Dickens's famous Christmas story embodies many of the characteristics of the masque tradition. Considers some of the implications of this tradition for the story, such as the foreshortening of character development.

Carey, John. *The Violent Effigy: A Study of Dickens' Imagination*. London: Faber and Faber, 1979. The number of works about Dickens and the various aspects of his career is enormous. Carey, in one insightful Dickens study, focuses on Dickens's fascination with various human oddities as a spur to his artistic inspiration.

Connor, Steven, ed. *Charles Dickens*. London: Longman, 1996. Part of the Longman Critical Readers series, this collection of essays provides a good reference for interpretation and criticism of Dickens.

Davis, Paul B. *Charles Dickens A to Z: The Essential Reference to His Life and Work*. New York: Facts On File, 1998. An excellent handbook for the student of Dickens.

Epstein, Norrie. *The Friendly Dickens: Being a Good-Natured Guide to the Art and Adventures of the Man Who Invented Scrooge*. New York: Viking Press, 1998. An interesting study of Dickens. Includes bibliographic references, index, and filmography.

Erickson, Lee. "The Primitive Keynesianism of Dickens's *A Christmas Carol*." *Studies in the Literary Imagination* 30 (Spring, 1997): 51-66. A Keynesian reading of Dickens's story that shows how Scrooge is an economic hoarder because of his fear of the financial future and his need for complete financial liquidity. Claims that Dickens correctly diagnoses the economic depression of Christmas, 1843.

Flint, Kate. *Dickens*. Brighton, England: Harvester Press, 1986. Looks at paradoxes within Dickens's novels and between his novels and his culture. Includes a select bibliography and an index.

Ford, George H., and Lauriat Lane, Jr., eds. *The Dickens Critics*. Ithaca, N.Y.: Cornell University Press, 1961. This collection consists of more than thirty essays concerned with various aspects of Dickens's literary life. Represented are notables such as Edgar Allan Poe, Henry James, Anthony Trollope, George Bernard Shaw, T. S. Eliot, Aldous Huxley, George Orwell, Graham Greene, and Edgar Johnson.

Frank, Lawrence. *Victorian Detective Fiction and the Nature of Evidence: The Scientific Investigations of Poe, Dickens, and Doyle*. New York: Palgrave Macmillan, 2003. Looks at the models of evidence at play in the detective fiction of Dickens, Edgar Allan Poe, and Sir Arthur Conan Doyle, comparing them to one another, as well as to the very different models of evidence that took hold in the twentieth century. Bibliographic references and index.

Haining, Peter. *Introduction to Hunted Down: The Detective Stories of Charles Dickens*. Chester Springs, Pa.: Dufour Editions, 1996. Extremely useful overview of Dickens's contribution to the detective genre and comparison of his various stories to one another.

Hawes, Donald. *Who's Who in Dickens*. New York: Routledge, 1998. The Who's

Who series provides another excellent guide to the characters that populate Dickens's fiction.

Hobsbaum, Philip. *A Reader's Guide to Charles Dickens*. Syracuse, N.Y.: Syracuse University Press, 1998. Part of the Reader's Guide series, this is a good manual for beginning students.

Jacobson, Wendy S., ed. *Dickens and the Children of Empire*. New York: Palgrave, 2000. A collection of fourteen essays focusing on child images and colonial paternalism in the work of Dickens.

Johnson, Edgar. *Charles Dickens: His Tragedy and Triumph*. 2 vols. New York: Simon & Schuster, 1952. This work was perhaps the first major scholarly biography of Dickens. The author integrates into his study an excellent discussion and analysis of Dickens's writings. It remains a classic.

Jordan, John O., ed. *The Cambridge Companion to Charles Dickens*. New York: Cambridge University Press, 2001. Useful resource from the Cambridge Companions to Literature series. Includes bibliographic references and index.

Kaplan, Fred. *Dickens: A Biography*. New York: William Morrow, 1988. Published a generation later than Edgar Johnson's study of Dickens, Kaplan's biography is more forthright about Dickens's family life and personal qualities, especially his relationship with the actress Ellen Ternan. An interesting and well-written work.

Newlin, George, ed. and comp. *Every Thing in Dickens: Ideas and Subjects Discussed by Charles Dickens in His Complete Works—A Topicon*. Westport, Conn.: Greenwood Press, 1996. A thorough guide to Dickens's oeuvre. Includes bibliographic references, index, and quotations.

Newsom, Robert. *Charles Dickens Revisited*. New York: Twayne, 2000. From Twayne's English Authors series. Includes bibliographic references and index.

Newton, Ruth, and Naomi Lebowitz. *The Impossible Romance: Dickens, Manzoni, Zola, and James*. Columbia: University of Missouri Press, 1990. Discusses the impact of religious sensibility on literary form and ideology in Dickens's fiction.

Reed, John Robert. *Dickens and Thackeray*. Athens: Ohio University Press, 1995. Discusses how beliefs about punishment and forgiveness affect how Dickens and William Makepeace Thackeray told their stories. Discusses Dickens's major fiction in terms of moral and narrative issues.

Smiley, Jane. *Charles Dickens*. New York: Viking Press, 2002. A Dickens biography by a noted American novelist. Includes bibliographic references.

Smith, Grahame. *Charles Dickens: A Literary Life*. New York: St. Martin's Press, 1996. A strong biography of Dickens.

Tytler, Graeme. "Dickens's 'The Signalman.'" *The Explicator* 53 (Fall, 1994): 26-29. Argues that the story is about a man suffering from a type of insanity known in the nineteenth century as lypemania or monomania; discusses the symptoms of the signalman.

Weliver, Phyllis. *Women Musicians in Victorian Fiction, 1860-1900: Representations of Music, Science, and Gender in the Leisured Home*. Burlington, Vt.: Ashgate, 2000. Includes a chapter on Dickens's use of the tropes of fugue and dissonance in *The Mystery of Edwin Drood*. Bibliographic references and index.

Wilson, Angus. *The World of Charles Dickens*. New York: Viking Press, 1970. The author, an Englishman, has been a professor of literature, has published a major work on Rudyard Kipling, and has written several novels. This relatively brief study is enriched by many period illustrations ranging from George Cruikshank to Gustave Doré.

the PARIS
REVIEW

The *Paris Review* Perspective _____

Elizabeth Gumport for *The Paris Review*

In his biography of Charles Dickens, G. K. Chesterton called the author "a great event in English history." Images attach themselves to events: the French Revolution is the guillotine; George Washington is a cherry tree. Dickens is an uneaten wedding cake, tablefuls of chanting orphans, Scrooge in his nightcap. The English-speaking world is so steeped in Dickens that anybody who does not claim to be on intimate terms with Dickens counts him, at least, as an acquaintance.

The reality, however, is nothing like the event. One expects a diorama but finds moving parts instead. To read Dickens is to encounter, as Chesterton put it, "the first of all democratic doctrines, that all men are interesting." His small men loom large and his dull men cannot help but entertain, but above all they are men, round and whole. "A wonderful fact to reflect upon," Dickens writes in *A Tale of Two Cities*, "that every human creature is constituted to be that profound secret and mystery to every other." Wonder is the fundamentally Dickensian attitude, the source of the democratic generosity observed by Chesterton. In Dickens's respect for the mystery of individuality, and in the great array of individuals his novels contain, one finds a kind of moral imperative. We cannot know others, Dickens suggests, but we can empathize, and through empathy we know them to be like ourselves, capable of pain and therefore deserving protection from it. If death is, as Dickens continues, "the inexorable consolidation and perpetuation of the secret that was always in that individuality," so is fiction, for in honoring the unknowable wholeness of the minds of others, Dickens makes them a little less unknown.

Reading Dickens, one is convinced: the world looks just like he says it looks. George Orwell, who rightly stated that nobody wrote so well about childhood as Dickens, confessed that when he first read *David Copperfield* he believed its early chapters to have been written by a child, so accurately did they evoke the sensitivity and terror of youth. For Dickens, whose own early years were unhappy ones, childhood imprisons children. Whether his subject is, as in *Hard Times*, the harassed students of Coketown who are instructed "Go and be somethingological already," or the likes of *Our Mutual Friend*'s Georgiana Podsnap, cosseted into hysteria by the unceasing inanity of her parents, Dickens captures the helplessness of childhood, and the child's frightening discovery that his destiny is controlled by the whims of distracted, and often lunatic, adults.

Unable to act, children remain free to think. Dispatched to Pumblechook's shop, *Great Expectations*' Pip discovers "a singular affinity between seeds and corduroys. Mr. Pumblechook wore corduroys, and so did his shopman; and somehow, there was a general air and flavor about the corduroys, so much in the nature of seeds, and a general air and flavor about the seeds, so much in the nature of corduroys, that I hardly knew which was which." These associations seem arbitrary at first; in the child's contained world, each thing relates to the next simply by virtue of proximity.

Yet Pip is correct: there is a connection between seeds and corduroys, at least in the dream logic of childhood. Children, as powerless as we all are in nightmares, must build a private system to explain the inexplicable images that swoop down upon them. Just as one enters a dark room and intuits the presence of another person without being able to see him, one reads Dickens and perceives, in flashes, the happy, hidden unity of the world.

This fullness of vision is why Dickens's writing transcends realism. "His art is like life," Chesterton wrote, "because, like life, it cares for nothing outside itself, and goes on its way rejoicing. . . . Art indeed copies life in not copying life, for life copies nothing. Dickens's art is like life because, like life, it is irresponsible, because, like life, it is incredible." His novels are not representations of the world but worlds unto themselves.

When David Copperfield—a mostly autobiographical portrait of Dickens himself, the differences between author and character as subtle as the reversal of the first letters in their first and last names—reads as a child, he imagines the Murdstones as the villains in his stories and he as their heroes; fiction and fact, entwined so early, can never be untangled. Recalling his youth, Copperfield pictures himself in bed on a summer evening, "reading as if for life." Reading *is* for life, Dickens suggests, for words and stories give shape to our minds. More than describe us to ourselves, they make us who we are. Dickens does not simply depict the world in words: his words invent the world.

Works Cited

Chesterton, G. K. *The Collected Works of G. K. Chesterton*. Vol. 15, *Chesterton on Dickens*. Fort Collins, CO: Ignatius Press, 1990.

Orwell, George. *Dickens, Dali, and Others*. New York: Mariner Books, 1970.

CRITICAL
CONTEXTS

Charles Dickens in His Times_____

Shanyn Fiske

> Paradox though it may seem . . . it is none the less true that Life imitates Art
> far more than Art imitates Life.
> > —Oscar Wilde, "The Decay of Lying: An Observation" (1889)

Despite Oscar Wilde's scorn for Victorian sentimentalism in general and Dickensian melodrama in particular,[1] the above lines might have been penned with the author of *The Old Curiosity Shop* (1840-1841) in mind. Hardly an image of Victorian London appears to us now clear of the fog, soot, and mud that seep through Dickens's landscapes and transfix his at once unfathomable and indelible characters. As one critic wrote in a 1976 study of the author and his times, "[Victorian] history is today largely reconstructed from the scenes [Dickens] depicts and the human beings he perpetuates" (Chancellor 13). Aside from shaping the historical reality of his time for later readers, Dickens also presented narrative pathways, perspectival frames, and models of behavior that guided his contemporary audience toward understanding and finding their places within a newly developed, rapidly changing, industrial age in which factories, workhouses, poverty, pollution, crime, and disease confounded traditional values and practices. As the "first great novelist of the industrial city" (Ackroyd, *London* 11), Dickens urged his readers to leaven their lives with humor, assume critical agency, and look beyond their isolation to see their part in a common struggle against violations of justice and human dignity. If, as Lynda Nead has argued, modernity is "a set of processes and representations that were engaged in an urgent and inventive dialogue with their own historical conditions of existence" (8), Dickens was one of the most active facilitators of that dialogue, consulting with the immutabilities of emotional experience while recording the cacophony of cultural change. Testimonies to the success of his orchestration abound. "It is so graphic, so individual, and so true, that you could curtsey to all the people as you met them in the streets," the novelist and Dickens contemporary Mary Russell Mitford remarked upon the appearance of *Pickwick Papers* (1836-1837). "I did not think there had been a place where English was spoken to which 'Boz' had not penetrated. All the boys and girls talk his fun . . . and yet they who are of the highest taste like it the most" (qtd. in Ford 7). Mitford's comment indicates not only Dickens's widespread popularity (the sales totals of his serialized fiction averaged 40,000 copies per issue) but also the extent to which his narratives wove themselves into his readers' daily lives. Victorians of various social classes at once recognized Dickens's imagination of the absurd and found in it a fitting expression of their experiences. Indeed, when critics—Wilde among them—fault Dickens's realism, pointing out the caricaturish nature of his depictions, they overlook the fact that reality often did not seem real to the Victorians and that they were frequently required to make leaps of imagination in order to function in their phenomenal world.

"London created Dickens just as Dickens created London" (*London* 7), writes Dickens biographer Peter Ackroyd. The London that Dickens brought to life in his fiction is one fraught with ambivalence—a place at once of thrilling adventure and deadening monotony; of high hopes and plunging disappointments. Such contradictory impressions of the city first made their mark in the mind of ten-year-old Dickens himself, whose relocation with his family from the port town of Chatham to the outskirts of London in 1822 marked an abrupt transition from childhood tranquility to humiliation and neglect:[2] "It is wonderful to me how I could have been so easily cast away at such an age," Dickens wrote of the abrupt end to his formal education upon moving to Bayham Street, Camden Town. "It is wonderful to me that, even after my descent into the poor little drudge I had been since we came to London, no one had compassion enough on me—a child of singular abilities: quick, eager, delicate, and soon hurt, bodily or mentally—to suggest that something might have been spared, as certainly it might have been, to place me at any common school" (Forster I: 21).

Displaced by the pressures of his father's accumulating debts, the young Dickens traded the classroom for the spectacle of a teeming metropolis whose rhythms and geography would prove fascinating objects of study. Dickens's first biographer and close friend John Forster notes that the move to London gave the author his "first impression of that struggling poverty" (I: 12) and deprivation that would texture all of his novels, but Dickens's writings also indicate his seduction by the streets and sights that would become the playground and prison of his adult imagination. "I wandered about the City, like a child in a dream, staring at the British merchants, and inspired by a mighty faith in the marvellousness of everything," Dickens wrote in his 1853 article "Gone Astray," which recalls an early experience of being lost in London.

> Up courts and down courts—in and out of years and little squares—peeping into counting-house passages and running away . . . ever staring at the British merchants, and never tired of the shops—I rambled on, all through the day. In such stories as I made, to account for the different places, I believed as devoutly as in the City itself. (*Selected Journalism* 39)

This description of his early wandering encapsulates much of Dickens's fiction, which continually strives to "account for" sights that challenge comprehension. Indeed, the boy's dream-shrouded journey through London replayed multiple times in Dickens's adult life as he roamed the streets in periods of insomniac sympathy with the "restlessness of a great city" (*Selected Journalism* 73) that not only formed the backdrop for almost every one of his novels but also took on a life of its own as distinctive as any of the characters the novels housed.

That London should play a central role in Dickens's writings is hardly surprising given both his intimate, lifelong connection with the place and its vibrant, multifaceted, and protean nature during the author's lifetime (1812-1870). From the beginning of the century to its end, London's population grew more than fourfold from 1 million to

4.5 million (Ackroyd, *Dickens* 17). Areas such as Camden Town, which were still developing and considered semirural when Dickens first came to the city, had been consumed in the burgeoning overflow of Greater London by the 1850s. Streets that flickered fitfully under oil lamps at the century's start glowed steadily under gas lighting by the 1840s and, by the century's close, shown brilliantly beneath electricity. Sewage that poured into the Thames and mixed with the city's supply of drinking water in the 1820s had been contained and regulated by an underground sewer system by the 1860s.

But as modernity took shape over, around, and in the crevices of the city, it also spurred an aggregate of competing architectures, values, and time periods. Commercial buildings arose among the crumbling ruins of older, Elizabethan houses. The railway, which wound through the city by midcentury, created major schisms between old and new, order and chaos, while also connecting the urban center with suburban enclaves and wreaking havoc in settled areas. "Houses were knocked down; streets broken through and stopped; deep pits and trenches dug in the ground," chronicles Dickens in *Dombey and Son* (1846-1848). "Everywhere were bridges that led nowhere; thoroughfares that were wholly impassable; Babel towers of chimneys, wanting half their height. . . . There were a hundred thousand shapes and substances of incompleteness, wildly mingled out of their places, upside down, burrowing in the earth, aspiring in the air, mouldering in the water, and unintelligible as any dream" (120-21). Attempting to theorize the pandemonium of growth and disintegration that characterized Victorian London, Nead ventures that

> the spaces of improvement were caught up in a ceaseless exchange with the
> spaces of the city's historical past. London's past had to be endlessly re-
> written and re-imaged; contained through the conventions of text and im-
> age and assimilated within a manageable lexicon of the metropolitan pic-
> turesque. (8)

With his descriptions of Babel towers and dead-end thoroughfares, Dickens never did—or, more likely, never even aspired to—dispel his hallucinatory vision of an industrialized London. Instead, his portrayals recall to readers a common vocabulary of childhood illusion and dream-logic in which they might contextualize—if not fully comprehend—the unnavigable spaces opening out and closing in around them.

Alterations to the city's physical surfaces were but one visible manifestation of greater changes to the ethos and operation of the country as a whole. These changes included the First Reform Act (1832), which made extensive changes to the country's electoral system; the abolition of slavery in British possessions (1833); the Factory Act (1833), which limited work hours for women and children; the first government grant in support of elementary education (1833); and the enactment of the New Poor Law Amendment Act (1834). The first and last of these were particularly contentious legislations with widespread repercussions. The former—the first of three Reform Acts during the nineteenth century—acknowledged the growing powers of the middle classes and the inadequacy of aristocratic patterns of governance. The Act extended the vote to upper-middle-class men, thereby increasing the percentage of adult males who were voters from 13 percent to 18 percent; reapportioned Parliamentary representation to more accurately reflect the constituent body; and eliminated "rotten boroughs"—those districts with so small an electorate that they did not warrant individual Parliamentary representation. In contrast to this move toward social equality, the New Poor Law Amendment Act deepened class divides. Intended to dissuade the poor from dependence on government aid, the Act included such measures as the prohibition of outdoor relief (i.e., relief for the poor from sources outside of workhouses); the stipulation that conditions in workhouses should be less preferable than those of the lowest-paid worker; and the abolition of rate-in-aid (i.e., grants to supplement low wages). Both of these acts contributed to the mobilization of the Chartist movement, which began in 1836 as a radical campaign in direct opposition to the New Poor Laws and demanded further Parliamentary reforms such as universal male suffrage and the abolition of property qualifications for members of Parliament.

Working in the 1820s and 1830s as an independent shorthand reporter in Doctors Commons (a society of civil lawyers), as a Parliamentary reporter for *The True Sun*, and later as a freelance journalist for the ultraliberal daily *The Morning Chronicle*, the young Dickens honed his observational and writing skills while situated at the heart of these debates between the haves and the have-nots, the Whigs and the Tories. As Ackroyd notes, "Dickens was becoming deeply involved in the reporting of political affairs at precisely the time when the life of the nation was undergoing a profound change" (*Dickens* 135). His ambivalent political stance in later life testifies, perhaps, to his early journalistic exposure and attentiveness to all sides of an issue. On the one hand, he strongly opposed the New Poor Laws from the outset, thoroughly lambasting the system for its inhumanity in *Oliver Twist* (1837-1839) and, in an 1850 article for his journal *Household Words*, implying that a workhouse's conditions can reduce its denizens to an animalistic state. "They slunk about, like dispirited wolves or hyaenas; and made a pounce at their food when it was served out, much as those animals do," he noted of the inhabitants of the youth ward. And later: "Groves of babies in arms; groves of mothers and other sick women in bed; groves of lunatics; jungles of men in stone-paved down-stairs day rooms, waiting for their dinners; longer and longer groves of old people, in up-stairs Infirmary wards, wearing out life" (*Selected Journalism* 242). A distaste for the animality latent in humankind is apparent in these condemnations of misguided government policy; however, it is this same disgust with primitivism that underlies Dickens's objection to the Chartists, whose agenda would seem—on its surface—to correspond with Dickens's own. "Although Dickens understood the grievances of those at the rough end of this new industrial age, he never sympathised with those who tried to create a revolutionary movement in England" (*Dickens* 326), observes Ackroyd. The Chartist movement too closely resembled the specter of mob rule that had haunted the British consciousness since the French Revolution and that Dickens continually condemned both in his private writings and in novels such as *Nicholas Nickleby* (1838-1839), *Barnaby Rudge* (1841), and *A Tale of Two Cities* (1859) as monstrous, malicious, and barbaric.

These conflicting sentiments toward the revolutionary politics of his age have frustrated readers and critics who look in Dickens's writing for a viable alternative to the institutions he critiques. But, as Andrew Sanders has stated: "Dickens was not primarily a social reformer or even a particularly sharp analyst of how and why reform was necessary" (49). And Ackroyd has noted: "His judgments were never formulated into a coherent system . . . and were not meant as the basis for any kind of 'thought' on his part" (*Dickens* 174). It is precisely Dickens's ambiguity that invigorates his fiction and constitutes its synchronicity with the polyphony of his age. "In his novels, by that act of general identification which makes him so much the most powerful writer of his period, he infuses the whole of the struggling middle-class with his own life and animation, so that instinctively he embodies their concerns and expresses the changes which were even then altering the country beyond recognition," writes Ackroyd. "To say, therefore, that Dickens was 'radical' in any party sense or in any ideological sense would be to mistake the unique nature of his perceptions" (*Dickens* 138).

One issue, however, upon which Dickens might be considered "radical"—insofar as that term implies passionate commitment to an ideal—was the proper treatment of children and the preservation of childhood. His absorption in the topic stemmed from his own brief time working in a blacking factory as a twelve-year-old before and during his father's incarceration in the Marshalsea prison for nonpayment of debts. The experience has been documented so often that it has become legend, but Dickens no doubt tells it best in the fragmentary autobiography interpolated into Forster's text:

The blacking warehouse was the last house on the left-hand side of the way, at old Hungerford Stairs. It was a crazy, tumble-down old house, abutting of course on the river, and literally overrun with rats. Its wainscotted rooms and its rotten floors and staircase, and the old grey rats swarming down in the cellars, and the sound of their squeaking and scuffling coming up the stairs at all times, and the dirt and decay of the place, rise up visibly before me, as if I were there again. . . . My work was to cover the pots of paste-blacking: first with a piece of oil-paper, and then with a piece of blue paper; to tie them round with a string; and then to clip the paper close and neat, all around, until it looked as smart as a pot of ointment from an apothecary's shop. When a certain number of grosses of pots had attained this pitch of perfection, I was to paste on each a printed label; and then go on again with more pots. . . . No words can express the secret agony of my soul as I sunk into [the companionship of my fellow workers]; compared these everyday associates with those of my happier childhood; and felt my early hopes of growing up to be a learned and distinguished man, crushed in my breast. (I: 21-22)

While Dickens's tenure in the factory lasted less than a year, the humiliation and disgust associated with the experience reverberated throughout his life, striking mournful chords in his fiction. His novels echo with the suppressed cries of children prematurely confronted with the responsibilities of adulthood. Oliver Twist is, from his birth, "the orphan of a workhouse—the humble, half-starved drudge—to be cuffed and buffeted through the world—despised by all, and pitied by none" (20-21). Both Caddy Jellyby and Charley are victims of parental neglect and overwork in *Bleak House* (1852-1853). Jenny Wren—the crippled doll's dressmaker in *Our Mutual Friend* (1864-1865)—is almost unrecognizable as a little girl both to herself and everyone around her. "'What childhood did you ever leave me?'" (472) cries Edith Harker to her mother in *Dombey and Son*, voicing the plaint that any number of Dickens's characters might lament to the adults and society responsible for robbing them of their childhoods. Dickens had a very clear ideal of what childhood should be like—carefree, innocent, unencumbered—but so forcefully did the realities of his experiences and observations intrude upon this ideal that almost none of his child characters are granted these favors. Indeed, even his vision of an ideal childhood uninterrupted by extraordinary events was clouded by his knowledge of its mutability: "Childhood is usually so beautiful and engaging, that, setting aside the many subjects of profound interest which it offers to an ordinarily thoughtful observer . . . there is a mournful shadow of the common lot, in the notion of its changing and fading into something else" (*Selected Journalism* 30). For Dickens, who, some critics have argued, never outgrew his childhood perceptions, the poignancy and interest of childhood lay precisely in its fleeting nature and the incompletion inherent within it.

Dickens's vision of childhood was enforced not only by his personal experiences but also by the conditions and attitudes of his age. Throughout the nineteenth century, child labor was common in textile mills, coal mines, and factories, and, before the Factory Act of 1833, it was largely unregulated. A report on child labor in 1843 notes that "instances occur in which Children begin to work as early as three or four years of age; not infrequently at five, and between five and six; while, in general, regular employment commences between seven and eight; the great majority of the Children having begun to work before they are nine years old" (qtd. in Mitchell 43-44). Like Dickens, children were frequently employed to help support the family, and because small bodies could more easily maneuver in mine shafts, chimneys, and the tight spaces of machinery, they were particularly in demand in these dangerous occupations. However, as Sally Mitchell notes, "child labor was not invented by the Victorians. . . . What the Victorians did 'invent' was concern for working children, and ultimately the legal means to protect them" (43). Such legislation was prompted by a larger shift in attitudes toward children and childhood that enabled and was furthered by Dickens's imagination. James Kincaid—among others in the growing field of childhood studies—has argued that the phenomenon of the child is "contingent" and "determined" by historical circumstances (62), and it is largely agreed upon by critics that the nineteenth century witnessed a new focus on the child as a distinct entity from the adult. The child, states Kincaid, "became a conceptual and thus biological and social category . . . flowering in the nineteenth century" (61). As Kincaid and others such as Philippe Ariès point out, the Victorians busied themselves constructing, defining, and redefining this new category and institution of humanity. Discussing the extensive body of literature focused on this task, Kincaid states that "experts were not slow to complicate the complications, introducing, among other things, overlapping categories . . . where infancy extends through the first year; childhood, including that same period, advances to the end of the fourteenth year; boyhood and girlhood . . . cutting into that and running from age seven to twenty-one, a span that further takes in but is not limited to 'youth,' ages fifteen to twenty-one" (69). These new, often shifting and colliding, categories were reinforced—and further confused— by legislation that set specific age limits and work hours for children, established and reestablished the age of consent (from ten to twelve at first, and then to thirteen and then, in 1885, to sixteen), prescribed rules for how children should be and behave, and made education at first more accessible and then mandatory.

Such historical details allow us to contextualize further the elusive image of the child that haunts Dickens's fiction. On one hand, a plethora of children's books and magazines, manuals about child rearing and child psychology, children's clothing, and children's toys were constructing an ideal of the child that was physically and intellectually segregated from adult spaces. On the other hand, the demand for child labor, rampant poverty, and unregulated child abuse throughout the century suggest the impossibility of clear distinctions between the realms of child and adult. Dickens's uncannily mature children—Paul Dombey, Amy Dorrit, Jenny Wren—emphasize the tragedy of lost childhoods as well as reflect the ideological entanglements resulting from the Victorians' production of this new category of human experience.

The problem of prostitution—or "fallen women"—also highlights the ambiguous line between child and adult during the Victorian period as well as the instability of the Victorian "angel of the house"—the period's model woman, who is selflessly devoted to her children and husband. According to Ackroyd, the number of prostitutes in midcentury London was anywhere from 10,000 to 120,000 (*Dickens* 588), and a great number of them were what would now be considered grossly underage. According to Kincaid, streetwalkers were as young as eight or nine years of age. Quite often, these girls were born and raised in neighborhoods in which brothels were simply part of the landscape, and the sex industry presented itself to them as a viable means of income for supporting themselves and their families. While the youth of these women did not greatly concern the Victorians until late in the century, according to Kincaid, Victorians did recognize prostitution as a problem. The popular satirical weekly *Punch* identified it as "The Great Social Evil" in an 1857 cartoon; furthermore, literature and art of the period abound with "fallen women" who are duped into the profession (e.g., Marian Erle in Elizabeth Barrett-Browning's epic poem *Aurora Leigh* [1856]) or who succumb to their desires for love and money (e.g., Jenny in Dante Gabriel-Rossetti's eponymous poem [1870] and his painting *Found* [1859]). A number of modern critics have analyzed the nature of the threat prostitutes were perceived to pose to the ideal domestic woman, who was "'naturally' self-sacrificing and self-regulating [and] radiated morality because her 'substance' was love, not self-interest or ambition" (Poovey 8). Mary Poovey argues that the prostitute not only threatened this domestic ideal but also undermined the "consolidation of bourgeois power [and] economic success" (10) founded upon the sequestration of the domestic, female sphere. That not all women confined their activities to this idealized space is evident from the fact that prostitutes constituted an integral part of the urban scene. According to Judith Walkowitz, the prostitute was "a logo of the divided city itself . . . [and] brought into relief the class structure and general social distribution of London. . . . [Prostitutes] stood in stark opposition to the classical elite bodies of female civil statuary that graced the city squares: they were female grotesques, evocative of the chaos and illicit secrets of the labyrinthine city" (*Dreadful Delight* 21-22). Despite the physical, moral, and ideological threats posed by prostitution, however, Victorians hesitated to pass laws to curtail the sex trade. Two bills that would have done so—the Brothels Suppression Bill (1840) and the Bill for Protection of Females (1848)—failed to pass. Not until the Contagious Diseases Acts of 1864, 1866, and 1869 did prostitution come under legal oversight, and these highly controversial laws were instituted for the protection of military officials and their families from venereal diseases (primarily syphilis). By and large, then, prostitution was not illegal, and police had limited control over prostitutes' actions. Walkowitz notes: "Authorities were mainly concerned to impose a certain level of public decorum on prostitutes, to contain them within certain areas, and to break up collusions between prostitutes and thieves" (*Prostitution and Victorian Society* 14). Such reluctance to impose legislation could have stemmed, as Trevor Fisher suggests, from government unwillingness to interfere in individual affairs. Whatever the reason, this relatively unregulated social problem became a point of fascination for writers and artists whose depictions of prostitutes tended to combine prurient and philanthropic interests.

Dickens was among the most fascinated of these writers. His Home for Homeless Women, established in 1847 in partnership with the wealthy philanthropist Angela Burdett-Coutts, was Dickens's intimate concern for twelve years. His efforts on behalf of the Home—also called Urania Cottage—included researching similar institutions throughout England and France to determine the best system for such a venture; personally interviewing each of the residents before admission; and deciding on appropriate activities and clothing for the Home's thirteen wards. The early goal of the Home was to rehabilitate women criminals—primarily prostitutes—and prepare them for emigration, resettlement, and, preferably, marriage. Dickens firmly believed that the last was the best method of rehabilitation. He wrote: "I can certainly descry a kind of active repentance in their being faithful wives and mothers of virtuous children" (qtd. in Collins, *Dickens and Crime* 114). However, despite his enthusiasm for the project, Dickens's efforts were not as successful as he hoped. The first boatload of emigrants to Australia took up their trade again on the ship and by 1853 only about half of the girls who had been through the home had been successfully rehabilitated. Dickens's evaluation of the characters of the girls in his Home indicates the difficulty of the task he set himself. In a letter to Burdett-Coutts, he notes: "There is no doubt that many of them would go on well for some time, and would then be seized with a violent fit of the most extraordinary passion, apparently quite motiveless, and insist on going away. There seems to be something inherent in their course of life, which engenders and awakens a sudden restlessness and recklessness which may be long suppressed, but breaks out like madness" (qtd. in Collins, *Dickens and Crime* 108). It is possible to conjecture that in his portrayals of fictional prostitutes, Dickens attempted to counteract the frequent disappointments of his actual experiences with the Home. While fits of madness, relapses, and desertions were not uncommon at Urania Cottage, Dickens's fictional prostitutes are as a whole repentant, kindhearted, and excused from any responsibility for their downfalls. Nancy, in *Oliver Twist*, falls to prostitution after a childhood career as a pickpocket, but she gives her life saving Oliver. Alice Marwood in *Dombey and Son* is also a victim of childhood abuse, but as a grown woman, "there shone through all her wayworn misery and fatigue, a ray of the departed radiance of the fallen angel" (572). And *David Copperfield*'s little Em'ly is seduced by Steerforth but granted a new life in Australia under the doting care of Mr. Peggotty. Dickens's fictional fallen women thus serve as testaments to the resilient goodness of the human spirit in spite of corruptive environmental forces—as well as to their author's strong belief in the efficacy of the "angel of the house" as an ideal. While Dickens's optimistic outlook may not have been born out wholly by his experience—and

ies, and murders became uncommon [as the century progressed]. In London in the 1890s, with a population of five million people, there were only about twenty homicides per year" (96). These statistics pointing to decreasing crime rates are, however, frequently overshadowed by the public's hunger for sensational stories and the print industry's eagerness to deliver them.

The 1840 murder of Lord William Russell by his Swiss butler Francois Courvoisier, for example, created a media uproar that fed a countrywide fascination with the suave, charismatic murderer. Dickens himself was not immune to the excitement surrounding the case, and on the day of Courvoisier's execution, he joined the 40,000 spectators to watch the convict's hanging. "It was so loathsome, pitiful and vile a sight, that the law appeared to be as bad as he, or worse; being much the stronger, and shedding around it a far more dismal contagion" (qtd. in Diamond 157), Dickens reflected in an 1846 article for *The Daily News* that argued against the death penalty. But while he might have been repulsed by the vileness of prurient, public interest in such affairs, Dickens nevertheless frequently indulged his own fascination with crime and the criminal mind. "He readily identified himself, in imagination, with [criminals'] aggressive activities, but would also strongly repudiate this sympathy by extolling their adversaries, the police, and by demanding severe punishment for offenders against the law" (*Dickens and Crime* 1), Philip A. W. Collins notes. These conflicting impulses of sympathy and self-repudiation were acted out not only in his many fictional portraits of criminals and their apprehenders (for example, in *Oliver Twist*, *Bleak House*, *Our Mutual Friend*, and *The Mystery of Edwin Drood*) but also through his involvement with the Metropolitan Police—an institution established in 1829 by Home Secretary Sir Robert Peel that enacted a definitive tactical and philosophical shift from criminal apprehension to crime prevention. Dickens embarked on many nighttime excursions with Police Inspector Charles Field—a figure whom the author idealized in his writing and upon whom Inspector Bucket of *Bleak House* is based. "Inspector

Field's eye is the roving eye that searches every corner of the cellar as he talks," writes Dickens in his article "On Duty with Inspector Field":

> Inspector Field's hand is the well-known hand that has collared half the people here, and motioned their brothers, sisters, fathers, mothers, male and female friends, inexorably to New South Wales. Yet Inspector Field stands in this den, the Sultan of the place. Every thief here cowers before him, like a schoolboy before his schoolmaster. All watch him, all answer when addressed, all laugh at his jokes, all seek to propitiate him. This cellar company alone—to say nothing of the crowd surrounding the entrance from the street above, and making the steps shine with eyes—is strong enough to murder us all, and willing enough to do it; but let Inspector Field have a mind to pick out one thief here, and take him; let him produce that ghostly truncheon from his pocket, and say, with his business-air, "My lad, I want you!" and all Rats' Castle shall be stricken with paralysis, and not a finger move against him, as he fits the handcuffs on! (*Selected Journalism* 308)

The hyperbolic descriptions here reveal an underlying fascination with power—both the power of the criminal underground and the power of those capable of suppressing it. Indeed, it is precisely the charisma and tantalizing appeal of Dickens's imaginary criminals (Magwitch, Fagin, Orlick, John Jasper, Hortense) that necessitated his exaggerated portraits of authority figures like Field (and his fictional counterpart Bucket). For Dickens, confidence in the power of the police both enabled voyeuristic criminal fantasies and offered the reassurance of timely salvation.

For much of the eighteenth and nineteenth centuries, reform for criminals and the state's salvation entailed the transportation of offenders to penal colonies—first to America and then, after America gained independence, to penal settlements in Australia. While his fiction concerned itself primarily with England in general and London in particular, Dickens's fascination with criminal affairs, his involvement in

Urania Cottage, and the career removal of his sons to stations abroad brought him into contact with the greater panorama of England's imperial interests. These were considerable. Expanding to cover nearly a quarter of the world's landmass by the mid-twentieth century, England eventually developed into the largest empire in modern history. "The British Empire arose more through commerce than through planned conquest," notes Mitchell.

> Because it was the first country to industrialize, it had vast quantities of cheap manufactured goods to export. British ships, in return, brought back food and raw materials from countries around the world. Traders, merchants, bankers, investors, and immigrants settled wherever they discovered promising opportunities. (282)

Owing to its growing empire and the strength of its industrial advancements (extravagantly displayed by the Crystal Palace Exhibition of 1851), a sense of national pride worked its way into the British identity during the nineteenth century. As Pip wryly reflects in *Great Expectations*: "We Britons had at that time particularly settled that it was treasonable to doubt our having and our being the best of everything" (187).

Dickens's own participation in the celebration of Empire was measured. In his novels, England's foreign territories and involvements are continually shoved into margins that ambivalently hint at salvation and hope as well as danger and corruption. Magwitch is exiled to an unseen Australia, and Pip as well departs off-stage to make his fortune in a nebulous East. Little Em'ly and Alice Marwood are both transported to New South Wales, but their experiences there are left largely untold. Portraits of opium dens in *Edwin Drood* (1870) indicate Dickens's anxiety about the corruptive effects of intimate relations with strange, far-flung lands but also hint at a fascination with the unknown and unknowable. When characters express interest in colonial concerns—as does Mrs. Jellyby for Borrioboola Gha—they are criticized for sacrificing their duties to their homes in exchange for misguided philanthropic schemes. It was this fear of neglecting the center for the periphery that discouraged Dickens from focusing his fictional efforts on affairs abroad.

His belief in the necessity of a strong home nation and his increasing frustration with England's mismanagement of its foreign relations—as demonstrated by the Crimean War and the tragedy of the 1857 Indian Mutiny—is hinted at everywhere in his novels and voiced explicitly in his articles and letters. As Grace Moore explains, "While he [Dickens] supported the self-sufficient colonies of settlement, he deeply resented any involvement with independent colonies, requiring efforts that he felt could be put to better use at home and distracting bureaucrats from the ameliorative work necessary in the mother country" (3). For Dickens, as for many of his readers, the territories of the greater Empire were fantastical places that manifested in daily life only through marvelous imported objects, travelers' tall tales, and, sometimes, news of relatives either prospering or dying (Dickens's own son Walter died in India in 1863). The dubious sketches in Dickens's fiction of foreign places like India and Australia mirror the unclear conceptions of these spaces in the minds of his readers and vividly contrast with the clarity and detail of his accounts of London—a place that, for Dickens and his readers, was as marvelous, multifaceted, entertaining, and tragic as anything the wider world had to offer.

While, as Ackroyd claims, Dickens was "unmistakably an early Victorian" (*Dickens* 1080) in his values, temperament, and visions, his responses to the nineteenth century's political, social, and industrial changes reflect more broadly the psychological and philosophical difficulties of adjusting to rapidly changing external circumstances. Later Victorians and early-twentieth-century writers might (and did) scoff at Dickens's open emotionality and idealism, but the alternative of an age devoid of such impulses presents a bleak image indeed. The widespread, transatlantic mourning at Dickens's passing in 1870 indicates the loss not just of a man but also of the whole vision he represented—a vision of a world that, despite chaos and change, could still find meaning and cohesion, if only in the resilience of individual spirit and effort. "We have no doubt whatever that much of the active benevolence of the present day, the interest in humble persons and humble things, and the desire to seek out and relieve every form of misery is due to the influence of [Dickens's] works" (in Collins, *Critical Heritage* 508), stated a leading article in the *Times*, published soon after Dickens's death. While it would be a mistake to characterize Dickens unequivocally as a philanthropist, his efforts to "maintain a vision of the coherence of the world, a vision of some central human continuity," as Ackroyd puts it (*Dickens* 1082), urged his readers to maintain their humanity in an increasingly mechanized world. It is, no doubt, not only the panoramic representation of his times in his novels but also this same emphatic preservation of the human that constitutes Dickens's continued attraction for our own age.

Notes

1. Wilde famously commented, "You would need to have a heart of stone not to laugh at the death of Little Nell" (qtd. in Ellman 469). Nell Trent's death in Dickens's fourth novel, *The Old Curiosity Shop*, occasioned mass mourning among readers on both sides of the Atlantic.

2. Accounts of Camden Town in 1822 vary. Dickens's biographer and close friend John Forster describes Bayham Street as being in the "poorest part of the London suburbs . . . and the house was a mean small tenement" (I: 12). Peter Ackroyd, however, states that it was an "area agreeable enough" and "placid and genteel" (*Dickens* 57).

Works Cited

Ackroyd, Peter. *Dickens*. New York: HarperCollins, 1990.

_____. *Dickens' London: An Imaginative Vision*. London: Headline Book Publishing, 1987.

Altick, Richard D. *The English Common Reader: A Social History of the Mass Reading Public, 1800-1900*. Columbus: Ohio State UP, 1957.

Chancellor, E. Beresford. *Dickens and His Times*. London: Richards Press, 1976.

Collins, Philip A. W. *Dickens and Crime*. London: Macmillan, 1962.

_____, ed. *Dickens: The Critical Heritage*. London: Routledge, 1971.

Diamond, Michael. *Victorian Sensation: Or, the Spectacular, the Shocking, and the Scandalous in Nineteenth-Century Britain*. London: Anthem Press, 2003.

Dickens, Charles. *Dombey and Son*. 1846-1848. New York: Penguin, 1970.

_____. *Great Expectations*. 1860-1861. New York: Penguin, 1965.

_____. *Oliver Twist*. 2 vols. 1837-1839. New York: Hurd and Houghton, 1867.

_____. *Selected Journalism 1850-1870*. Ed. David Pascoe. New York: Penguin, 1997.

Ellman, Richard. *Oscar Wilde*. New York: Knopf, 1988.

Fisher, Trevor. *Prostitution and the Victorians*. New York: St. Martin's Press, 1997.

Ford, George. *Dickens and His Readers: Aspects of Novel-Criticism Since 1836*. Princeton, NJ: Princeton UP, 1955.

Forster, John. *The Life of Charles Dickens*. 2 vols. New York: Dutton, 1966.

Kincaid, James R. *Child-Loving: The Erotic Child and Victorian Culture*. New York: Routledge, 1992.

Mitchell, Sally. *Daily Life in Victorian England*. Westport, CT: Greenwood Press, 1996.

Moore, Grace. *Dickens and Empire: Discourses of Class, Race, and Colonialism in the Works of Charles Dickens*. Burlington, VT: Ashgate, 2004.

Nead, Lynda. *Victorian Babylon: People, Streets, and Images in Nineteenth-Century London*. New Haven, CT: Yale UP, 2000.

Poovey, Mary. *Uneven Developments: The Ideological Work of Gender in Mid-Victorian England*. Chicago: U of Chicago P, 1988.

Sanders, Andrew. *Authors in Context: Charles Dickens*. New York: Oxford UP, 2003.

Walkowitz, Judith R. *City of Dreadful Delight: Narratives of Sexual Danger in Late-Victorian London*. Chicago: U of Chicago P, 1992.

_____. *Prostitution and Victorian Society: Women, Class, and the State*. New York: Cambridge UP, 1980.

Charles Dickens's Critical Reputation_____

Laurence W. Mazzeno

In 2002 the novelist and critic Jane Smiley observed, "The literary sensibility of Charles Dickens is possibly the most amply documented literary sensibility in history" (1). In fact, over the past 175 years there had emerged in both the popular press and academic circles what Lyn Pykett and others have described as "the Dickens industry" (2), an enterprise in which a veritable army of critics have offered widely diverse judgments on the merits of Dickens's fiction. At one time or another Dickens has been variously celebrated as one of the greatest English novelists and vilified as a caricaturist who relied on contrived plots and sentimental stories for his success. Critics have declared him a genius and a sham.

Even before his death, the sky-high reputation Dickens garnered with his early novels had begun to fall; it reached its nadir after World War I, when his work was considered fit only for what Leslie Stephen called "the half-educated" (935). His work began to receive serious attention during the 1940s, and since that date his stock has steadily risen. Today it seems safe to say that his place among the giants of fiction is secure. Nevertheless, the circuitous path of Dickens criticism is noteworthy not only for what it says about the novelist but also for what it reveals about the path of literary criticism in the nineteenth and twentieth centuries.

The Opinion of Dickens's Contemporaries

Even before he published his first novel, Dickens was being heralded by the British reading public as a new voice in literature. His *Sketches by Boz* (1836) earned him praise for his keen wit and ability to depict the lower classes with startling fidelity. The serialized publication of *Pickwick Papers* (1836-1837) made him a household word, and reviewers compared his work with that of Henry Fielding, Tobias

Smollett, and even William Shakespeare and Miguel de Cervantes. The most extraordinary aspect of his popularity, one reviewer noted, was "the recognition" he received "from persons of the most refined taste, as well as from the great mass of the reading public" (Buller 55).[1] The appearance of *Oliver Twist* (1837-1839) and *Nicholas Nickleby* (1838-1839) helped that reputation grow even more, although reviewer Abraham Hayward did express reservations about the future: Dickens "has risen like the rocket," Hayward wrote, but if he continues to write so quickly and haphazardly, "he will come down like the stick" (62).

Some evidence of that falling off appears in reviews of his next two novels, *The Old Curiosity Shop* (1840-1841) and *Barnaby Rudge* (1841), and was not helped at all by his decision to publish his observations on his first trip to America, *American Notes* (1842), which some critics saw as mean-spirited. The general public continued to read him avidly, although sales slumped for *Martin Chuzzlewit* (1843-1844). Dickens's decision in 1843 to begin publishing shorter works for sale at Christmas eventually won back readers and drew numerous favorable comments. E. L. Blanchard warned other critics that the tale was "not to be talked about or written of according to ordinary rules" (86). William Makepeace Thackeray, not yet famous in his own right as a novelist, was in awe. "Who can listen to objections," he asked in a *Fraser's Magazine* review, "regarding such a book as this?" (166). However, Dickens's next novel, *Dombey and Son* (1846-1848), showed signs of a darker intelligence at work in its scrutiny of British society, and reviews were mixed. Dickens was able to recapture the hearts of his countrymen (and American readers) with his semiautobiographical *David Copperfield* (1849-1850), so much so that a reviewer for *Fraser's Magazine* could assert boldly that though "innumerable reputations have flared up and gone out," the "name and fame of Charles Dickens have been exempt from all vicissitude" ("Charles Dickens" 251).

Unfortunately, that euphoria did not last. The novels that followed *David Copperfield* were, like *Dombey and Son*, dark commentaries on

---

English society, and the public turned away from them. *Bleak House* (1852-1853) was pilloried for "absolute want of construction" (Brimley 295); *Hard Times* was dismissed by some as "stale, flat, and unprofitable, a mere dull melodrama" (Simpson 319). *Little Dorrit* (1855-1857) and *A Tale of Two Cities* (1859) fared no better, as evidenced by the particularly harsh judgments rendered by James Fitzjames Stephen, who remarked that the former novel is characterized by a "cumbrous and confused" plot and "rather uninteresting characters" presented in a style "often strained to excess" ("License" 378). The latter, he wrote in another review, demonstrates again how Dickens has been able to "infect the literature of his country with a disease" that corrupts long-held standards of literary taste ("*Tale*" 41). *Great Expectations* (1860-1861) marked something of a comeback for Dickens among the critics of his time. American critic Edwin Whipple asserted that it demonstrates that "Dickens is now in the prime, and not in the decline of his great powers" (442), while British reviewer E. S. Dallas thought the novel should be "ranked among his happiest" (443). Dallas also praised *Our Mutual Friend* (1864-1865) as "one of his finest works, and one in which on occasion he even surpasses himself" (6). Unfortunately, the novel prompted a return of harsh critical judgments, the most famous being that of the young Henry James, who complained about its loose organization and superficial characterization. James concluded his review by offering a summary judgment that would stand for nearly half a century: it would be "an offense against humanity to place Mr. Dickens among the greatest novelists" (159).

Nadir and Rebound

The growing feeling of revulsion toward the Victorians' sentimentality and moral earnestness greatly affected Dickens's reputation for nearly seventy years after his death in 1870. While a cadre of fans celebrated the publication of John Forster's three-volume *Life of Charles Dickens* (1872-1874), the trend in criticism was to dismiss Dickens as either intellectually shallow or technically inept. George Henry Lewes, in his 1872 essay "Dickens in Relation to Criticism," offers a representative opinion when he finds in the novels "the substitution of mechanisms for minds, puppets for characters" (148). "Thought," Lewes says, "is strangely absent" from Dickens's work (151). The prolific and respected critic George Saintsbury complained of Dickens's "lack of anything like real acquaintance or sympathy with great and high regions of thought" (743). Perhaps the best gauge of the shift in sensibility is Oscar Wilde's witty but insightful observation about the much-harassed heroine of *The Old Curiosity Shop:* "One must have a heart of stone to read the death of Little Nell without laughing" (qtd. in Beckson 163).

Among the few supporters of Dickens's fiction during this period who made lasting critical contributions were George Gissing and G. K. Chesterton, both novelists themselves, who defended the author against the growing body of detractors. In *Charles Dickens: A Critical Study* (1898) Gissing examines Dickens's novels not simply as social commentaries but as works of art, finding Dickens a great but flawed artist who "had not the tragic gift" (149). Chesterton goes even further in celebrating the convivial side of Dickens, suggesting in *Charles Dickens* (1906) that the author is "a mythologist rather than a novelist" (38) and should not be judged by the usual critical standards. For three decades Chesterton celebrated what might be called the "Christmas Dickens," whose innate sense of hope and good cheer sets him apart from his dour Victorian contemporaries. Chesterton was certainly not alone. In 1902 a group of devoted fans formed the Dickens Fellowship to perpetuate interest in his work. Much of what they initially published, however, is largely antiquarian and lacks critical rigor as most early Dickensians were content to accept Dickens's genius as a given and his humor as the mark of his greatness. A notable dissenter to that majority view was the Irish playwright George Bernard Shaw, who may be said to have initiated the strand of criticism that focuses on the "dark Dickens." Shaw detects a strand of earnestness in Dickens's work that evidences a deep discontent with the social order he ostensibly celebrates. Read carefully, Shaw says, one discovers that "*Little Dorrit* is a far more seditious book than *Das Kapital*" (51), and *Hard Times* reveals Dickens's realization that "it is not our disorder but our order that is horrible" (29). T. S. Eliot comes close to joining Shaw's camp when he declares that *Bleak House*, a searing exposé of society, is Dickens's best novel.

Most moderns found Dickens's novels too haphazardly constructed and too shallow in characterization to be worthy of serious consideration as literature. Ford Madox Ford dismisses them by observing, "My father thought Dickens was vulgar" (108). Aldous Huxley concludes even more caustically that "the quality of Dickens' sentimentality" is "truly pathological" (59). David Cecil claims his work contains "a great deal that is bad" (27), and, furthermore, that Dickens had "no sense of form" and an "uncertain grasp of character" (46). With the rise of psychoanalytic criticism in the 1920s, Dickens criticism took a turn toward *ad hominem* argument as these critical tools were often applied to discern the character and mental state of the novelist rather than elucidate fictional characters. Thomas Wright's *Life of Charles Dickens* (1935) publicized the novelist's late-life affair with the actress Ellen Ternan and spawned a handful of highly derogatory character studies that painted Dickens as a selfish hypocrite who, by extension, could not be relied upon for accurate portraits of his times. Hugh Kingsmill's devastating portrait in *The Sentimental Journey: A Life of Charles Dickens* (1934) presents Dickens as a vain, self-centered, immature, and mediocre writer.

At the end of the 1930s, however, two studies signaled a shift in temperament and ushered in a new wave of critical appreciation. George Orwell's essay on Dickens in *Inside the Whale* (1940) may seem at first to be another litany of the novelist's faults. But Orwell insists Dickens deserves to be read for both his technical ability to make use of "the unnecessary detail" (59) and for his moral ability to celebrate "the native decency of the common man" (65). Edmund Wilson's portrait in "Dickens: The Two Scrooges" (1941) suggests that the writer was a tormented soul alienated from society and that his novels are actually stinging critiques of the world that he is supposed to have celebrated. Wilson's readings paved the way for criticism that privileged the later, darker novels and that valorized Dickens as an artist estranged from the social order of his time.

Dickens's "Dark" and "Light"

In 1941, a breakthrough of sorts occurred in the history of Dickens criticism with the publication of Humphry House's *The Dickens World*, the first book on Dickens published by an academic press. But where House defends Dickens's place among the important novelists of his day, the iconoclastic and highly opinionated F. R. Leavis took specific pains to omit him from *The Great Tradition* (1948), declaring that Dickens's fiction lacks the high seriousness and sustained criticism of life necessary to rank with works by writers such as Jane Austen, George Eliot, or Henry James. Still, American critics of the time tended to follow House and Wilson in according Dickens high marks for his social criticism, and essayists such as Lionel Stevenson in "Dickens's Dark Novels" (1943) demonstrated how the later fiction presents a penetrating critique of Victorian society. Dorothy Van Ghent follows a similar line of reasoning in "The Dickens World: A View from Todgers's" (1950). Her groundbreaking analysis shows how the symbolic qualities of Dickens's style, particularly his use of reification, repetition, and metonymy, reflect his deepening concerns about "a world undergoing a gruesome spiritual transformation" (419). Especially in the later novels, she says, Dickens employs figurative language and various tropes to emphasize that "human separatedness" is the ordinary condition of life. In an oft-reprinted 1953 essay on *Little Dorrit*, the influential critic Lionel Trilling points out how the prison in this novel serves as a metaphor for the individual in society and encourages symbolic readings of Dickens's fiction. Biographies of the period, especially Una Pope-Hennessy's *Charles Dickens* (1945) and Edgar Johnson's more detailed two-volume *Charles Dickens: His Tragedy and Triumph* (1952), stress the psychological traumas that shaped Dickens's character and motivated his fiction, which Johnson characterizes as a continuing "critical analysis of modern society and its problems" (viii).

At the same time that arguments about Dickens's social criticism were prevalent, a new approach was developing that attempted to treat his work independent of its social content. Foremost among its exponents was J. Hillis Miller, a future leader of the American deconstructionist movement, who argues in *Charles Dickens: The World of His Novels* (1958) that the novels should be read not as social criticism but as the vehicles through which Dickens inscribed a vision of the complex urban reality he encountered in Victorian London. The "world" of the novels is a self-contained universe parallel to, but not identical with, the real world from which Dickens extracted the content of his tales in order to impose a new moral and artistic ordering upon them.

The controversy over the proper way to read Dickens's social commentary continued into the 1960s, as major studies appeared supporting both the "light" and "dark" views. Most influential among supporters of the former position was Steven Marcus, who argues in *Dickens: From Pickwick to Dombey* (1965) that during the first half of his career Dickens created powerful works that offer "a more balanced representation of society" (225) than the later works. Robert Garis's *The Dickens Theatre* (1965) is a more tendentious attack on the proponents of the dark Dickens. Garis claims that critical principles held in high esteem during the first half of the century, specifically moralist and formalist notions of disinterestedness and "the sympathetic imagination" (37), skewed judgments in favor of abstruse readings that do great injustice to Dickens. Emphasizing the theatricality of the novels, Garis claims Dickens often uses techniques from the stage in his fiction. His works are not meant to provide deep insight into character, nor are they appropriately judged by formalist standards, which demand unity of plot and theme. Instead his skills as a humorist and caricaturist make his works memorable and brilliant and demonstrate his comic genius.

The portrait of Dickens as an alienated artist was most prevalent during this time among psychoanalytical and formalist critics, who discovered a strong symbolic substratum in much of Dickens's work. Mark Spilka's articles and his discussion in *Dickens and Kafka: A Mutual Interpretation* (1963) argue that Dickens's grotesque comedy serves the author as a way to deal with the dehumanizing society in which he lived. Taylor Stoehr's Freudian reading of the novels in *Dickens: The Dreamer's Stance* (1965) privileges the later novels. The recurrent patterns of revenge and retribution coupled with the accumulation of detail, the use of literary techniques such as metonymy and alliteration, and the heavy reliance on coincidence, make these novels function in much the same way as Freud describes dreams operating in the human unconscious. Many critical studies at this time stressed the symbolic qualities of Dickens's fiction. Grahame Smith's conclusion in *Dickens, Money, and Society* (1968) sums up this approach quite well: Dickens's later novels, he writes, "are symbolic, transmutations of Victorian life" in which "character, setting, and action are consistently imbued with symbolic meaning" (206).

Dickens in an Age of Theory

By 1970, the centenary of Dickens's death, his reputation had reached a new high point. In that year the total number of scholarly journals devoted to the study of Dickens and his work rose to four as *Dickens Studies Annual* and *Dickens Studies Newsletter* (later retitled *Dickens Quarterly*) began publication, joining *The Dickensian* (founded 1903) and *Dickens Studies* (founded 1965). A dozen books and special issues of scholarly periodicals devoted exclusively to his works were published in that year alone. Nevertheless, critical practice was changing, and revaluations of Dickens's work soon revealed aspects of his fiction that had either been ignored or not noticed by generations entrenched in humanist or formalist critical approaches. Beginning in this decade, deconstructionists, feminists, new historicists, neo-Marxists, Lacanians, Foucauldians, neo-Freudians, and proponents of interdisciplinary cultural studies all took up Dickens's works and in the process reshaped critical opinion about his fiction both as art and as social commentary.

Of course, analyses using methodologies that were coming to be known as "traditional" (that is, humanist, moral, or formalist) continued to appear. Barbara Hardy's *The Moral Art of Dickens* (1970) is an extended assessment stressing the "moral concern" of his novels (xi). F. R. Leavis and his wife, Q. D. Leavis, offer an extensive defense of Dickens as a moral artist in *Dickens the Novelist* (1970), curiously reversing F. R. Leavis's earlier judgment that Dickens, despite his exceptional talent, was too much of an iconoclast and lacked the sustained seriousness of purpose to rank among the great English authors. One need only to scan Fred Kaplan's *Dickens and Mesmerism* (1975), an examination of Dickens's fascination with this subject that combines biographical analysis and close textual readings, or Robert Patten's *Charles Dickens and His Publishers* (1978) to see that works based on time-honored forms of scholarly inquiry were still being published. Two important new biographical studies, Kaplan's *Dickens: A Biography* (1988) and Peter Ackroyd's *Dickens* (1990), also appeared during these years of critical revaluation. Valerie Gager's *Shakespeare and Dickens: The Dynamics of Influence* (1996) is illustrative of critical studies that are sensitive to new, poststructuralist interpretations of Dickens but employ traditional methodologies—in this case, comparative analysis and influence study—to illustrate how Dickens's art was shaped by his understanding of an earlier writer.

Still, despite the continuance of these traditional methodologies, a definite shift toward newer ones can be seen beginning in the early 1970s with the publication of two works, both on the same topic. John Carey's *The Violent Effigy: A Study of Dickens's Imagination* (1973) first refutes earlier psychological and social critiques of Dickens's work before launching into an extended analysis of the novelist's symbolic use of imagery to reveal some essential qualities of the human character. In contrast, Garrett Stewart's *Dickens and the Trials of Imagination* (1974), which explores the way in which Dickens deals with the topic of imagination, employs a highly metaphoric and self-conscious method of analysis that applies theories of narratology to close readings of individual novels. While Carey's work received polite if reserved praise, Stewart's polarized the community of Dickens scholars who seemed unsure of how to respond to this new way of viewing fiction.

A sampling of studies suggests the extent to which these new approaches, characterized by extensive references to a host of theorists of language, literature, psychology, and society, now serve as the foundation for analysis of the novelist's canon. Dickens is of great interest to Robert Higbie in *Character and Structure in the English Novel* (1984), a study influenced by Vladimir Propp, Northrop Frye, Tzvetan Todorov, and A. J. Greimas, in which Higbie defends Dickens against charges that his characters lack complexity. In *Dickens and the Broken Scripture* (1985) Janet Larson applies the theories of Jacques Derrida and Mikhail Bakhtin to reassess Dickens's use of biblical imagery. The social theories of Michel Foucault shape the argument of D. A. Miller in *The Novel and the Police* (1988), in which he demonstrates how Dickens seeks through his fiction to impose social discipline on his readers just as he sought to impose discipline on his own life. Natalie McKnight blends Foucault's sociological theories with contemporary feminist approaches to fiction in *Idiots, Madmen, and Other Prisoners in Dickens* (1993), a work that presents Dickens as a kind of precursor to Foucault in recognizing how society isolates and attempts to reshape social outliers. Jeremy Tambling's *Dickens, Violence, and the Modern State* (1995) goes even further in combining Foucauldian social criticism with theories of European theorists such as Julia Kristeva, George Bataille, and Walter Benjamin in demonstrating how Dickens's later novels are a kind of crusade "against the forces of modernity which organize social and private life" (7).

Perhaps no aspect of Dickens's fiction underwent more serious scrutiny or prompted greater debate among critics during the last three decades of the twentieth century than his portrayal of women. Here again, judgments are mixed. Richard Barickman argues in *Corrupt Relations* (1982) that Dickens's fiction is a "complex, persistent, and radical critique of the Victorian system of sexual relationships" (vii). Michael Slater's *Dickens and Women* (1983) explains how the novelist's relationship with the real women in his life influenced his fiction. He concludes that Dickens was somewhat uneasy about the power women possessed and that his portraits of women reveal his apprehensions about their potential to cause harm to men and to society at large.

Avowed feminists were not quite as gentle as Slater. The feminist revisionist reading of the Dickens canon can be said to have begun with Kate Millett's brief comments about him in *Sexual Politics* (1970). Here, she writes that even a "nearly perfect indictment of both patriarchy and capitalism" (89) such as *Dombey and Son* is marred by Dickens's lifelong penchant to present even his most serious women as "insipid goodies" (90). Writing a few years later, Françoise Basch asserts in *Relative Creatures* (1974) that Dickens cannot portray women realistically. In her influential study *Uneven Developments* (1988), Mary Poovey argues that Dickens's portraits of women reveal his willingness to fulfill the role expected of him as a male novelist in Victorian England. In "'Who Is This in Pain?': Scarring, Disfigurement, and Female Identity in *Bleak House* and *Our Mutual Friend*" (1989), Helena Michie explains how Dickens's heroines, "remarkable for their insubstantiality," become realized for readers only "through illness, scarring, and deformity" (199).

Near the close of the century, however, later feminist critics began to challenge earlier readings that had been highly critical of Dickens's portrayal of women. Notable among them is Sandra Hopkins, who argues in "'Wooman, Lovely Wooman': Four Dickens Heroines and the Critics" (1990) that early feminists often employed double standards in critiquing Dickens and his female contemporaries. Similarly, Alison

Milbank suggests in *Daughters of the House* (1992) that feminists have misunderstood and misinterpreted Dickens. What feminists do not want to acknowledge, she writes, is that Dickens understood that both women and men could be cut off from the sources of power and marginalized in society. Brenda Ayres's eloquent defense of Dickens in *Dissenting Women in Dickens' Novels* (1998) also challenges earlier feminist readings of his work, claiming that Dickens actually wrote against the dominant ideology of his day to produce work that is in fact subversive, a quality admired by feminists in women writers.

Two other intriguing groups of reinterpretations that appeared during the last decades of the century are those by Marxists and New Historicists. Earlier Marxists such as Raymond Williams were generally positive in their assessments of Dickens, finding that his method of dramatizing modern urban life "relates very precisely to his historical period" (*The English Novel* 40). However, later ones tend to follow the lead of Terry Eagleton, who insists in *Criticism and Ideology* (1976) that Dickens was too tied to bourgeois ideology to write truly revolutionary critiques. Hence, important Marxist works such as Steven Connor's *Charles Dickens* (1985) stress the internal disconnectedness of Dickens's novels, finding the author unable to provide closure to his novels because by doing so he would have endorsed the dominant capitalist ideology of his day, an ideology with which he was discernibly uncomfortable.

Postcolonial critics have been concerned with Dickens's attitudes toward another dominant ideology of Victorian England, imperialism. Among many such studies, Wendy S. Jacobson's collection *Dickens and the Children of Empire* (2000) provides a representative sampling of modern critical judgments of Dickens's support of Britain's colonial empire. Contributors to Jacobson's volume who are themselves from former British colonies generally find Dickens a man of his time who did not possess a universal humanitarian outlook, as many critics of earlier generations had suggested.

Evidence of Enduring Reputation

There is no doubt that Dickens will continue to attract critical attention at least for the foreseeable future. Since 2000, a number of important studies have appeared, some employing new theoretical approaches, others using more traditional methods of literary analysis. Some retrace old ground to offer new readings, such as John Bowen's *Other Dickens: "Pickwick" to "Chuzzlewit"* (2000), a reprise of Steven Marcus's 1965 study of the early novels that uses poststructuralist theory to celebrate the ambiguity and open-endedness of the early fiction. David Parker's *The Doughty Street Novels* (2002) also focuses on the earlier novels and seeks to explain how events in Dickens's life shaped this work. Several studies tackle Dickens's interest in literary tradition; for example, both Julian Wolfreys's "'I Wants to Make Your Flesh Creep': Notes Toward a Reading of the Comic-Gothic in Dickens" (2001) and Peter K. Garrett's chapter on Dickens in *Gothic Reflections* (2003) go beyond cataloging gothic elements in the novels to explain how this tradition shaped Dickens's narratives.

There has also been a renewed interest in Dickens's nonfiction. For decades the study of Dickens's journalism had interested a small group of scholars, but few extended discussions had been published. As cultural studies prompted an expanded interest in the entire Dickens canon, this lacuna began to be filled. John M. L. Drew's *Dickens the Journalist* (2003) is perhaps the best work to date detailing Dickens's career as a writer and editor for periodical publications. At the same time, Drew and David Paroissien, editor of the *Dickens Quarterly*, are spearheading a project to make the weekly magazines Dickens edited, *Household Words* and *All the Year Round*, accessible to scholars on the Internet.

Among the more innovative approaches to Dickens has been that of cultural studies specialists, who aim to examine Dickens as a kind of cultural phenomenon. Jay Clayton's *Charles Dickens in Cyberspace* (2003) is one such study. Here, Clayton uses Dickens's career and his continuing reputation as a vehicle for explaining relationships between the Victorians and their twenty-first-century descendants. In a similar vein, Grahame Smith offers provocative commentary on the relationship between Dickens and twentieth-century filmmakers in *Dickens and the Dream of Cinema* (2003).

Each year in the past decade has been marked by the publication of a handful of new books on Dickens that point out how much can yet be discovered when new theoretical principles are applied to careful textual analysis. For example, Lynn Cain's *Dickens, Family, Authorship* (2008) reminds scholars that psychoanalytical approaches to the study of the novelist and his work can still yield fruitful insights into the fiction. Chris Loutitt's *Dickens's Secular Gospel* (2009) challenges received opinion that Dickens was in accord with his contemporaries in his views on the subject of work. The essayists contributing to Eileen Gilooly and Deirdre David's *Contemporary Dickens* (2009), among them some of the most important Victorian scholars of recent years, point out how much Dickens has to say to twenty-first-century readers on issues such as gender, sexuality, human relationships, the environment, and the creation of personal and national identity. And perhaps nowhere is the richness of Dickens's achievements or the reasons for his continuing appeal explained with greater clarity than in Michael Slater's *Charles Dickens* (2009), a biography that includes detailed commentary on the novels as well as sage observations on Dickens's journalism and short fiction. The Dickens that emerges from the pages of these critical commentaries is likely to engage scholars for decades to come.

Note

1. Many early reviews of Dickens's work appeared in popular magazines or journals no longer in print, posing problems in finding these materials. The same might be said of essays published in journals available only in major research libraries. Fortunately, a representative sample of important commentary has been made available in a number of anthologies. Whenever possible, I have cited these reprints to facilitate my own readers' ability to locate material. Extensive discussions of Dickens's critical rep-

utation can be found in George H. Ford's *Dickens and His Readers* (1955), Philip A. W. Collins's *Dickens: The Critical Heritage* (1971), and my own study, *The Dickens Industry* (2008).

Works Cited

Ackroyd, Peter. *Dickens*. London: Minerva, 1990.

Ayres, Brenda. *Dissenting Women in Dickens's Novels: The Subversion of Domestic Ideology*. Westport, CT: Greenwood, 1998.

Barickman, Richard, Susan MacDonald, and Myra Stark. *Corrupt Relations: Dickens, Thackeray, Trollope, Collins, and the Victorian Sexual System*. New York: Columbia UP, 1982.

Basch, Françoise. *Relative Creatures: Victorian Women in Society and the Novel, 1837-1867*. Trans. Anthony Rudolf. London: Lane, 1974.

Beckson, Karl. *I Can Resist Everything Except Temptation, and Other Quotations from Oscar Wilde*. New York: Columbia UP, 1996.

Blanchard, E. L. Rev. of *A Christmas Carol*, by Charles Dickens. *Ainsworth's Magazine* Jan. 1844: 86.

Bowen, John. *Other Dickens: "Pickwick" to "Chuzzlewit."* New York: Oxford UP, 2000.

Brimley, George. Rev. of *Bleak House*, by Charles Dickens. *Spectator* 24 Sept. 1853: 923-25. Rpt. in *Dickens: The Critical Heritage*. Ed. Philip A. W. Collins. London: Taylor & Francis, 2005. 295-99.

Buller, Charles. "The Works of Charles Dickens." *London and Westminster Review* 29 (July 1837): 194-215. Rpt. in *Dickens: The Critical Heritage*. Ed. Philip A. W. Collins. London: Taylor & Francis, 2005. 55-59.

Cain, Lynn. *Dickens, Family, Authorship: Psychoanalytical Perspectives on Kinship and Creativity*. Burlington, VT: Ashgate, 2008.

Carey, John. *The Violent Effigy: A Study of Dickens's Imagination*. 1973. London: Faber and Faber, 1991.

Cecil, David. *Early Victorian Novelists*. London: Constable, 1934.

"Charles Dickens and David Copperfield." *Fraser's Magazine* Dec. 1850: 698-700. Rpt. in *Dickens: The Critical Heritage*. Ed. Philip A. W. Collins. London: Taylor & Francis, 2005. 251-55.

Chesterton, G. K. *Charles Dickens*. London: Methuen, 1906.

Clayton, Jay. *Dickens in Cyberspace: The Afterlife of the Nineteenth Century in Postmodern Culture*. New York: Oxford UP, 2003.

Collins, Philip A. W., ed. *Dickens: The Critical Heritage*. 1971. London: Taylor & Francis, 2005.

Connor, Steven. *Charles Dickens*. Oxford: Blackwell, 1985.

Dallas, E. S. Rev. of *Great Expectations*, by Charles Dickens. *The Times* 17 Oct. 1861: 6. Rpt. in *Dickens: The Critical Heritage*. Ed. Philip A. W. Collins. London: Taylor & Francis, 2005. 443-47.

_____. Rev. of *Our Mutual Friend*, by Charles Dickens. *The Times* 29 Nov. 1865: 6.

Drew, John M. L. *Dickens the Journalist*. London: Palgrave Macmillan, 2003.

Eagleton, Terry. *Criticism and Ideology: A Study in Marxist Literary Theory*. Rev. ed. London: Verso, 2006.

Eliot, T. S. "Wilkie Collins and Dickens." *Times Literary Supplement* 4 Aug.1927: 525-26.

Ford, Ford Madox. *The English Novel: From the Earliest Days to the Death of Joseph Conrad*. London: Lippincott, 1930.

Ford, George H. *Dickens and His Readers: Aspects of Novel Criticism Since 1836*. Princeton, NJ: Princeton UP, 1955.

Ford, George H., and Lauriat Lane, Jr., eds. *The Dickens Critics*. Ithaca, NY: Cornell UP, 1963.

Forster, John. *The Life of Charles Dickens*. 3 vols. London: Chapman & Hall, 1872-74.

Gager, Valerie. *Shakespeare and Dickens: The Dynamics of Influence*. New York: Cambridge UP, 1996.

Garis, Robert. *The Dickens Theatre: A Reassessment of the Novels*. Oxford: Clarendon Press, 1965.

Garrett, Peter K. *Gothic Reflections: Narrative Force in Nineteenth-Century Fiction*. Ithaca, NY: Cornell UP, 2003.

Gilooly, Eileen, and Deirdre David, eds. *Contemporary Dickens*. Columbus: Ohio State UP, 2009.

Gissing, George. *Charles Dickens: A Critical Study*. London: Blake, 1898.

Hardy, Barbara. *The Moral Art of Dickens*. London: Athlone, 1970.

Hayward, Abraham. Rev. of *Pickwick Papers* and *Sketches by Boz*, by Charles Dickens. *Quarterly Review* 62 (Oct. 1837): 484-518. Rpt. in *Dickens: The Critical Heritage*. Ed. Philip A. W. Collins. London: Taylor & Francis, 2005. 59-65.

Higbie, Robert. *Character and Structure in the English Novel*. Gainesville: UP of Florida, 1984.

Hopkins, Sandra. "'Wooman, Lovely Wooman': Four Dickens Heroines and the Critics." *Problems in Feminist Criticism*. Ed. Sally Minogue. London: Routledge, 1990. 199-244.

House, Humphry. *The Dickens World*. New York: Oxford UP, 1941.

Huxley, Aldous. "The Vulgarity of Little Nell." *Vulgarity in Literature*. London: Chatto & Windus, 1930. 54-59.

Jacobson, Wendy S., ed. *Dickens and the Children of Empire*. New York: Palgrave, 2000.

James, Henry. "*Our Mutual Friend*." *Nation* 1 (Dec. 1865): 786-87. Rpt. as "The Limitations of Dickens." *Views and Reviews*. Boston: Ball, 1908. 153-61.

Johnson, Edgar. *Charles Dickens: His Tragedy and Triumph*. 2 vols. New York: Simon & Schuster, 1952.

Kaplan, Fred. *Dickens: A Biography*. 1988. Baltimore: Johns Hopkins UP, 1998.

_____. *Dickens and Mesmerism: The "Hidden Springs of Fiction."* Princeton, NJ: Princeton UP, 1975.

Kingsmill, Hugh. *The Sentimental Journey: A Life of Charles Dickens*. London: Wishart, 1934.

Larson, Janet. *Dickens and the Broken Scripture*. Athens: U of Georgia P, 1985.

Leavis, F. R. *The Great Tradition*. London: Chatto & Windus, 1948.

Leavis, F. R., and Q. D. Leavis. *Dickens the Novelist*. New York: Pantheon, 1970.

Lewes, George Henry. "Dickens in Relation to Criticism." *Fortnightly Review* 17 (Feb. 1872): 141-54.

Loutitt, Chris. *Dickens's Secular Gospel: Work, Gender, and Personality*. New York: Routledge, 2009.

McKnight, Natalie. *Idiots, Madmen, and Other Prisoners in Dickens*. New York: St. Martin's Press, 1993.

Marcus, Steven. *Dickens: From Pickwick to Dombey*. New York: Basic Books, 1965.

Mazzeno, Laurence W. *The Dickens Industry: Critical Perspectives 1836-2005*. Rochester, NY: Camden House, 2008.

Michie, Helena. "'Who Is This in Pain?': Scarring, Disfigurement, and Female Identity in *Bleak House* and *Our Mutual Friend*." *Novel* 22 (1989): 199-212.

Milbank, Alison. *Daughters of the House: Modes of the Gothic in Victorian Fiction*. New York: St. Martin's Press, 1992.

Miller, D. A. *The Novel and the Police*. Berkeley: U of California P, 1988.

Miller, J. Hillis. *Charles Dickens: The World of His Novels*. Cambridge, MA: Harvard UP, 1958.

Millett, Kate. *Sexual Politics*. Garden City, NY: Doubleday, 1970.

Orwell, George. *Inside the Whale*. London: Gollancz, 1940.

Parker, David. *The Doughty Street Novels*. New York: AMS Press, 2002.

Patten, Robert. *Charles Dickens and His Publishers*. Oxford: Clarendon Press, 1978.

Poovey, Mary. *Uneven Developments: The Ideological Work of Gender in Mid-Victorian England*. Chicago: U of Chicago P, 1988.

Pope-Hennessy, Una. *Charles Dickens*. London: Chatto & Windus, 1945.

Pykett, Lyn. *Charles Dickens*. London: Palgrave, 2002.

Saintsbury, George. *A Short History of English Literature*. London: Macmillan, 1898.

Shaw, George Bernard. *Shaw on Dickens*. Ed. Dan H. Laurence and Martin Quinn. New York: Frederick Ungar, 1985.

Simpson, Richard. Rev. of *Hard Times*, by Charles Dickens. *The Rambler* n.s. 2 (Oct. 1854): 361-62. Rpt. in *Dickens: The Critical Heritage*. Ed. Philip A. W. Collins. London: Taylor & Francis, 2005. 319-21.

Slater, Michael. *Charles Dickens*. New Haven, CT: Yale UP, 2009.

_____. *Dickens and Women*. London: Dent, 1983.

Smiley, Jane. *Charles Dickens*. New York: Viking Press, 2002.

Smith, Grahame. *Dickens and the Dream of Cinema*. Manchester, England: Manchester UP, 2003.

_____. *Dickens, Money, and Society*. Berkeley: U of California P, 1968.

Spilka, Mark. *Dickens and Kafka: A Mutual Interpretation*. Bloomington: Indiana UP, 1963.

Stephen, James Fitzjames. "License of Modern Novelists." *Edinburgh Review* 106 (July 1857): 124-56. Rpt. in *Dickens: The Critical Heritage*. Ed. Philip A. W. Collins. London: Taylor & Francis, 2005. 377-85.

_____. "*A Tale of Two Cities*." *Saturday Review* 8 (17 Dec. 1859): 741-43. Rpt. in *The Dickens Critics*. Ed. George H. Ford and Lauriat Lane, Jr. Ithaca, NY: Cornell UP, 1963. 38-46.

Stephen, Leslie. "Dickens, Charles." *Dictionary of National Biography*. Vol. 5. 1885. London: Smith, Elder, 1908. 925-37.

Stevenson, Lionel. "Dickens's Dark Novels, 1851-1857." *Sewanee Review* 51 (Summer 1943): 398-409.

Stewart, Garrett. *Dickens and the Trials of Imagination*. Cambridge, MA: Harvard UP, 1974.

Stoehr, Taylor. *Dickens: The Dreamer's Stance*. Ithaca, NY: Cornell UP, 1965.

Tambling, Jeremy. *Dickens, Violence, and the Modern State*. London: Macmillan, 1995.

Thackeray, William Makepeace. "A Box of Novels." *Fraser's Magazine* Feb. 1844: 166-69.

Trilling, Lionel. "*Little Dorrit*." *Kenyon Review* 15 (Autumn 1953): 57-90.

Van Ghent, Dorothy. "The Dickens World: A View from Todgers's." *Sewanee Review* 58.3 (1950): 419-38. Rpt. in *The English Novel: Form and Function*. New York: Holt, 1953.

Whipple, Edwin. "*Great Expectations*." *Atlantic Monthly* Sept. 1861: 380-82. Rpt. in *Dickens: The Critical Heritage*. Ed. Philip A. W. Collins. London: Taylor & Francis, 2005. 441-43.

Williams, Raymond. *The English Novel: From Dickens to Lawrence*. New York: Oxford UP, 1970.

Wilson, Edmund. "Dickens: The Two Scrooges." *The Wound and the Bow*. Boston: Houghton Mifflin, 1941.

Wolfreys, Julian. "'I Wants to Make Your Flesh Creep': Notes Toward a Reading of the Comic-Gothic in Dickens." *Victorian Gothic: Literary and Cultural Manifestations in the Nineteenth Century*. Ed. Ruth Robbins and Julian Wolfreys. New York: Palgrave, 2000. 31-59.

Wright, Thomas. *The Life of Charles Dickens*. London: Jenkins, 1935.

Order in Disorder:
Surrealism and *Oliver Twist*_____

Nancy M. West

Several critics have used the term surrealist to describe the blend of fantasy and realism found in Dickens's novels: the interspersion of Gothic supernaturalism and fairy-tale elements with intensely realistic descriptions, the dream-like or hallucinatory style of many of his passages, and the psychological and metaphysical concern Dickens had with dreams. However, these critics hesitate to discuss his work in specific terms of surrealist techniques and concepts. Unwilling to associate him with as radical a movement as that of André Breton and his followers, they do not take their discussions much beyond the term itself.

Dickens's novels anticipate the surrealist movement in much more concrete and conceptual ways than most scholars may realize. While even early critics such as George Henry Lewes have noted the hallucinatory strain of his work, most will discuss this quality only in terms of mood or atmosphere rather than as evidence of Dickens's concern with probing the unconscious. Even Taylor Stoehr, whose extensive study *The Dreamer's Stance* posits that Dickens's style and narration create a governing vision that is often dreamlike, emphatically maintains that the author's work is not surrealist. His argument is based on the questionable assumption that Dickens, unlike the later artists, did not consciously set out to imitate dreams. The distinction, for him, thus lies in artistic intention.

Stoehr is undoubtedly correct in refraining from labeling Dickens a surrealist per se. It is quite unlikely that the novelist whose works are so finely interwoven and whose artistic control is so apparent would have completely agreed, for example, with surrealist notions about the function of the artist and methods of style and composition. Dickens was too concerned with the aesthetic, too conscious of his craftsmanship, to release the artistic control surrealists considered an obstacle to art. Dickens, though, did share a much more central concern with the movement, that is, he used his art to explore the role that dreams and fantasy play in our understanding of external reality and what lies beyond it. His novels therefore contain a substantial number of elements that are strikingly similar to those present in surrealist painting and fiction. A close study of the many similarities between Dickens's work and the later movement, rather than simply providing a trendy means of approaching the novels, elucidates the surprisingly modern concern he had with the unconscious and the innovative means he used to explore it.

A study of *Oliver Twist* will be particularly fruitful, as readers generally have criticized the novel as poorly constructed, inconsistent, and overly sentimental. However, a comparison with surrealist practices suggests that what are usually thought to be infelicities and weaknesses in characterization, structure, and plot are perhaps instead signs of Dickens's modern experimentation with examining dreams. Moreover, a likening of elements in the novel to those of surrealist painting will emphasize the pictorial quality of his work: his attention to images, objects, lighting, shading, and spatial arrangements. Finally, a comparison should reveal the complexity of those passages on dream states, passages that readers have generally found to be among the most interesting yet puzzling aspects of the novel.

Mary Rohrberger has been the only scholar to argue that a comparison to surrealism is a valid means of approaching Dickens's work, and she also chooses *Oliver Twist* as the focus of her study. While her article points to some important connections between the novel and surrealist and Freudian theory, it is not inclusive. There is no mention of such important concepts as critical paranoia, hallucinatory realism, or surrealist ideas about the object. Nor does Rohrberger discuss surrealist fiction, some of which is remarkably similar to Dickens's novels in terms of characterization and setting. Her major omission, however, is that she fails to discuss surrealism as a visual art. Since it is primarily through painting that the surrealists expressed their fascination with the unconscious, such neglect of paintings and the techniques used to create them seriously weakens an understanding of the movement and its relation to Dickens. Finally, a study of the novel still needs to take into account the context of other Dickens novels that are replete with surrealist elements. References to other novels will clarify how this "apprentice" work launched Dickens's fascination with dreams and the unconscious.

Surrealism has as its essence a desire to draw upon and even imitate dream experience; ideally, its followers wished their art to be an expression of imagination as realized in dreams. Adopting Freud's theory that the unconscious is the domain where real motivations of conscious thought are to be discovered, the surrealists believed that human beings achieve self-discovery through exploring the unconscious as manifested in the dream state.

What most attracted the surrealists to the unconscious is its blending of the fantastical with external reality, a synthesis that they regarded as fundamental to human understanding. Contrary to popular notions, surrealism's basic aim was not a rejection of the material world but its reconciliation with dreams and the imagination. In fact, the surrealists ultimately strived for a reconciliation of all that appears to be contradictory. Breton elaborates in his *Second Manifesto of Surrealism*: "Everything leads us to believe there exists a certain point in the mind in which life and death, real and imaginary, past and future, communicable and incommunicable, high and low cease to be perceived as contradictions" (*Manifestoes* 123). Reaching this point is their ultimate aim, which can be realized through exploring the seemingly disparate nature of dreams.

Oliver Twist comprises many conflicting or incongruous elements and forces. The most obvious of these is, of course, the two "camps" of good and evil as represented by the Maylies and Brownlow on the one hand and Fagin and his gang on the other; others include realism and supernaturalism, dream and reality, darkness and light, open pastoral and crowded city, anguish and contentment, youth and old age, birth and death or near-dying, and innocence and corruption. As Steven

Marcus observes (67), at first glance it seems that there is a distinct separation between most of these pairs of opposites, so much so that a traditional reading of the novel posits a clear demarcation between the realms of goodness and wickedness. A close study, however, challenges this black-and-white approach, and reveals that *Oliver Twist* attempts a reconciliation of seemingly contradictory elements similar to those found in dreams.

To begin with, there is the merging of realism characterized by precision and detail with unbridled fantasy: a fusion that is a significant characteristic of the dream. As Stoehr observes, one of the main similarities between Dickens's work and dreams is a predilection for detail. Dickens's vision, which deals with the familiar detail rather than the unfamiliar, complex abstract, and which often dwells on apparently insignificant objects, has much in common with the vision of a dreamer: "The fragmentation of perception and the displacement of feeling to the isolated inanimate parts has a leveling effect, so that everything is somehow of equal emotional weight; thus, as in dream or magic, the smallest irrelevancy has talismanic force" (Stoehr 88).

Acknowledging the importance of detail in dreams, many surrealists painted with a surprising exactness and concern for detail. This emphasis on accuracy was an important part of what they termed "hallucinatory realism," defined as "a careful and precise delineation of detail, yet a realism which does not depict an external reality since the subjects realistically depicted belong to the realm of dream or fantasy" (Osborne 529). Thus, painters such as René Magritte, Salvador Dalí, and Victor Brauner tempted the viewer into a feeling of familiarity engendered by recognition of forms while simultaneously usurping this familiarity by rendering their landscapes with a strangeness, sense of displacement, or fantastical quality.[1] Similarly, the vivid detail of the London scenes in *Oliver Twist* works to transform ordinary streets and places into an alien, sometimes magical, often horrific world. The heavy use of detail with no focal point, as in surrealist collages, disorients and assaults the reader so that realistic images become hallucinations or fantasies.

Dickens achieves this same disorienting blend of detail and fantasy in *Martin Chuzzlewit*. In this early novel, Dickens carefully delineates objects while simultaneously infusing them with animation. The passage that describes the view from the roof of Todger's boarding-house exemplifies this technique most clearly:

> After the first glance, there were slight features in the midst of this crowd of objects, which sprung out from the mass without any reason, as it were, and took hold of the attention whether the spectator would or no. Thus, the revolving chimney-pots on one great stack of buildings, seemed to be turning gravely to each other every now and then, and whispering the result of their separate observation of what was going on below. Others, of a crook-backed shape, appeared to be maliciously holding themselves askew, that they might shut out the prospect and baffle Todger's. . . . (130)

The purpose here, as in many other passages from the novel, is to force the reader to observe objects closely: "We cannot dismiss them with our usual unseeing recognition, a recognition that identifies but does not perceive" (Stone 96). In *Martin Chuzzlewit*, the magical quality of objects that are so carefully described causes the viewer to question his own reactions to external reality since what he normally regards as mere background suddenly moves to the forefront of his perception and assaults his senses. This manipulation of the viewer through emphasis on objects is a distinctive feature of many surrealist paintings. In Giorgio de Chirico's work, such as *The Anxious Voyage*, objects that are traditionally represented as background (pillars, columns, statues) appear prominently in the landscape while human figures are faintly represented in the distance. Even more interesting is that these figures seem to be in a state of motionless anonymity; we have no idea who these people are or for what they are waiting, only that they are part of a landscape where objects tower over and, in fact, seem to paralyze them. Interestingly, this relationship between objects and persons is also an important aspect of *Martin Chuzzlewit*. The objects that can be viewed from Todger's render the observer absolutely passive. Their magical presence exerts such force that the viewer has no control over perception or consciousness.

Of course, *Oliver Twist* differs from *Martin Chuzzlewit* in that it places a child at the center of detailed yet fantastical visions. As a child, Oliver perceives his experience and surroundings in very concrete terms; he is not yet able to apply rational or philosophical explanations to them. The overwhelming sense of terror he feels through much of the novel acts upon his childish sensations, and therefore transforms detail into exaggerated or phantasmagoric forms. Being an orphan, Oliver feels a profound sense of isolation and helplessness that causes him to perceive the world as a domain where continual threats and surprises await him, where there is no comforting sense of certainty. Since we often assume Oliver's point of view, we too see the detail of London as alien and fantastic.

The perspective of the child—combining a capacity for exaggeration, emphasis on detail, and primordial sense of fear and helplessness—is one that many surrealists tried to convey in their art. As Breton explains, men in the world of dreams are like very small children, still unable to classify, situate, or interpret the elements of the outside world. Hence, Joan Miró uses the child's perspective as the governing vision for most of his art. This perspective is also present in some surrealist fiction. René Crevel employs a child as the central figure in his novel *Babylone*. Her outlook, juxtaposed to the rational and flat perspective of the adult world, infuses the external world with hidden possibilities, transforming ordinary objects into elements of wonder. Similarly, Oliver's perspective transmutes such seemingly insignificant objects as trees and wooden boards into phantoms and turns definite, oft-traveled places into unknown and dangerous domains, as this passage in chapter 16 describing Oliver's journey with Sikes conveys:

It was Smithfield that they were crossing, although it might have been Grosvenor Square, for anything Oliver knew to the contrary. The night was dark and foggy. The lights in the shops could scarcely struggle through the heavy mist, which thickened every moment and shrouded the streets and houses in gloom; rendering the strange places still stranger in Oliver's eyes, and making his uncertainty the more dismal and depressing. (159)

This helpless position of a child promotes paralysis: stricken with terror and uncertainty, Oliver cannot exert control over his experience. Consequently, he remains passive through most of the novel and emerges as a fragile symbol of innocence rather than a believable character. Critics have generally maintained that Dickens's portrayal of Oliver is a major defect of the work. On a realistic level, Oliver's character is an artistic failure. However, if we compare Oliver to the figures of many surrealist novels, his passivity becomes not only excusable but necessary. The essentially passive role of a dreamer was one of the most significant aspects of dreams for the surrealists. Acknowledging that in dreams man submits without questioning and what he appears to see and experience offers him little surprise until he returns to the waking world, surrealists tried to adopt that position for themselves as artists and for their viewers. This approach also applies to surrealist novels. J. H. Matthews explains that the "protagonist" in a surrealist novel is, or becomes, listless as a result of despair and frustration with the external world and consequently seeks refuge in dreams (*Surrealism and the Novel* 38). He thus achieves self-discovery not through action in the external world but through submission to the dream state, a surrender of the will to the unconscious.

As Rohrberger notes, Oliver's desire to escape an anguish-filled reality causes him to submit easily to either a hypnogogic or dream state. In fact, Oliver spends more time hallucinating, fainting, or sleeping than he does anything else. Moreover, the descriptions of these dreams or dream-like states add to the novel's complexity and help refute a judgment of Oliver as simply another of Dickens's "flat" characters.

Catherine Bernard explains that Dickens's psychological approach to dreams differed markedly from the contrived dream usage of his Victorian contemporaries or the Gothic novelists who preceded him. Unlike those found in Gothic novels, for example, Dickens's dreams are generally designed not to "promote plot or heighten atmosphere" but to reveal the underlying conflicts or desires within his characters. Nor did his employment of dreams conform to Victorian literary conventions or ideas of morality: "Forfeiting the popular Victorian tenet that dreams serve as a type of moral index to character, he permitted his loathsome villains like Headstone and Orlick to sleep away in peaceful slumber, while he assigned long troubled dreams to his pure innocents, those who seem totally shut off from dark imaginings of any sort" (Bernard 207). Bernard points to Esther Summerson's dreams during her illness in *Bleak House*, visions that reveal the altruistic heroine's reticent desire to be released from social responsibility. Notable also in Esther's dreams is the focus on the objects of the necklace and staircase. This focus is another indication of Dickens's surprisingly sophisticated knowledge of dreams; according to Freud, the meaning of dreams is primarily expressed through the symbolic objects that they contain.

Bernard's observation, however, also applies to the "simple" character of Oliver himself. The opening episode of chapter 5 in *Oliver Twist* exemplifies her argument most clearly. Alone for the first time in the basement of Sowerberry, the undertaker, Oliver timidly surveys the room before going to sleep. There are several noteworthy elements in this episode: foremost among them is the revelation of Oliver's death-wish. Dickens conveys this desire in terms that are close to surrealist philosophy:

An unfinished coffin on black tressels, which stood in the middle of the shop, looked so gloomy and death-like that a cold tremble came over him, every time his eyes wandered in the direction of the dismal object, from which he almost expected to see some frightful form slowly rear its head, to drive him mad with terror. . . . The shop was close and hot. The atmosphere seemed tainted with the smell of coffins. The recess beneath the counter in which his flock mattress was thrust looked like a grave. . . . he wished, as he crept into his narrow bed, that that were his coffin, and that he could be lain in a calm and lasting sleep in the churchyard ground. . . . (75)

Though not actually in the dream state, Oliver is close to it. And as he approaches the unconscious, Dickens reveals the disturbing, seemingly anomalous desire for death in childhood: a wish the surrealists would have considered one of those "contradictions" that should be reconciled.

Another noteworthy element in this description is the close, stifling atmosphere of the basement that suggests the feeling of suffocation that is often characteristic of the nightmare. Fear of suffocation runs throughout *Oliver Twist*, emphasizing the fine line Oliver (as well as Nancy, Sikes, Fagin, and Rose) walk between life and death. The motif is present in other novels, most notably in *The Mystery of Edwin Drood*. The fictional world of Cloisterham is remarkably still and constrictive—almost as if it were sinking into the cathedral crypt that lies beneath it. Interesting too is Dickens's withholding the name of the village until the third chapter. Rather than immediately establishing a location for the reader and thus rendering a sense of reality to his setting, he begins the novel with a dream in which the dreamer cannot locate where he is: "An ancient Cathedral town? How can the ancient English Cathedral town be here!" (37). Hence Dickens forces the reader to question the reality of his world right from the beginning. This technique of using an unnamed and hermetic setting resembles the effect of Chirico's novel *Hebdomeros*: "What these people are doing is not made clear. We do not even know where 'here' is, nor why Hebdomeros wishes to escape. Chirico leaves us with the impression—which becomes clearer and clearer as the novel progresses—that we are reading a novel which can only be described as obstinately closed and hermetic" (Matthews; *Surrealism and the Novel* 75). This is of course the sensation we experience in *Oliver Twist* and, with even more eerie intensity, in Dickens's last novel, *The Mystery of Edwin Drood*. Perhaps the most striking surrealist element in the above passage from *Oliver Twist* is the death-wish the boy expresses as he focuses on the coffin, an object to which Oliver responds with the antithetical feelings of attraction and fear. This conflicting and intense reaction to an object exemplifies the surrealist perception of how an object should affect its viewer. Marcel Jean and Arpad Mezei explain:

> . . . the surrealists, and Chirico himself in particular, rediscovered the object: a new object containing a large admixture of subjectivity, in the shape of Desire. But desire also implies resistance, is a limited, defined tendency, and by its very nature presupposes a certain degree of restraint. So that an object, in the surrealist sense of the word, is a complex of fantasy and restraint, of desire and resistance, which possesses a material substance. (243)

The coffin is at once a concrete expression of Oliver's primordial fear of and desire for self-destruction, a desire that Freud argues is shared by all men. In this sense as well, the coffin is a surrealist object, since the surrealists attempted to create an object as a sort of Jungian archetype, an "image in which each of us can recognize his own desire" (Jean and Mezei 243).

Dickens takes other modern approaches to dreams in *Oliver Twist* that anticipate surrealism. Chapter 28, for example, relates how a dazed, semiconscious Oliver stumbles blindly alone after the attempted robbery and hallucinates that he is reliving the events of the previous night. A montage of "rapid visions" focusing on Sikes, Crackit, and gunfire flashes across his mind. This visual condensation of experience is, according to Freud, characteristic of a dream or hallucination. Dickens anticipates Freud's theory in his depiction of Esther Summerson's dreams as well. As she describes them, her dreams compress past experiences of childhood and adulthood together, making it impossible for her to distinguish individual time periods. All the past becomes merely one small part of her dreams: "I had never known before how short life really was, and into how small a space the mind could put it" (431). Understanding the compressive nature of dreams, surrealist painters such as Max Ernst tried to imitate condensation in collages or frottages where apparently unrelated or disjunctive elements or objects illustrate a condensation of dream thoughts.

Oliver's hallucinations, as the Sowerberry episode illustrates, also cause him to attribute other dimensions to elements of external reality—a sort of reverse of dream condensation. His childish sensations act upon objects and thus present the reader with a host of possible realities. The intensity of these sensations is so keenly described that external reality seems to lose a definite value since objects are continually subject to alteration through Oliver's imagination. Dickens also explores this technique in the second chapter of *Great Expectations* where Pip, frightened on his nighttime journey to the graveyard, transforms his surroundings into phantasmagorical shapes (14). The intensity of Pip's imagination leaves such a distinct impression as to establish initially a confusion for the reader over what is illusion and what is reality: a dominant concern of the novel and, in fact, most of Dickens's novels. *Martin Chuzzlewit* also presents objects that are constantly undergoing change. In this novel, however, the change does not stem from the viewer's perception but is an inherent part of the object. In fact, the viewer himself is subject to the same change that occurs in the external objects he perceives. J. Hillis Miller offers a fascinating interpretation of the relation between object and viewer in the novel:

> He is at the mercy of these things and especially at the mercy of their motion. There is no stability in the world he sees, but more astonishingly, he discovers that to this constant metamorphosis of things there corresponds a metamorphosis of himself. When something changes in the scene outside himself, he too changes. The perpetual change in things imposes itself on the spectator until, in the end, he exists as the same person only in the infinitesimal moment of an enduring sensation. (117)

The surrealists defined and implemented a concept strikingly similar to what we see in Dickens's work; crucial to their art was the concept of "critical paranoia." Jean and Mezei elaborate on this term: "A given reality suggests two, three or more different ones (depending on the individual's imaginative capacity), each one as acceptable as the original since each variation can be perceived and accepted as real by others. . . . From which the proposed conclusion is that it is impossible to concede any value whatsoever to immediate reality, since it may represent or mean anything at all" (207). Certainly, the external world of *Oliver Twist* has little "immediate value" if we take the novel only on a realistic level, since Dickens encourages the same confusion between fantasy and reality in his reader that Oliver experiences. In fact, Harry Stone observes that in no other novel does Dickens so strongly suggest supernatural explanations of realistic events. Stone points to two scenes to support his thesis. The first is the episode in chapter 32 when Oliver sees the Chertsey house where he had been taken before the robbery and that has now been transformed completely. Dickens never explains the reason for this transformation, leaving the reader to wonder whether a supernatural cause is at work.

This fairy-tale illogic is precisely what the surrealists considered as part of reality along with the physical world. As Anna Balakian explains, what attracted the surrealists to the fairy tale was the fact that it had been "the only form of art that reconciled the contradictions which even the most imaginative adult mind found to exist between reality and the dream" (83). Similarly, by leaving no rational explanation for his reader, Dickens encourages a vision of reality that, like the fairy-tale world, presents realistic detail side by side with fantasy, finding its illogic in the logic that creates it.

Stone also refers to the scene in chapter 34 in which Oliver at twilight (symbolic of the threshold between dream and reality) falls into the same half-waking, half-dreaming state in which he saw Fagin gazing over his jewels. This episode is particularly noteworthy not only for its fairy-tale structure but also for its surrealist approach toward the dream state. As in other episodes where terror overtakes him and presages the approach of the nightmare world, Oliver feels the air grow close and confined as he dreams that he is back in Fagin's den. Dickens's description here of the dream state is unusual because it emphasizes a sleep in which the conscious and the unconscious work upon each other—again, a surrealist reconciliation of opposites:

> So far as an overpowering heaviness, a prostration of strength, and an utter inability to control our thoughts or power of motion, can be called sleep, this is it; and yet, we have a consciousness of all that is going on about us, and, if we dream at such a time, words which are really spoken, or sounds which really exist at the moment, accommodate themselves with surprising readiness to our visions, until reality and imagination become so strangely blended that it is afterwards almost a matter of impossibility to separate the two. . . . (309)

The idea of external reality working with the unconscious to form a new vision clearly anticipates surrealism. Moreover, the description of how an object unapprehended by consciousness can affect our visions resembles the surrealist notion of the object's or image's function. Generally scornful of traditional symbolism that was based on the obvious and logical representative nature of objects, the surrealists created their objects to appeal to the unconscious; hence, their meaning or value in external reality or consciousness is, to use Dickens's word, "silent."

Oliver's vision in this episode is of Fagin and Monks standing within touching distance, a vision that lasts "but an instant." And when Oliver, Ralph Maylie, and Mr. Losberne pursue these intruders, they discover only that they have vanished. There are no marks of the criminals' flight, even though they covered terrain that would normally have left tell-tale signs. Their disappearance seems magical.

Certainly on a rational level, one could argue as Ralph Maylie does that Oliver was simply dreaming, which he was in part. However,

Dickens strongly encourages us to believe in the reality of that dream vision—to forego rationality, reconcile the workings of the unconscious with the conscious, and accept Fagin and Monk's appearance as more than a projection of Oliver's imagination. At the novel's end, in fact, their appearance is confirmed by Brownlow. Dickens, though, never closes up the question of the unmarked ground, thereby encouraging the reader to accept the apparent illogic of an actual event with supernatural characteristics. And an event, moreover, that marks the intrusion of evil into the pristine world of the Maylies, making the demarcation of opposites even more blurred.

Dickens's use of shadows and light, his emphasis on darkness, and his employment of liminal imagery are also important to an understanding of how he deliberately blurs the line between fantasy and reality in *Oliver Twist*. Surrealist painters used shadows frequently to give a supernatural aura to their landscapes; the early work of Picasso (for example, *Factory, Horta del Ebro* [1907]) uses deep, menacing shadows in which hard lights gleam, visual representations that disturb the viewer with their unreality. Similarly, Dickens played with the dramatic possibilities of light and shadow to instill confusion in his characters and his readers. In chapter 18, he describes how the dim light afforded in Fagin's den "made the rooms more gloomy, and filled them with strange shadows" (179); these shadowed rooms provoke a sense of fear and disorientation in Oliver. Shadows, in fact, abound in *Oliver Twist*, functioning visually as expressionist projections of Oliver's terror. This use of light and shadow to create an alien, unreal atmosphere occurs more frequently and is much more developed in his later novels such as *Bleak House*, particularly in the Dedlock scenes where Dickens so vividly describes "The Ghost's Walk" in terms of shadows and bright lighting (498-99). In fact, many of the physical descriptions in *Bleak House* are in harsh tones of black and white. Noteworthy also is that much of *Oliver Twist* takes place at night, a mystical time for the surrealists. As Breton explains: "During the night hours man, like the child and the primitive, faces all his fears and his feelings of the infinite. . . ." (63). As in numerous surrealist paintings and novels, darkness pervades *Oliver Twist*. Many of the events associated with the world of Fagin occur at night or in dark rooms where day never enters. Darkness, however, suggests uncertainty and mystery as well as evil, for it is also the time when Oliver faces his fears of the supernatural.

A surprising number of the scenes in *Oliver Twist*, as in surrealist painting, also occurs at dawn: Nancy's murder, Oliver's embarkation for London, the departure of Sikes and Oliver for the robbery, and so on. In these scenes we can also see how Dickens played with the suggestive power of light and darkness to create an unreal and often menacing atmosphere. In the episode where Sikes and Oliver depart for the robbery, for example, Dickens presents the dawn as a time of uncertainty and confusion—a reversal of the traditional notion of dawn bringing the light that symbolizes understanding or direction: "There was a faint glimmering of the coming day in the sky; but it rather aggravated than relieved the gloom of the scene: the sombre light only serving to pale that which the street lamps afforded, without shedding any warmer or brighter tints upon the wet house tops and dreary streets" (202).

The visual quality of *Oliver Twist* has, admittedly, been recognized by Dickens scholars as one of the novel's merits. While they are quick to praise the pictorial nature of the work, they have far more problems with its structure. Most readers tend to see the extreme coincidences and highly improbable plot as detracting from the novel's realism.[2] A surrealist approach, however, helps refute such judgments in that we can examine the coincidences not strictly in terms of plot and structure but as part of a thematic whole emphasizing the reconciliation between fantasy and reality.

Oliver's world, including both "camps" of wickedness and goodness, is a world of chance. Practically everything that happens to Oliver is fortuitous: his encounter with Brownlow, who just happens to be the best friend of his dead father; his accidental arrival at the Maylies', where his unacknowledged sister Rose just happens to be; his chance meeting with the "artful Dodger," and so on. Admittedly, these coincidences seem contrived and inconsistent with Dickens's realistic, often naturalistic, depictions. If, however, we attempt to see these apparently opposing elements as a logical whole, we can conclude that they are yet further examples of the surrealist world of *Oliver Twist*, a world that has its logic in its very illogic.

At the heart of surrealism lies the concept of objective chance, defined as the belief that "inexplicable coincidence is central to reality, which is not an orderly system of events apprehensible by logical thought" (Osborne 529). The surrealists, in fact, considered chance to be the governing universal force rather than an order created by an omnipotent being or scientific determinism. In a surrealist world "disorder becomes the real God and providence which is generally revered as the manifestation of the mystical order of things, gives way to the worship of hazard, or chance, the mystical manifestation of the inconceivable but extant disorder of things" (Balakian 11). This is why, of course, the surrealists were fascinated by the irrational and seemingly random workings of the dream that they saw as an analogy to the irrational workings of coincidence. If we therefore accept Stoehr's thesis that Dickens tried to present a reality that was dreamlike, we must accept these coincidences as consistent with that reality.

Dickens represents this world governed by chance primarily through the image of the labyrinth, an important image for the surrealists as well. His London streets are narrow, winding mazes that hold the continual possibility of threat or surprise. Such labyrinths abound in *Martin Chuzzlewit*, *Bleak House*, and *The Mystery of Edwin Drood*. In these novels, however, it is the adults who are lost or subject to terror. The surrealists also saw the street as a terrain of discovery, disorder, and confusion. Chirico created maze-like porticoes and streets in many of his paintings, for example, in *The Anxious Voyage*. These mazes imply to the viewer the presence of something beyond what the painting depicts—perhaps an apparition that waits to be discovered. Paul Delvaux's night-enshrouded winding streets also suggest a haunted domain. Similarly, the labyrinthine passageways of *Oliver Twist* create anticipation in Oliver and, arguably, in the reader as well, of some hidden terror or marvel. Oliver's initial journey to London, for example, is marked by an emphasis on the dark, narrow streets that seem filled with continual threats and surprises:

> The street was very narrow and muddy, and the air was impregnated with filthy odours. There were a good many small shops; but the only stock in trade appeared to be heaps of children, who, even at that time of night, were crawling in and out of doors, or screaming from the inside. . . . Covered ways and yards, which here and there diverged from the main street, disclosed little knots of houses, where drunken men and women were positively wallowing in filth; and from several of the doorways, great ill-looking fellows were cautiously emerging. . . . (103)

Among the threats that exist in this world where anything can happen are phantoms, the reality of which is reinforced by Dickens's subjecting the adult mind of Sikes to them as well. As Sikes flees from the scene of the murder and journeys to London, he is haunted by a persistent vision of Nancy. The ghost is, on the realistic level, a projection of Sikes's guilt; yet on a deeper level, it is also a fruition of the supernatural sense that pervades the landscape. Like Dickens, the surrealists intended to bring to life within the subjective human experience and ordinary reality the active presence of a haunted domain. Hence Breton and many others were drawn to the Gothic novel in much the same way as Dickens was. The typical Gothic trappings of ghosts, castles, romance, and nightmare intrigue appealed to the surrealists because they seemed to be drawn largely from the realm of dream and nightmare. *Oliver Twist*, like many surrealist novels, employs Gothic devices not simply to advance plot or heighten atmosphere, but also to incorporate the supernatural within a realistic setting and give a reality to the visions of the unconscious.

In order to heighten an anticipation of supernatural discovery, many surrealist painters invested their landscapes with a suggestive stillness. Chirico's landscapes, for example, are often set in the slumberous quiet of late afternoon. Their very absence of motion indicates to the viewer that they contain something that, although not visible, is nevertheless present and perhaps about to be revealed. Dickens does this as well. Though *Oliver Twist* employs an active and crowded plot, there is still the frequent sense of an uncanny cessation of movement. The London streets and Fagin's den are close and hot and therefore restrict freedom and force one to wait passively for discovery. Moreover, Dickens's emphasis on night, twilight, and dawn, generally times of silence and depopulation, powerfully evokes the supernatural: "It was a cold, dark night. The stars seemed, to the boy's eyes, farther from the earth than he had ever seen them before; there was no wind; and the sombre shadows thrown by the trees upon the ground, looked sepulchral and death-like, from being so still" (95).

This cessation of movement is particularly important for the surrealists because it is a characteristic of what they term the absolute. At this point, the infinite becomes reality; man has transcended the barriers of life and death and all contradictions cease to be perceived as such. Unlike the Romantics, who regarded movement as the traditional symbol of escape from the physical world to the infinite, the surrealists believed man can realize eternity by getting at the essence of material reality; movement is therefore an antithesis of the absolute. A key to achieving the infinite was stripping objects of their physical nature; thus, the surrealists had a "tendency to disregard the natural phenomenon and to refuse to imitate it in art: by divesting it of the concepts of time, space, and movement" (Balakian 97). Similarly, Dickens suggests in *Oliver Twist* that a landscape divorced from movement holds some sort of revelatory power. There are several scenes where Oliver senses something unearthly—something suggestive of another, hidden reality—when he is left alone in the stillness of a landscape at night or dawn.

However, for both *Oliver Twist* and surrealist works the realm of the unconscious or fantasy is not entirely comprised of nightmare elements. As there is an insistence by Dickens on the reality of such horrific elements as phantoms, so too is there an insistence on a paradise lost. Children such as Oliver and Little Dick, who have that state of grace so important to the surrealists and the Romantics that enables them to perceive the infinite, are allowed to glimpse this paradise through dreaming. In a description of Oliver's initial sleep at the Maylie home that has Platonic overtones, Dickens posits the existence of a "former and happier life which no voluntary exertion of the mind can ever recall" (268).

At the center of Oliver's dreams is Agnes, who emerges, despite her illicit affair with Oliver's father, as a sort of divine mother and woman. Interestingly, the surrealists also regarded woman as a mystical being, the very projection of the marvelous into our dreary existence. Paul Delvaux's paintings, for example, portray women who are ethereally lovely; the largeness and haunted expression of their eyes as well as the translucent fairness of their skin recall, for example, Edgar Allan Poe's "Ligeia" who also functioned as a catalyst between man and an unknown world. Woman, for these artists, is man's key to reclaiming that paradise lost, one of their fundamental motivating impulses. Without pressing the point too far, perhaps it is possible to see Dickens's treatment of Agnes as anticipatory of how the surrealists view women. Though Agnes dies at the beginning, her presence is nevertheless felt throughout the novel by Oliver and Brownlow. For both boy and adult, her image conjures up thoughts of a higher, spiritual reality in which all anxiety and suffering will be gone. Hence Agnes functions as an intermediary between men and the unknown. To a limited extent, we may view Rose Maylie this way as well. Her role is not so much to participate actively in the plot of the novel as to fulfill the symbolic function of representing goodness in an unfair, confusing, and often evil world. Her near-death, an aspect of the novel that has often been criticized, thus signifies the precariousness of goodness' existence in material reality rather than Dickens's weak attempt at a twist in plot. Similarly, women in surrealist fiction are often passive characters, serving only to bring the male protagonist to some sort of recognition of the divine. Their end in fact is often a sudden or violent death; in Julien Gracq's novel *Au Chateau d'Argol*, Heide, the woman who acts as the catalyst for the self-discovery of other characters, is the victim of a sadistic and brutal attack that ends in her death. Her tragedy is Gracq's statement that the woman who acts as intermediary to the unknown world has no lasting place in material reality—that indeed she is too good for this world.

To reclaim this lost paradise in *Oliver Twist*, one must, as Oliver does, surrender to the unconscious as well as the conscious and to the fantastical as well as external world. Rationality and logic that place trust only in what is known to external reality hold little value and meaning in *Oliver Twist*. Dickens's novels illustrate the belief that it is not in our disorder but in our order that confusion and terror lie, a belief that culminates in his later novels, particularly *Bleak House*, where system equals chaos and human truth is often spoken in the voices of the insane. However, it also applies to the early novel *Oliver Twist*, where a complex world of apparent opposites cannot be grasped by logic, but through submission to dreams and our unconscious, wherein the magical mysteries of unknown worlds await.

From *South Atlantic Review* 54, no. 2 (May 1989): 41-58. Copyright © 1989 by the South Atlantic Modern Language Association. Reprinted by permission of the South Atlantic Modern Language Association.

Notes

I would like to thank Dr. Charles Edge for his comments and his kindness.

1. Dali's *The Persistence of Memory*, Brauner's *The Inner Life*, and Magritte's *The Human Condition* are definitive examples of this technique.

2. See George Gissing's chapter on *Oliver Twist* (43-57) and Angus Wilson's "Introduction" (13).

Works Cited

Balakian, Anna. *Literary Origins of Surrealism: A New Mysticism in French Poetry.* New York: New York UP, 1947.

Bernard, Catherine A. "Dickens and Victorian Dream Theory." *Annals of the New York Academy of Sciences* 360 (1981): 197-216.

Bigsby, C. W. E. *Dada and Surrealism.* London: Methuen, 1972.

Breton, André. *Manifestoes of Surrealism.* Trans. Richard Seaver and Helen R. Lane. Ann Arbor: U of Michigan P, 1969.

Cardinal, Roger and Robert Stuart Short. *Surrealism: Permanent Revelation.* London: Studio Vista, 1970.

Chirico, Giorgio de. *Hebdomeros.* London: Owen, 1968.

Crevel, René. *Babylone.* Paris: Simon Kra, 1927.

Dickens, Charles. *Bleak House.* 1852-1853. New York: Norton, 1977.

_____. *Great Expectations.* 1860-1861. London: Oxford UP, 1953.

_____. *Martin Chuzzlewit.* 1843-1844. London: Oxford UP, 1951.

_____. *The Mystery of Edwin Drood.* 1870. New York: Penguin, 1974.

_____. *Oliver Twist.* 1837-1839. New York: Penguin, 1966.

Freud, Sigmund. *The Interpretation of Dreams.* 1913. Trans. A. A. Brill. New York: Modern Library, 1950.

Gissing, George. *Critical Studies of the Works of Charles Dickens.* New York: Greenberg, 1924.

Gracq, Julien. *Au Chateau d'Argol.* Paris: José Corti, 1967.

Jean, Marcel and Arpad Mezei. *The History of Surrealist Painting.* Trans. Simon Watson Taylor. London: Weidenfeld and Nicholson, 1960.

Lewes, George Henry. "Dickens in Relation to Criticism." *Literary Criticism of George Henry Lewes.* Ed. Alice R. Kaminsky. Lincoln: U of Nebraska P, 1964.

Marcus, Steven. *Dickens: From Pickwick to Dombey.* New York: Basic Books, 1965.

Matthews, J. H. *An Introduction to Surrealism.* University Park: Penn State UP, 1965.

_____. *Surrealism and the Novel.* Ann Arbor: U of Michigan P, 1969.

Miller, J. Hillis. *Charles Dickens: The World of His Novels.* Cambridge: Harvard UP, 1958.

Osborne, Harold, ed. *The Oxford Companion to Twentieth Century Art.* Oxford: Oxford UP, 1981.

Rohrberger, Mary. "The Daydream and the Nightmare: Surreality in *Oliver Twist.*" *Studies in Humanities* 6 (1978): 21-28.

Stoehr, Taylor. *Dickens: The Dreamer's Stance.* Ithaca: Cornell UP, 1965.

Stone, Harry. *Dickens and the Invisible World.* Bloomington: Indiana UP, 1979.

Wilson, Angus. "Introduction." *Oliver Twist.* New York: Penguin, 1966. 11-27.

CRITICAL
READINGS

Another Version of Pastoral:
Oliver Twist

Joseph M. Duffy, Jr.

> "What is your name?"
>
> "Got none."
>
> "Where do you live?"
>
> "Live! What's that?"
>
> *—The Haunted Man*

The question of how men are to live in a world which seems so little geared to their accommodation is of primary concern in all Dickens' novels. The depth and heaviness of the way in which the majority of men are compelled to live make up the travail of the actual which is variously confronted by major characters from Samuel Pickwick at the moment of his entry into Fleet Street Prison to Eugene Wrayburn in *Our Mutual Friend* who would prefer an existence "on an isolated rock in a stormy sea" (I, xii, 145)[1] over the exacerbating boredom of his present vassalage to society. It is not a matter of physical or economic survival that is at issue, though failure in both may also occur, but it is rather the human need to reconcile a widely cherished dream of what life ought to be like with the apprehension of what it really is. By the nineteenth century the world which had once seemed a sphere turning in accord with some celestial music had become a battleground where the forces of order and chaos appeared locked in tenebrous conflict. The gap between the individual and the universal appeared to be un-bridgeable, for there was, as the narrator in *Our Mutual Friend* observes, an "immensity of space between mankind and Heaven" (IV, vi, 689).

Such as it was, the busy, discordant world of the nineteenth-century English might be evaluated as an unconvincing counterfeit of a treasured Platonic ideal or as a place of rayless exile from some abandoned glory. One of the most affecting images of the forlorn child in nineteenth-century literature is that of "the lovely Boy" in Book VII of *The Prelude*, isolated at a tavern among "dissolute men and shameless women," who appears to the speaker to be in his innocent childhood "Like one of those who walked with hair unsinged/ Amid the fiery furnace." By the end of the century the early death which Wordsworth had in charity wished for the yet uncorrupted London boy is grimly accorded Sorrow, the illegitimate baby in *Tess of the D'Urbervilles*, who is buried according to merciless church custom among the "unbaptized infants, notorious drunkards, suicides, and others of the conjecturally damned. . . ." The inhospitableness of this earthly environment is dramatized by the plight of the child who feels the poignancy of his own condition, who like Arnold's "Gipsy Child by the Sea-Shore" has a dream sadder than any exile's and a sorrow more forlorn than any angel's. Nowhere is this helpless awareness of the world-besieged child manifested with more contrasting detail than in the account of the "adventures" of Oliver Twist.

In *Oliver Twist* the disparity between the real and the ideal is delineated in the simple, and often simplistic, lines of the moral fable. Even the reader who knows the tale well experiences in rereading the obsessive appeal of a fabulous recital which defines antinomies of black and white in human affairs. Since the characters of *Oliver Twist* are unmistakably stamped with marks of good and bad, the audience is not perplexed by subtleties of motive and action in the story. In order to achieve this effect of simplicity, the representation does not include any significant ambiguity of character or incident. For modern readers who are attached to the craft of character development, such a figure as Oliver may seem stiff and sentimental and Fagin hysterical and grotesque. These representations are as stylized, however, as the masks of tragedy or, better still, as the masks of tribal dancers. Because Oliver does not speak in the ordinary manner of children (or anyone else), his portrayal may seem to be preposterously stilted:

'So lonely, sir! So very lonely!' cried the child. 'Everybody hates me. Oh! sir, don't don't pray be cross to me!' The child beat his hand upon his heart; and looked in his companion's face, with tears of real agony. (IV, 23)

But Oliver is not an imitation of a real child in his speech and action; like the children in Blake's poems whose songs are equally removed from natural speech, he is an emblem of vulnerable and threatened innocence.

Oliver is the reverse of the idealized figure in Keats' letters who would, from the spark of divinity within him, create his soul amid the circumstances of this world. But this is the heroic and tragic destiny that Keats so readily confronted and that novelists rarely engage themselves with: the destiny of the Lear-inspired man who must "burn through" "the fierce dispute/ Betwixt damnation and impassion'd clay." Similar to many worthy characters in art and life, Oliver is minor in every detail of his being including his geniality of spirit. The boy's spark of divine fire needs to be protected against the inundation of the world, and his soul is made for him by others, particularly by Brownlow, so that he does not create his destiny as much as he inherits and accepts it.

Even more passively tugged through the labyrinthine ways of his life than K. in Kafka's fiction, Oliver is like an object that is taken up, handled, and put in place rather than an individual who controls his own movement. He is introduced to this world "of sorrow and trouble" as an "item of mortality" who will be "a new burden" (I, 1-2) for the parish; in boyhood he is advertised as a commodity with a five pound bounty attached available to the businessman who will relieve the public of his presence. Society with its money ethic recognizes the orphan in no other terms than as a liability or an asset, for as a pauper he has nothing to do "'with soul or spirit'" (VII, 41). This is the voice of the world speaking through Mr. Bumble and announcing its own narrow system of election and damnation. And the world, according to the narrator in *Nicholas Nickleby*, is "a conventional phrase, which, being interpreted, often signifieth all the rascals in it. . . ." (III, 41).

In novel after novel, Dickens traced the effects of this system on those who suffered from the world's great exclusion. Initially not at all lacking in "soul or spirit," the children of poverty are, like most children, susceptible to adult influence and adult experience for the development or erasure of that spirit. If they have been completely isolated and have never had comprehensible acquaintance either with cruelty or affection, they become what would now be called "autistic" like the unnamed boy in *The Haunted Man*. In some cases they may be trained to become part of the social organization: they are passed through a rigidly practical and emotionally insensitive educational process and are turned out as frosty moral and emotional geldings like Bitzer in *Hard Times* who is appropriately light-eyed, light-haired, and pale or like Charley Hexam in *Our Mutual Friend* who advises his sister, Lizzie, to "control" her "fancies" and look into "the real world" (II, i, 128). Or, already shunned by the respectable world, these children may become outcasts like the derisive goblins who enjoy the perverse freedom of Fagin's postlapsarian Eden. Sometimes a nearly dehumanized child, a Jo in *Bleak House* who "lives—that is to say, Jo has not yet died—in a ruinous place, known to the like of him by the name of Tom-all-Alone's" (XVI, 219-220), is exalted by the personal care of Allan Woodcourt and made fit, if not for life in this world, at least for human passage out of it. These children become, then, the product of what is done for or to them. To a great extent Oliver's history is determined by the accident of his birth which accounts both for Fagin's persecution and Brownlow's concern. In addition, during the time of the novel he is faced with the threat of Fagin's malign influence and he also enjoys the protective affection of the Maylies and of Brownlow. As an unesteemed orphan the boy may, to the official mind, have nothing to do "with soul or spirit." At the same time the circumstances imposed upon him in the city and the country are so unique and extreme that his person is potentially a rare environment for the cultivation or the blighting of such spirit.

Except for his flight from the Sowerberrys' which he initiates, Oliver is subjected to adventitious experience, and the contest for his life seems to be waged outside of himself. His early survival under the "protecting care" of the aptly named Mrs. Mann is accidental since the majority of her charges "sickened from want and cold, or fell into the fire from neglect, or got half-smothered by accident . . ." (II, 4). When

Oliver is put out into the world as a piece of chattel for exploitation, he is saved by the authorities from Gamfield, the chimney-sweep, as fortuitously as he is handed over by Bumble to Sowerberry, the undertaker. On the road after his flight Oliver meets up with John Dawkins who leads him to Fagin; he is in turn taken from Fagin through Brownlow, abducted back by Nancy, and finally rescued by the Maylies. Managed almost by anyone who comes in contact with him, the boy is like a puppet plucked by strings manipulated above and beyond his view. But a puppet has both the security and bondage of his strings while Oliver does not know who he is or, often, where he is. At both the literal and the metaphorical level he can not find his way on his own. He is lost within the strangeness of Fagin's den, wakes up baffled in Brownlow's home, and falls unconscious at the Maylie threshold. Nor is he able to chart a course through the maze-like passages of London and even loses himself on the brief errand for Brownlow by "accidentally" turning "down a by-street" (I, 95). Although children usually have minimal freedom in settling the direction of their lives, Oliver seems more liable than most to the caprice of circumstance, to the chance benevolence or cruelty of his elders, and, importantly, to the uncommon helplessness of his own nature.

Oliver's latent humanity is used with rough indifference by those who represent the rule and custom of the social order. At the workhouse he is one among many charges who are confined and abused by supervising moral derelicts; and at the Sowerberrys' he is fed a dog's leavings, bedded down among the coffins, and persecuted for his social inferiority by the charity-boy, Noah Claypole, who at least is not an orphan. The cruelty of the Fagin world is much sharper and more personal but also more confusing because it is ambiguously mingled with the expression of boyish fellowship and with comic affection as well as suddenly fervid tenderness on Fagin's part. Oliver's position is so strange that there seem to be no advances he can make either of language or gesture that will enable him to communicate to others his dimly-felt identity or to understand and define theirs. Although Nancy warns him accurately that he is "hedged round and round" (XX, 131), the orphan can find in the dingy men who surround him and in their soiled habitat nothing that will give off a reflection of the danger he knows is impending. He only feels the profundity of his isolation from the ordinary world, the numbing quality of his ignorance, and the undefinable danger in his weakness. Oliver gazes drearily out at a world which mirrors nothing of himself that will help him to know it better or his own disposition:

> In all the rooms, the mouldering shutters were fast closed: and the bars which held them were screwed tight into the wood; the only light which was admitted, stealing its way through round holes at the top: which made the rooms more gloomy, and filled them with strange shadows. There was a back-garret window, with rusty bars outside, which had no shutter; and out of this, Oliver often gazed with a melancholy face for hours together; but nothing was to be descried from it but a confused and crowded mass of house-tops, blackened chimneys, and gable-ends. Sometimes, indeed, a ragged grizzly head might be seen, peering over the parapet wall of a distant house: but it was quickly withdrawn again; and as the window of Oliver's observatory was nailed down, and dimmed with the rain and smoke of years, it was as much as he could do to make out the forms of the different objects beyond, without making any attempt to be seen or heard,— which he had as much chance of being, as if he had lived inside the ball of St. Paul's Cathedral. (XVIII, 115)

Because of its dimness, its stillness, and its silence, the city outside appears shut in, and empty. Alone in the quarters to which he had been so mysteriously confined, Oliver glimpses a shadowy chaos of forms which seem to be a dismal extension of the already sombre object world within Fagin's tenement where the weaving of indefatigable spiders and the scampering of terrified mice are the only evidence of life. What living elements exist outside are probably more portentous than reassuring: the quick surreptitious appearance and withdrawal of the "ragged grizzly head" is a rodent-like movement. Life in the city so diminishes its inhabitants that the slum-dwellers are like rats and Fagin like a reptile and man like a dog or dog like a man in the Sikes relationship with his cur. In Wordsworth's "Westminster Bridge" sonnet the city is beautiful in its quietness and seems "asleep" with its "mighty heart lying still" while here it appears inert and "heartless" with all its usual tormented energy suppressed. As a composition of molecules occupying space Oliver must have some conviction of his reality, but otherwise, melancholy in appearance, his thoughts still, usually crouched "in the corner of the passage by the street-door, to be as near living people as he could," the boy is experiencing a lack of relationship to other beings so complete as to annihilate his personal identity. He is undergoing a psychic testing prepared by Fagin so that he will "prefer any society to the companionship of his own sad thoughts in such a dreary place. . . ." (XVIII, 120).

Another aspect of this record of Oliver's lonely vigil is its dreamlike quality. Oliver in his observatory is as unreal as the world upon which he looks—or as real. Again and again in the novel the dream as fact or metaphor is used to describe the insubstantial character of Oliver's existence. The dream state may be actual as is the case during the boy's illness at Brownlow's when it is benign and peaceful and so like death as to make death seem a gracious release from care:

> Gradually, he fell into that deep tranquil sleep which ease from recent suffering alone imparts; that calm and peaceful rest which it is pain to wake from. Who, if this were death, would be roused again to all the struggles and turmoils of life; to all its cares for the present; its anxieties for the future; more than all, its weary recollections of the past! (XII, 69-70)

Here, as elsewhere in Dickens, death, the ultimate insubstantial state, is a temptation to a man in the midst of life: it is not a summons to perfected being, a portal to the irrefragable now, which Keats sometimes celebrates (although it does include the Keatsian forgetfulness of chaffing circumstance), but a deliverance from consciousness which always nags man into knowing his present misery. Because reality is so vivid, so energetic, so much larger and more powerful than human feeling, and so indifferent to it, a man—or a boy—is apt to break his heart against the hardness of the actual world—and he is always tempted to seek an anodyne rather than submit to this heavy fate. The dream of heaven, the careless life of childhood, sleep, and death are all corresponding modes of security in Dickens' fiction. Emerging from sleep to the consciousness of Fagin's room, Oliver watches through half closed eyes the old man examining his stolen wealth:

> Although Oliver had roused himself from sleep, he was not thoroughly awake. There is a drowsy state, between sleeping and waking, when you dream more in five minutes with your eyes half open, and yourself half conscious of everything that is passing around you, than you would in five nights with your eyes fast closed, and your senses wrapt in perfect uncon-sciousness. At such times, a mortal knows just enough of what his mind is doing, to form some glimmering conception of its mighty powers: its bounding from earth and spurning time and space: when freed from the re-straint of its corporeal associate. (IX, 51)

It is better to lie in bed, safe from the urgencies of time and dreamily suspended above the menace of the actual. When Oliver creeps into his "narrow bed" at the Sowerberrys', he wishes "that that were his coffin; and that he could be laid in a calm and lasting sleep in the churchyard ground: with the tall grass waving gently above his head: and the sound of the old deep bell to soothe him in his sleep" (V, 26). The quiet orderly routine of the Brownlow household resembles the peace of heaven:

> They were happy days, those of Oliver's recovery. Everything was so quiet, and neat, and orderly; everybody so kind and gentle; that after the noise and turbulence in the midst of which he had always lived, it seemed like Heaven itself. (XIV, 83)

At the end of the novel a visit to the workhouse recalls the boy's old painful life so vividly that all the intervening pleasant days seem like a dream: "there was nearly everything as if he had left it but yesterday, and all his recent life had been but a happy dream" (LI, 349).

When, therefore, Oliver stands observing the city from his confinement at Fagin's, the claustral moodiness of this scene is complexly relevant to the point of view of the novel. Unlike the Malloy-Malone-Unnamable complex of characters (or character) in Beckett's fiction who have their thickly oppressive consciousness and their strong bodily awareness to assert against the obscurity and insubstantiality of the external world, Oliver has only his thin and splintered layer of past memory and murky apprehension of the present to serve him in identifying himself and in relating that self to the object world outside. But here the solitary orphan can only be identified as another object and not defined as a person; he too is opaque as are the grotesque shapes he sees. Perhaps no more can be said of the real world of people and places than that it is a jumble of objects which can be ordered only as in a dream arranged and shaped by the imagination.

Such an ordering occurs tentatively in the pastoral setting of the Maylie residence and finally in the little society presided over by Brownlow at the end of the novel. In his perplexed captivity, Oliver can only wait to be moved from the limbo of his present by some external force. At this point in the novel that force is Fagin who restores the boy to the company of thieves. Oliver's laugh sounds "heartily" at the capers of this frolicsome group and at Fagin's stories of his own career. By his laughter Oliver implicates himself in a world which had been remote and baffling to him, and the narrator observes sententiously but accurately that Fagin was "now slowly instilling into his soul the poison which he hoped would blacken it, and change its hue forever" (XVIII, 120). In giving Oliver over to Bill Sikes for the Maylie burglary, however, Fagin frustrates his own design. For it is this final exploitation of the boy that leads almost to his death and then to his renewal to a new life in the country environment.

II

Whereas the city in *Oliver Twist* is always viewed as grimy, lurid, or festering, the country is always fair and blossoming. The Maylies live at Chertsey on the upper Thames, one of those "pleasant little towns" described in *Our Mutual Friend* where "you may hear the fall of water over the weirs, or even, in still weather, the rustle of the rushes; and from the bridge you may see the young river, dimpled like a young child, playfully gliding away among the trees, unpolluted by the defilements that lie in wait for it on its course, and as yet out of hearing of the deep summons of the sea" (III, viii, 504). During Oliver's recovery "when the fine warm weather had fairly begun, and every tree and flower was putting forth its young leaves and rich blossoms," the group move to "a cottage some distance in the country" (XXXII, 209-10). Here the narrator describes the natural scene with Wordsworthian awareness of nature's power to evoke primal memories. An act of human love, a work of art, a glimpse of nature are related in Dickens' estimation as they are in Wordsworth's by their power to link the human imagination with eternal consciousness:

> The boy stirred, and smiled in his sleep, as though these marks of pity and compassion had awakened some pleasant dream of a love and affection he had never known; as a strain of gentle music, or the rippling of water in a silent place, or the odour of a flower, or even the mention of a familiar word, will sometimes call up sudden dim remembrances of scenes that never were, in this life; which vanish like a breath; and which some brief memory of a happier existence, long gone by, would seem to have awakened, for no voluntary exertion of the mind can ever recall them. (XXX, 191)

The beauty and harmony of the natural order may touch with life the ennobling dreams of men and influence them to leave off the glum and minor grievances that rust their fretting days:

Who can describe the pleasure and delight: the peace of mind and soft tran-
quillity: the sickly boy felt in the balmy air, and among the green hills and
rich woods of an inland village! Who can tell how scenes of peace and qui-
etude sink into the minds of pain-worn dwellers in close and noisy places,
and carry their own freshness, deep into their jaded hearts! . . . The memories which peaceful country scenes call up, are not of this world, nor its
thoughts and hopes. Their gentle influence may teach us how to weave
fresh garlands for the graves of those we loved: may purify our thoughts,
and bear down before it old enmity and hatred; but beneath all this, there
lingers, in the least reflective mind, a vague and half-formed consciousness
of having held such feelings long before, in some remote and distant time;
which calls up solemn thoughts of distant times to come, and bends down
pride and worldliness before it. (XXXII, 210)

With Coleridge, however, who emphasized that "in our life alone
does Nature live," Dickens does not posit an intrinsic life in nature nor
does he see in it any organic correspondence with the gaiety or pain of
individual men:

A knell from the church bell broke harshly on these youthful thoughts. Another! Again! It was tolling for the funeral service. A group of humble
mourners entered the gate: wearing white favours; for the corpse was
young. They stood uncovered by a grave; and there was a mother: a mother
once: among the weeping train. But the sun shone brightly, and the birds
sang on. (XXXIII, 219)

Indeed, for all its apparently solicitous beauty, nature is fundamentally
separate from and indifferent to human affairs. In *Nicholas Nickleby*, at
the death of Lord Frederick Verisopht in the duel with Sir Mulberry
Hawk, the minutely particularized and peaceful regularity of nature
mocks the shocking discord of the human trespassers as the "clean
earth smiling" and the butterfly do man's reckless enterprise after
Stein's ambush by the rebels in *Lord Jim*:

The sun came proudly up in all his majesty, the noble river ran its winding course, the leaves quivered and rustled in the air, the birds poured their cheerful songs from every tree, the short-lived butterfly fluttered its little wings; all the light and life of day came on; and, midst it all, and pressing down the grass whose every blade bore twenty minute lives, lay the dead man, with his stark and rigid face turned upward to the sky. (L, 666)[2]

Nevertheless, the fresh country surroundings, where, in Hopkins' words, all is not "seared with trade; bleared, smeared with toil," foster self-respecting behavior by encouraging in men the most elevated responses to themselves and to others. Even the poor are idealized so that they seem like Arcadian rustics:

There was the little church, in the morning, with the green leaves fluttering at the windows: the birds singing without: and the sweet-smelling air stealing in at the low porch, and filling the homely building with its fragrance. The poor people were so neat and clean, and knelt so reverently in prayer, that it seemed a pleasure, not a tedious duty, their assembling there together; . . . Then, there were the walks as usual, and many calls at the clean houses of the labouring men. . . . (XXXII, 211)

Countrymen, though usually not of the lowest class, are celebrated for their health of spirit—but in considerably more candid color tones—in English fiction from Jane Austen's Robert Martin in *Emma* through George Eliot's Caleb Garth in *Middlemarch* to Forster's Stephen Wonham in *The Longest Journey* and Lawrence's Tom Brangwen in *The Rainbow*. The language used by Dickens to describe country persons and places in *Oliver Twist* is often exaggerated—that is, unsatisfactory if close imitation of reality is the standard—but all the scenes of the novel are drawn to accommodate the imaginative bias inherent in a fable. In a novel where no serious attempt at realistic depiction is made and where stylization—and consequently distortion of nature is a prevailing technique, the idealized representation of life in the country, which is consistently carried out, is no more arbitrarily or tendentiously done than the mephitic descriptions of the city which seem to cause little critical complaint on grounds of lack of verisimilitude.

Early in the novel Sowerberry and Oliver approach a slum dwelling where a young woman has recently died:

> They walked on, for some time, through the most crowded and densely inhabited part of the town; and then, striking down a narrow street more dirty and miserable than any they had yet passed through, paused to look for the house which was the object of their search. The houses on either side were high and large, but very old; and tenanted by people of the poorest class: as their neglected appearance would have sufficiently denoted, without the concurrent testimony afforded by the squalid looks of the few men and women who, with folded arms and bodies half doubled, occasionally skulked along. A great many of the tenements had shopfronts; but these were fast closed, and mouldering away: only the upper rooms being inhabited. Some houses which had become insecure from age and decay, were prevented from falling into the street, by huge beams of wood reared against the walls, and firmly planted in the road; but even these crazy dens seemed to have been selected as the nightly haunts of some houseless wretches; for many of the rough boards, which supplied the place of door and window, were wrenched from their positions, to afford an aperture wide enough for the passage of a human body. The kennel was stagnant and filthy. The very rats, which here and there lay putrefying in its rottenness, were hideous with famine. (V, 30-31)

In the country scene the poor are described as neat and clean; and they are reverently attentive in the church which is fragrant from the air outside and happy with the sound of birds' song. The entire description is meant to convey an "impression" of a wholesome environment where simple virtue flourishes. But decay, disorder, and viciousness are equally "impressions" of the slums and these qualities are epitomized in the view of the bent humans skulking amid crazy and mouldering buildings. The final sentence of the paragraph is unnecessary for the effect since the rodent-like existence of the people has been sufficiently denoted to establish the analogy without need of excessive specification.

The conclusion from these contrasting descriptions is that evidently only outside the city can men define their own worth and dignity as human persons whereas in the gloom of the tenement world they sink almost inevitably to the most contemptible animal level. When the facts of life are so hard, these facts resist and shatter the values of the spirit from which men customarily take their pride of self-identification and absorb, instead, only the instinctive predatory twitches of the human animal. The mother of the dead woman whose funeral Sowerberry arranges triumphs in her own survival and finds the ironic juxtaposition of young death and old merriment "'as good as a play—as good as a play!'" (V, 32) Since a choice must be made between the two environments, all the "good" figures in the novel are removed from the contaminating influence of the city. Oliver finds his true home in the country remote from London and the vicissitudes of his previous life (for it is another life altogether that he leads at the Maylies and at last under the guardianship of Brownlow). The boy's dream of happiness—and redemption—is realized at last when the mystery of his birth is explained and he is adopted by Brownlow and taught the ways of filling out his new identity. In the city Oliver had undergone great unhappiness and his potential integrity had been endangered by Fagin. Nevertheless, because of the particularity of his birth as the child of deepest love, he had passed through this experience like a disguised prince amid a host of his enemies or like one of the elect unsinged by the inferno.

Except in the mechanical sense of transit, the rescue of Oliver does not reveal the opening of any moral passage between the reality of the world and the pastoral ideal. The orphan is never essentially touched by the evil around him since even Fagin is cowered by his innocence as a wicked spirit is said to be intimidated by holy water:

The boy was lying, fast asleep, on a rude bed upon the floor; so pale with anxiety, and sadness, and the closeness of his prison, that he looked like death; not death as it shews in shroud and coffin, but in the guise it wears when life has just departed; when a young and gentle spirit has, but an instant, fled to Heaven: and the gross air of the world has not had time to breathe upon the changing dust it hallowed.

'Not now,' said the Jew, turning softly away. 'To-morrow. To-morrow.' (XIX, 128)

Nancy is too implicated emotionally in the wretchedness of her world to be "saved" by Brownlow's offer of assistance. "Chained" to her old life, she is released from this bondage by her prayer for mercy only at the moment when Sikes' club descends upon her. One character alone from Fagin's group is redeemed to a better life, and that is Charley Bates who "appalled by Sikes's crime, fell into a train of reflection whether an honest life was not, after all, the best" (LIII, 367). Appropriately for the design of the novel he retires to the country where he becomes "the merriest young grazier in all Northamptonshire."

III

The antagonists in their novel are not Oliver and Fagin, but Brownlow and Fagin. Oliver is the trophy for whose possession they contend. As in the descriptive passages where the city seems the dominant reality, Fagin seems to be more powerful than Brownlow. Certainly his energy is always visible in his physical gestures whether he is sorting through his stolen property or writhing through the tortuous streets of London or frantically working his hands in impatience or covetousness or hate. Brownlow, however, has his forcefulness as well although it is less overtly conveyed; and his character is too strong to be confused with the impulsive boyishness of Losberne or the gentle, almost otiose benevolence of Mrs. Maylie. Losberne's perpetual youthfulness and his impetuosity, which are like Pickwick's, have won him "the warmest respect and esteem of all who knew him" (XXXII, 208), but he is not toughly reliable, as Rose Maylie realizes when she chooses to confide Nancy's story to Brownlow rather than to the Doctor. And the effectiveness of Mrs. Maylie's kindly nature is circumscribed by a limited imagination and limited energy. The obscurity of Rose's birth, for example, inspires in Mrs. Maylie reservations, which are prudent but ungenerous, about the propriety of a marriage between her son and the girl.

Brownlow and Fagin are both mature bachelors which is probably a necessary uncircumstanced condition for the role either of savior or destroyer. Losberne is also a bachelor but he is a spasmodic innocent like a hearty child. But Brownlow has suffered disappointment in love, and Fagin whose dislike for women is made clear in his attitude towards Nancy appears to be at least latently homosexual in his relationship with his protégés. As much as disinterestedness is possible in man, Brownlow has such a disinterested attachment for order and virtue while Fagin is equally disinterested in his love of chaos—his physical surroundings are in no way improved nor is he made personally comfortable by his successful "business." Unlike the Sowerberrys, the Bumbles, or Noah Claypole all of whom are stung by greed and covet status in the morosely selfish way of their society, Fagin is no Conradian "flabby devil" but an ascetic destroyer indifferent to his own aggrandizement and passionately devoted to the extension of evil.

The school of crime over which Fagin presides has a mock Edenic freedom about it—it is the false pastoral environment of the novel—, for his pupils, merry as schoolboys on perpetual holiday, need never turn away from their games and can always be playful in their relationship with each other. As in all the gestures of his life, Fagin is extraordinary in his dealings with his boys, a man of character who can dominate the fancies of the young and win their attachment with his perverse charm. But Fagin's pupils are also cavorting in a despoiled Eden, and their master is like "some loathsome reptile, engendered in the slime and darkness through which he moved. . . ." (XIX, 120-21). The gang are always in danger of apprehension, and their argot contains many references to transportation, hanging, and other impending punishments. Moreover, the lack of love and consequently of loyalty in their relationship is shown by their desertion of Oliver after Brownlow's pocket had been picked. Fagin is a corrupting authority figure who has depraved Nancy and who furiously prods Sikes to murder her. He is worse than his pupils and yet greater than any one around him. Even in his despair in the condemned cell, Fagin, under the eyes of Brownlow, still attempts to persuade Oliver to become one with his evil by having him. Fagin's last "cry upon cry" marks his terror but not his remorse; it is the clamor of a stricken giant untimely stopped in his vocation to multiply disorder in the world. Brownlow, like God with Job before Satan, brings Oliver before his antagonist to permit Fagin a last trial for the prize which they had both sought. And Fagin's confinement, it might be noted, gives Brownlow an advantage about equal to that possessed by the Lord with his dimensionless power.

From the time of his appearance in court before the police magistrate, Fang, Brownlow shows that he is not intimidated by brute power—whether it appear in the form of an overbearing minion of society or of a dark Satanic fury. Nor, though a bachelor, is Brownlow an inexperienced man whom life has not touched. An undefinable memory of another's countenance is strangely signalled by Oliver's presence and figures from Brownlow's past are called up:

> He wandered over them again. He had called them into view; and it was not easy to replace the shroud that had so long concealed them. There were the faces of friends, and foes: and of many that had been almost strangers: peering intrusively from the crowd; there the faces of young and blooming girls that were now old women; there were faces that the grave had changed and closed upon, but which the mind, superior to its power, still dressed in their old freshness and beauty. . . . (XI, 61-62)

"Strongly disposed" as he is to trust Oliver, Brownlow, who is cut from a more complicated pattern than the Cheeryble brothers, does not yield to soft and undiscriminating benevolence. Grimwig, that dogged and saturnine sceptic, is like another aspect of Brownlow's character with which he must contend and whose prerogatives he must acknowledge—the deeply withdrawn self who suspects that life will always disappoint him but who is gratefully surprised when, on rare occasions, it does not. And although in his trial of Oliver urged by Grimwig and in the visit to Fagin's cell as well as in his attitude towards Nancy, Brownlow, like "the old fantastical Duke of dark corners" in *Measure for Measure*, may seem to display a remote and ambiguous mode of behavior, his standard of justice is high and consistent and allows the individual freedom to acknowledge or resist it. Grimwig is useful because he can remind his friend that although personal life is short the annals of human corruption are so extensive and varied that no specific instance of betrayal can be considered remarkable. It is hard but reasonable—and indicative also of a larger trust—for Brownlow to submit to Grimwig's wager and permit Oliver to be tested through the errand to the bookseller. At the same time, even in his disappointment over the boy's disappearance with the books and the five pound note, Brownlow continues to seek him in order to discover the facts of his case; only when he feels the search is hopeless does he travel abroad to the West Indies.

Throughout the investigation into Oliver's background, Brownlow is firm and assured and metes out justice with both magnanimity and a clear-eyed apprehension of the possible. Having offered Nancy the hope of asylum from her criminal companions but not necessarily a guarantee of "peace of heart and mind," Brownlow understands almost at once, as Rose Maylie does not, that Nancy will not accept the offer. In commemoration of his friendship with Monks' father, Brownlow extends to that corrupt young man at least the freedom to end his life as he chooses. He does not spare the Bumbles for their aimless cruelty and greed: they are removed from their parish posts and are permitted to sink to the position of inmates in the workhouse over which they had formerly presided. Brownlow is not a Nobodaddy in the novel, an ineffectual patriarch exercising bogus influence over those with whom he is involved. Instead he is a man of organized experience who reacts in a vigorous personal manner to any affront to human order he encounters and who brings together into "a little society" those individuals most fit to enjoy a condition as near "to one of perfect happiness as can ever be known in this changing world" (LIII, 365).

The conclusion of *Oliver Twist* may well be a disappointment to those readers whom experience has led to expect at best a wavering line of demarcation between joy and pain in this life—who indeed suspect, and perhaps rightly, that the upright life not only does not bring success but that it is not even, as Plato would have it, its own reward. It is true that the final chapter looks pretty naive to the sceptical eye when the wicked die of "old disorders" like Monks or "far from home" like the remnants of Fagin's tribe while the good fish and garden and carpenter, listen to the edifying Sunday sermons of their friend, and meditate with luminous sadness upon the past. But this is the conclusion of a type of romance and everything in the hitherto stylized contrast between the two worlds prepares for the equally stylized close.

IV

In the great world nothing has evidently changed as a result of the elimination of one evil and the departure of some individuals to a life of modified contentment in the country. Dickens had no prophetic message of deliverance as did Blake in Plate 27 of *Jerusalem*:

> In my Exchanges every Land
> Shall walk, & mine in every Land,
> Mutual shall build Jerusalem:
> Both heart in heart & hand in hand.

The good in Dickens' novels do not inherit England or the world, for there is little left worthy of inheritance. This denial of customary values and expression of hopelessness before the world as it is—as even its most energetic and potentially most able inhabitants have made it—are basic to *Oliver Twist* and to the development of Dickens' treatment of society in his later fiction. As much as Brownlow and his friends do at the conclusion of the novel, Fagin exists outside society and he is no more the author of its corruption than Brownlow is a contributor to its amelioration. In an industrial, financial, and governmental organization so large, complex, and impersonal as the one depicted here and elsewhere in Dickens' novels, the term social good is without meaning because society is an unprincipled network of mutual hostility, exploitation, and betrayal. That the audience can sympathize with Fagin in his besetment and see him as another victim of society and even that it can feel pain at the death of Sikes slung from the tenement roof in a noose of his own making are not the perverse reactions of readers stupefied by the craft of the artist. For although both these men are murderers of the body and of the spirit, their exercise of this terrible human power has its source in great personal rage and hatred that demand respect from the beholder: not admiration but respect for the evidence of tormented humanity these feelings represent. The Bumbles in their indolent and haphazard cupidity, the London mob in its faceless anger, Henry Maylie's friends in their anonymous snobbishness are impersonal but corrosive executioners of the human spirit, and their subversion prevails. Fagin can be overcome by Brownlow, but society remains unvanquished; it is enduringly blank and corrupt like the slums it lets moulder around its members. Ironically the only "successful" member of Fagin's group is Noah Claypole who with the help of his wife becomes an agent of society by turning informer.

The view of the world is more allegorically defined in *Oliver Twist* with fewer consoling ambiguities than in the other novels by Dickens, but from Pickwick's retirement to "some quiet pretty neighbourhood in the vicinity of London" (LVII, 796) to the use of the paper mill on the upper Thames operated by the conventionally perfidious—yet here charitable—Jews in *Our Mutual Friend*, the rejection of the ambitions and standards of contemporary society—its church, its state, and its business—is everywhere apparent in Dickens. The questions and answers of the Stranger in Eliot's "Choruses from 'The Rock'" are relevant to the depleted world of *Oliver Twist*:

> When the Stranger says: 'What is the meaning of this city?
> Do you huddle close together because you love each other?'
> What will you answer? 'We all dwell together
> To make money from each other'? or 'This is a community'?

And in that most Dickensian of Conrad's fiction, *The Secret Agent*, Stevie, the retarded boy, the damaged Christ-Apollo figure, sighs for the plight of those around him: "'Bad world for poor people.'" A bad world is depicted there and in *Oliver Twist* not only for the economically poor but for all men impoverished in their hearts by the false pieties of society. The most explicitly pastoral retreat in the novel is made by Henry Maylie who elects to become a shepherd of country people and announces his decision in the conventionalized language of the enamored swain:

> if my world could not be yours, I would make yours mine; that no pride of birth should curl the lip at you, for I would turn from it. This I have done. Those who have shrunk from me because of this, have shrunk from you, and proved you so far right. Such powers and patronage: such relatives of influence and rank: as smiled upon me then, look coldly now; but there are smiling fields and waving trees in England's richest county; and by one village church—mine, Rose, my own—there stands a rustic dwelling which you can make me prouder of, than all the hopes I have renounced, increased a thousandfold. This is *my* rank and station now, and here I lay it down. (LI, 357)

It is only personal evil that can be defeated, this novel announces, and personal love that can triumph. And a life of "mercy to others" in which Brownlow instructs Oliver and of "mutual love" among a few people is not so dispirited an adventure as some critics suppose nor is it defenceless and sentimental reverie as close to the celebration of "the happy summer days" of childhood in *Alice in Wonderland* as they might imagine.

From *ELH* 35, no. 3 (1969): 403-421. Copyright © 1968 by The Johns Hopkins University Press. Reprinted with permission of The Johns Hopkins University Press.

Notes

1. All quotations from *Oliver Twist* are from *The Clarendon Dickens* ed. Kathleen Tillotson (Oxford, 1966). All other quotations from the novels are from *The New Oxford Illustrated Dickens*. Where a novel is divided into books, upper case Roman numerals indicate the books, lower case Roman numerals the chapters, and Arabic numerals the pages; otherwise, upper case Roman numerals indicate the chapters and Arabic numerals the pages.

2. The day was fair as Stein rode along: ' " 'the face of the earth was clean; it lay smiling to me, so fresh and innocent-like a little child.' " ' After the ambush Stein describes the scene and the appearance of the butterfly: ' " 'And then I sit alone on my horse with the clear earth smiling at me, and there are the bodies of three men lying on the ground. One was curled up like a dog, another on his back had an arm over his eyes as if to keep off the sun, and the third man he draws up his leg very slowly and makes it with one kick straight again. I watch him very carefully from my horse, but there is no more—*bleibt ganz ruhig*—keep still, so. And as I looked at his face for some sign of life I observed something like a faint shadow pass over his forehead. It was the shadow of this butterfly.' " ' Riverside Edition ed. Morton D. Zabel (Boston, 1958), XX, 150-51.

Mourning Becomes David:
Loss and the Victorian Restoration of Young Copperfield_____

Alan P. Barr

David Copperfield is familiarly discussed as a novel about growing up and putting away the frivolities of childhood, including a toy or child-wife. A celebrated Victorian *Bildungsroman*, it has attracted a long shelf of critical commentary analyzing its concern with maturation, its very Dickensian proliferation of deaths and problematical loves, and its intertwined themes of memory, discipline, and the craft of writing. The novel's imagery and structure, the parallels (both internally within its narrative and to the contemporary literature), its characterizations, and its humor have been richly chronicled. While exploring the growth and maturation of the eponymous figure who so diligently reconstructs his past, only incidentally or tangentially, however, have scholars of *Copperfield* spoken of David's embedded elegy to lost innocence, his transcription of his mourning for it. Bert Hornback encapsulates this critical tradition: "David's 'progress' is, in one sense, quite a simple one. As a child, David is required to relinquish his innocence, and the world which he meets beyond this innocence contains all the evil which the novel describes" (78). The actual experience of relinquishing this innocence, certainly significant, is simply overlooked or summarily regarded. I would like to argue that it is interesting, appropriate, and rewarding to examine *David Copperfield* as a novel that mourns and elegizes the loss of innocence and its enthusiasms.

The novel focuses on the development of David, which parallels his progress as a writer, and it emphasizes the centrality of memory in the evolution of its hero and the telling of his tale. But peel back that surface and coexisting with or underpinning the forward-looking story of success is the backward-glancing narration of a detailed mourning (four chapters are called "Retrospect"). For all of the deaths that punctuate *David Copperfield*, the determining, overarching loss that David experiences and mourns is the world of innocence, a loss he confronts repeatedly and that is periodically refracted in other figures.

David Copperfield is the novel in which Dickens was probably most attentive to the surrounding literature of the nineteenth century, poetry as well as fiction. This makes perfect thematic and psychological sense, considering that it is the first person narrative of someone who develops (much like his author) into a notably successful novelist. The specific allusions and echoes accumulate to reveal a pervasive concern with the process of mourning and of how one deals with loss. It may be only one of the tidy coincidences of literary history that Wordsworth's *Prelude*, Tennyson's *In Memoriam*, and Dickens's "autobiographical" fiction were all published in 1850, but that convergence (as Carl Dawson, among many, has examined) remains striking.

Wordsworth's "Tintern Abbey" (1798) hones to poignant lyric a diminished reality; the "dizzy rapture," William's bounding "o'er the mountains" wherever "nature led" are gone; "That time is past." In his "Growth of a Poet's Mind," he elaborated this theme into transcendent Romantic epic. Dickens implicitly acknowledges his predecessor. David experiences and has to deal with the sense of lost innocence that Wordsworth so resonantly described. Just as Dorothy remained a fixed image of what was, a point to which the speaker can return at the end of "Tintern Abbey," so does David find Agnes Wickfield stalwartly waiting, pillar-like. Even the initial repetition of the five long years that have passed since William has returned to the Wye anticipates David's awareness of having been away from England for three years. More tellingly, the place that memory and "spots of time" occupy in *The Prelude* is analogous to the emphasis on memory in the novel, in both instances serving as an artistic driving force.

The theme of loss at the center of Wordsworth's poetry (whether in the Lucy poems or in *The Prelude*) is comparatively abstract; it reexamines the stability of individual identity, the continuity of experience from the past to the present, and the security of one's place in nature. Blake's contemporary *Songs*, famously progressing from Innocence to

Experience, though they abound in precise (engraved) images, are similarly abstract in their focus. By contrast, the loss and mourning in *In Memoriam* are sharply identified; the poem is in memory of A. H. Hallam. The psychological dynamics in Tennyson's quintessential Victorian elegy are perhaps closer to the comparatively universalized experience that David records. The poem and the novel (again) share a pattern of evoked memories, a process of grief and mourning leading to recovery, and even a comparable three-year convalescence.

The interspersed references to or echoes of Carlyle, Ruskin, Byron, Coleridge, et al. make the notion of a *Zeitgeist* seem more than just a catchy Germanism. Nineteenth-century writers expressed their acute awareness of this sense of loss and explored, sometimes agonizingly, the possibility of restoration. Whether the issue was lost faith (with its "melancholy, long, withdrawing roar"), lost/enclosed commons, dehumanizing (industrial) labor and its products, society's smudge and ugliness, or love that has withered, this period that contributed so much to the modern notion of childhood returned over and again to that which was disappearing. Accompanying this manifold alertness to loss, is an attempt to grieve and come to terms with it. The most obvious analyst of this process was Freud, writing "Mourning and Melancholia" in 1917 and amplifying and modifying it in such later essays as "The Ego and the Id" (1923). He described himself as merely a codifier of what poets had long before understood and rendered, but his codifying analyses can still be useful in unraveling a work of art.

The nineteenth century was also the classic period of the art of the fairy tale, a genre that scholars like Bruno Bettelheim and Marina Warner have taught us to appreciate for its interwoven cultural and psychological insights. The web of fairy tale-like images and references in *David Copperfield* is yet another indicator of how the subtext is one of surviving the loss of innocence in a world that confusingly resembles a dark, uncertain, and dangerous woods.

Common alike in fairy tales, quest stories, and *Bildungsromane* are journeys, and a significant pattern or motif in *David Copperfield* is that of a journey. The principal or overarching journey is David's, from his birth to his marriage to Agnes. Subsumed within this are the literal journeys of David—to Yarmouth, to London, to Dover and Canterbury, and to the salubrious Alps and back,—Dan Peggotty's dogged pursuit of Emily, Emily's elopement with Steerforth and her voyage back to London, and the Micawber entourage's emigration to Australia. There are also the psychological or emotional and the professional-artistic trajectories: David's transformation both as a lover-husband and as a writer (imaged in his moving away from and then back to Agnes).

Within David's personal journey is an almost classic depiction of his losing his sense of innocence, the necessary initial stage of his evolving maturation. With unobtrusive propriety, the periodic fairy tale-like references, parallels, and images reinforce this process. The Murdstones resemble the evil stepparents who disrupt childhood paradises. As threatening monsters, they anticipate Creakle and Uriah Heep. David's consignment to Murdstone and Grinby's warehouse—besides consciously recalling Dickens's blacking factory stint—brings to mind Cinderella's posting to the ash heap. David's own comments occasionally invoke the world of fairy tales. About to embark for Yarmouth, he wondered, if Peggotty "were employed to lose me like the boy in the fairy tale, I should be able to track my way home again by the buttons she would shed" (76; ch. 2). Visiting Spenlow's house in Norwood, he "was wandering in a garden of Eden all the while, with Dora" (452; ch. 26). He subsequently determined, "What I had to do, was, to take my woodman's axe in my hand, and clear my own way through the forest of difficulty, by cutting down the trees until I came to Dora" (582; ch. 36). Having hewn his way through the forest to his love, he felt like a "Monster who had got into a Fairy's bower," frightening her and making her cry (607; ch. 37). With some chagrin, he describes their domestic arrangement as "this make-belief of housekeeping" (715; ch. 44). Rosa Dartle has, David feels, an air "worthy of a cruel Princess in a Legend" (735; ch. 46). He overhears Rosa concede, in her tirade, that the undeniably lovely Emily is "an ill-used innocent, with a fresh heart full of love and trustfulness . . . [a] fairy spirit" (789; ch. 50). And in the aptly named chapter, "Absence," David bemoans the loss of "the whole airy castle of [his] life" (886; ch. 58).

If the occasional fairy-tale quality spaced across the novel provides a vaguely fabular aura to David's journey, his path is much more dramatically punctuated by a series of deaths—deaths that are entangled with love. It is tempting to take at face value the griefs he experiences as fundamentally deriving from the loss of those he has loved. I suggest it is more coherent and useful to see his story as one of lost innocence, in which the specific losses (these deaths—of his mother, infant brother, Dora, Steerforth, Ham) are reiterations of this loss. He of course began life in the shadow (and psychological luxury) of his father's having already died, a death subsequently associated by Betsey Trotwood with an emotionally unequal marriage; Clara was endearing but immature and weak, grist, as it turns out, vulnerable to Murdstone's lethal mill wheels. David's arrival and childhood were almost defined by death; it is preeminently a paradise shattered by losses. Loved ones, like idylls, tend to die or to disappear into the distance. His infatuation with Emily, so engrossing, was doomed by its unreality to fade:

> Ah, how I loved her! What happiness (I thought) if we were married, and were going away anywhere to live among the trees and in the fields, never growing older, never growing wiser, children ever. . . . Some such picture, with no real world in it, bright with the light of our innocence, and vague as the stars afar off, was in my mind all the way. (202; ch. 10)

As in the seminal creation story in our literature, David's expulsion from this carefree bliss is associated with mortality. Various monsters intrude upon it (one notoriously described as serpentine), and their intrusions threaten catastrophe. Murdstone's hardness (he advertises it as firmness) distances David from his mother and the love she represents. It also leads to the deaths of Clara and of David's brother. Reflecting back, David comments, "The mother who lay in the grave, was the mother of my infancy; the little creature in her arms, was myself, as I had once been, hushed for ever on her bosom" (187; ch. 9).

Clara's character and her love for David are particularly associated with innocence and a childlike naiveté. Betsey had objected to her marriage to David's father, "a favourite of hers," because Clara was "a wax doll" (51; ch. 1). Her devotion and her death also importantly foreshadow the subsequent death of Dora. David's marriage to Dora was facilitated by the sudden death of her father, Mr. Spenlow—a comic variant of the ogres who would obstruct young love. But the elimination of this (adult) impediment only allows David to reconstitute in his adored wife the figure of his mother. Dora resembles Clara in her frailty and incapacity before the demanding rigors of the practical world. Ultimately, she prevails in making David—admonished by Aunt Betsey—accept her as the plaything, the child-wife, she declares herself to be. Clara and Dora, like Emily, were unprotected, defenseless orphans. (As if to underscore the parallel, just as Clara's infant died shortly after she did, so Jip, Dora's lap dog, expires in his Chinese house as Dora passes away upstairs.)

Steerforth, another of David's youthful loves, also dies— "drowndead" along with Ham, Emily's abandoned love. But long before "The Tempest," David accepted Steerforth's death (to him), almost philosophically musing on his continued strong, if ambivalent attachment to the romantic, suave, commanding aspect of his school idol. "The Beginning of a Long Journey" opens:

> What is natural in me, is natural in many other men, I infer, and so I am not afraid to write that I never loved Steerforth better than when the ties that bound me to him were broken. In the keen distress of the discovery of his unworthiness, I thought more of all that was brilliant in him, I softened more towards all that was good in him, I did more justice to the qualities that might have made him a man of a noble nature and a great name, than ever I had done in the height of my devotion to him. Deeply as I felt my

own unconscious part in his pollution of an honest home, I believed that if I had been brought face to face with him, I could not have uttered one reproach. I should have loved him so well still—though he fascinated me no longer.... I felt, as he had felt, that all was at an end between us.... [My remembrances] of him were as the remembrances of a cherished friend, who was dead. (516; ch. 32)

We can understand why the alluring friend, whom Agnes warned was his "evil angel," had to be cleared out from David's forest—at least physically.

Besides these actual deaths, David experienced figurative deaths, the disappearances of such early loves as Emily and the transitory attractions of Miss Shepherd and Miss Larkins. Even his early love for Agnes necessarily goes underground for years, until he has recovered and matured sufficiently to perceive it. But all of these losses, physical and psychological, are recurrences of the fundamental, scarring loss of innocence David experiences and observes in the world. They re-enact the loss he mourns and surmounts.

Modern European literature about the process of mourning, like the literature portraying the process itself, is substantial. The primary text or starting point remains Freud's "Mourning and Melancholia," but extensions and elaborations continue, with the appearance as recently as 2004 of Tammy Clewell's, "Mourning Beyond Melancholia: Freud's Psychoanalysis of Loss." The process, as Freud described it and others seek to refine and clarify it, illuminates the extent to which the psychological trajectory that David labors to make transparent falls into a recognizable pattern.

Freud was careful not to limit the loss that occasioned the subject's mourning to a beloved person. "Mourning is regularly the reaction to the loss of a loved person, or to the loss of some abstraction which has taken the place of one, such as one's country, liberty, an ideal, and so on" (243). This accommodates the sense of a lost paradise elegized by Wordsworth in "Tintern Abbey" and still more decidedly in the "Intimations Ode" ("Whither is fled the visionary gleam?"). Freud's formulation helps to reframe David's grief. It is not simply the prelude to his maturation in the face of Dora's death, but also—importantly—his reaction to the disruption of his vision of innocence, manifested in the series of deaths of those he loves.

Freud summarized the psychological work of mourning:

> Reality-testing has shown that the loved object no longer exists, and it proceeds to demand that all libido shall be withdrawn from its attachment to that object. This demand arouses understandable opposition—it is a matter of general observation that people never willingly abandon a libidinal position, not even, indeed, when a substitute is already beckoning to them. . . . The fact is, however, that when the work of mourning is completed the ego becomes free and uninhibited again. (244-45)

If, as I have been urging, David's lost "love-object" is a carefree, exuberant response to the world, then the repeated buffetings that have forced him to abandon this attachment are the deaths of his mother (preceded by that of his father), of Steerforth, and of Dora. The process of yielding accomplished, he (his ego) is then "free and uninhibited" and can turn to Agnes.

David, in fact, becomes increasingly introspective and articulate about his sorrow towards the end of his history. After Dora's death, he lets us glimpse his despondency: "I came to think that the Future was walled up before me, that the energy and action of my life were at an end, that I never could find any refuge but in the grave. I came to think so, I say, but not in the first shock of my grief. It slowly grew to that" (839; ch. 54). He looks to change and travel for restoration. Abroad, alone with his "undisciplined heart," he had not yet any "conception of the wound with which it had to strive" (885; ch. 58). In tones approaching the lugubriousness of Coleridge's "Dejection Ode" or the plaints of Byron's world-weary wanderers, he writes of his "desolate feeling," the "heavy sense of loss and sorrow" that dominated his mood (885; ch. 58).

The first pages of "Absence" go on to present an extraordinary self-analysis of his misery, a compilation of images drawn from well-known Romantic novels and poems on loss and death. David has become despairingly conscious of all that he has lost:

> love, friendship, interest; of all that had been shattered—my first trust, my first affection, the whole airy castle of my life; of all that remained—a ruined blank and waste, lying wide around me, unbroken, to the dark horizon.
>
> If my grief were selfish, I did not know it to be so. I mourned for my child-wife, taken from her blooming world, so young. I mourned for him who might have won the love and admiration of thousands, as he had won mine long ago. I mourned for the broken heart that had found rest in the stormy sea; and for the wandering remains of the simple home, where I had heard the night-wind blowing, when I was a child.
>
> From the accumulated sadness into which I fell, I had at length no hope of ever issuing again. I roamed from place to place, carrying my burden with me everywhere. I felt its whole weight now; and I drooped beneath it, and I said in my heart that it could never be lightened.
>
> When the despondency was at its worst, I believed I should die. . . . Listlessness to everything, but brooding sorrow, was the night that fell on my undisciplined heart. (886; ch. 58)

This remarkable catalog of emotional distress makes eloquently clear that no single incident is bedeviling him. What follows is the slow, initially dark-clouded pilgrimage to rejuvenation. Like Wordsworth and Shelley, he found "sublimity and wonder in the dread heights and precipices, in the roaring currents" (887; ch. 58). Like Wordsworth, Tennyson, and Mill, he would find psychological healing in Nature and beauty: "All at once, in this serenity, great Nature spoke to me; and soothed me to lay down my weary head upon the grass, and weep as I had not wept yet, since Dora died!" (887). The process of mourning and recovery that Dickens renders is not only artful, it simulates the realism of a personal experience.

Freud emphasized the primacy of memory in the letting go that mourning requires, and Tammy Clewell elaborates, explaining that mourning

> entails a kind of hyperremembering, a process of obsessive recollection . . . [that] comes to an objective determination that the lost object no longer exists. With a very specific task to perform, the Freudian grief work seeks, then, to convert loving remembrances into a futureless memory. Mourning comes to a decisive and "spontaneous end" according to Freud, when the survivor has detached his or her emotional tie to the lost object and reattached the free libido to a new object. (43-4)

Over and over again, the mature, authorial David asserts that his "Personal History" derives from his fruitful memory. This is insisted upon at the beginning of the second chapter, "I Observe." He claims to know himself well: he was "a child of close observation," and, as a man, he has "a strong memory" of his childhood (61; ch. 2). In "Another Retrospective," his "child-wife . . . is a figure in the moving crowd before [his] memory" (834; ch. 53). Recollections of his young love, Emily, he tells us, are "Ever rising from the sea of my remembrance" (838; ch. 53).

Besides being suffused with memory, *David Copperfield* also very much follows the pattern Clewell abstracts from Freud. The hoarded, studied, and artistically shaped memories coalesce into a rapid emotional reorientation for David; "decisive" and "spontaneous" are accurate descriptors. Agnes's letter arrives almost like an epiphany, concluding David's agonizing; reading it, he claims, "night was passing from my mind" (888; ch. 58). He quickly resumes his career as a writer, now alert to the romantic possibilities in Agnes. Reestablishing himself artistically is preparatory to returning to England and Agnes.

As Peter Homas argues, memory is pivotally linked with mourning and recovery: "In the case of mourning, the giving up of the lost object proceeds gradually through repeated remembrances of it, each contradicted by reality. This can occur because the mourner is psychologically separate from the lost object" (17). As David accomplishes this separation, his view of a fairy world becomes increasingly remote.

David's earliest recollected image includes the picture of his mother, "with her pretty hair and youthful shape" (61; ch. 2). David Kellogg effectively indicates how David merges the cherished image of his mother with that of his first wife, invoking the mourner's characteristic initial response of denial in the process:

> In marrying Dora, David refuses to recognize the death of his mother, creating a substitute for her in his wife. Dora's death devastates David not because of his love for Dora but because he has recreated his mother in Dora. The loss of a parent is likely to destabilize anyone's identity; but for David, whose sense of self is repeatedly threatened from a number of quarters, the death of Dora comes as the last in a series of traumas. (61)

Memory, mourning, and his quest for identity all converge. As Jerome Buckley observed, "To David, memory reaching back is in fact the strongest sanction of identity, for the present consciousness is constantly colored by the remembered or never quite forgotten past." In likening Dickens's use of memory to the "central theme of the two greatest autobiographical poems in the language, *The Prelude* and *In Memoriam*," Buckley specifically points out that "The curious wind from the past recurring throughout the novel, 'the wind going by me [David] like a restless memory' is reminiscent of the elegy's 'wind/ Of memory murmuring the past'" (232-33).

Coincident with the question of identity, remembering who you are—so as to achieve the transition from innocence and its loss to experience and its stability—is Dickens's delight in names. Some are overtly comic—the "pagan" Peggotty, Wilkins Micawber, Miss Mowcher—some metaphoric or onomatopoetic—Murdstone, Uriah Heep, Creakle, Rosa Dartle, and Steerforth—some, like Blunderstone, Traddles, Dora, Agnes, and Spenlow, accrue meaning as the tale progresses. David's is an especially suggestive onomastic romp. He enters life misnamed; "Betsey" emerges as David, variously to be called Daisy (by Steerforth) and Doady (by Dora). He is importantly rebaptised Trotwood (by Betsey), which he then earns and retains through his maturity, along with his reassumed professional name of David.

Dickens's delight in playing with names is here, as is generally true of his fictions, palpable. In *David Copperfield*, he cannily charts the stages of David's growth, the way people respond to him, and his ultimate resignation of his grief, through his various names. He is always "David," but in his more guileless youth, that name often yields to others. His mother and Peggotty naturally refer to him as Davy or little Davy. It's more pointed for the dominating, six-year-older Steerforth to call him Daisy at Creakle's school and then reassert it (permission granted by David) seven or eight years later when David is seventeen and they meet up again. This clearly identifies the juvenile side of the narrator (who admits to never entirely relinquishing his romantic image of Steerforth). It is also congruent with Dora's nickname for him, Doady. David may have been stripped, reclothed, and renamed Trotwood by Aunt Betsey when he arrived at Dover, soon to be cast free by Murdstone, and he may have chronologically reached his majority when he married Dora, but Dickens astutely shows that dispensing with a blissful innocence is not a simple or clear-cut, one-step event. David's desire for the earlier world and its allure, evoked with seeming charm by "Daisy" and "Doady," persists; he must struggle to make his rechristening prevail, just as he must go through the pains of grief and mourning before he can relinquish his mother, Dora, and even little Em'ly. He may have felt, at nine, "The mother who lay in the grave" to have been the mother of his infancy, but his "infancy" was not so expeditiously interred. It would require repeated steps for the "Young Innocent," as Steerforth and Littimer call him, to put it at a secure distance.

This play of names associated with David is also a minor comic motif in the novel. Murdstone's shady associates befuddle the young visitor by puzzling allusions to a Brooks of Sheffield. An increasingly insinuating Uriah Heep has awful difficulty making the switch from Master to Mister. And, with some prescience, Micawber chides David that he had unquestionably thought his favorite letter was A not D (630; ch. 39), a preference David is not yet cognizant of. Blunderstone itself, the rookery without rooks, extends the play upon names, reflecting David's experience of loss. The rooks are gone, lost, or a cheat—another meaning of rook—indicating that the illusion of a rookery or nest was a blunder; it was more petrific than nest-like.

In retrospect, David discloses, with self-deprecating irony, that returning home from Yarmouth was a fantasy: "It touches me nearly now, although I tell it lightly, to recollect how eager I was to leave my happy home; to think how little I suspected what I did leave for ever" (76; ch. 2). Under the new domestic arrangement, he is greeted by an angry dog and finds his room relocated far from his mother. When he visits for the school holiday, David feels it strange "to be going home when it was not a home, and to find that every object I looked at, reminded me of the happy old home, which was like a dream I would never dream again!" (161; ch. 8). David is only one of the characters, like Emily, Dan Peggotty, the Micawbers, the Wickfields, and even the Steerforths, Heeps, and Spenlows, whose home is lost or threatened.

Even more pronounced than Dickens's use of names and the alienated home as markers in David's development is the theme of writing. Writing, for the young David, has its roots in reading. To escape from the oppressive Murdstone regime, he retreats to the trove of fables, from the *Tales of the Arabian Nights* to *Peregrine Pickle*, bequeathed by his father. These not only offer a refuge from the puritanical, Gradgrindish regimen, they also turn him into a story teller, initially providing private entertainments for Steerforth and ultimately fashioning him into a novelist of renown. Not surprisingly, as Juliet McMaster discovers, "His vision of a lost paradise is intimately bound up with the art of reading" (297). Beginning as a desperate escapee into a world of fables, he comes to forge his own tale of loss and resolution.

David's mourning can be seen as mirrored in the struggle he has with writing. He must literally escape from under the damning sign pinned to his back, *"Take care of him. He bites"* (130; ch. 5). His correspondence with Dora Spenlow, espied by Jane Murdstone, temporarily derails his romantic hopes. He sets out to earn his way by mastering the inscrutable code of shorthand. Incrementally, with continued diligence and application (both of which he is careful to make the reader aware), David not only vanquishes "the noble art and mystery of stenography" (608; ch. 38), he establishes a career in creative writing—first desultorily with short pieces, then with acclaimed novels. But David's current, most advanced prose is the memoir before us (paradoxically announced as not for publication). He has labored to achieve a style that is efficient, persuasive, precise, sophisticated, and, most important, transparent. This well-wrought prose presents itself as the authentic voice of the author, denuded of anything fabulous or sensational, equally distant from the Arabian tales, the undisguised sadism of Creakle's sign, and the euphuistic epistles of Micawber. It correlates wonderfully with the speaker who has lost his illusions of a paradisial bliss, weathered his mourning, and is trenchantly recording the successful process—to a placid domesticity. Significantly, it coincides with the arrival of Agnes's similarly guileless letter effectively summoning him back toward England and terminating his mourning. The imaginative style, like Dora, like his ebullient, youthful innocence, like Blunderstone and Yarmouth, has slipped from his life—along with his grieving.

David's loss of innocence has, expectedly, a notable sexual dimension. At about eight, when he first encountered little Em'ly, he was young enough to indulge in all of the enthusiasms of prepubescent crushes and fantasies. Thinking back, David is "sure I loved that baby quite as truly, quite as tenderly, with greater purity and more disinterestedness, than can enter into the best love of a later time of life" (87; ch. 3). Though seemingly safe, warnings loom. There are hints at the kind of cautionary figure she would later become, abandoning Ham for an erotic sojourn with Steerforth. Emily lets slip that she is afraid of the sea and that she wants "to be a lady." The sea, associated with open danger and the allure to which she later succumbs (partly for wanting to be made a lady), suggests the sexual or erotic figures David would warily encounter.

On first meeting Emily, David ironically describes how he and his mother "had always lived by ourselves in the happiest state imaginable, and lived so then, and always meant to live so" (84-5; ch. 3). Unsuspected by him, the very reason for his holiday jaunt, as we (and he) soon discover, is so that his mother can remarry, thus cashiering his happy existence. Leaving Emily, he claims, left a void, if he ever had one, in his heart. The void proved to be premonitory.

Much like Emily, Steerforth embodies the memoirist's ambivalence about eroticism. David readily admits, when Steerforth is most calumnious, to his attraction. He finds him as beguiling as he had while watching him (innocently) asleep at Creakle's. In his seduction of Emily and general drifting, we see the dangerous side of his sensuality. One of the casualties in Steerforth's past is Rosa Dartle, whose temperamental scar (her inner, wasting fire of passion) compounds her fascination for David—a fascination he recognizes to be dangerous—even before he overhears her berating Emily (ch. 50).

Among the most comically exuberant of the novel's passages is when David recounts his early infatuation with Dora, how engrossingly he loved her. What a "beautiful name," he exults; "I was a captive and a slave. I loved Dora Spenlow to distraction!" (450; ch. 26). The intrusion of her confidential friend Miss Murdstone does not diminish his rapture. Not only does he feel himself "wandering in a garden of Eden," but with Olympian humor, the adult stenographer of his youth reports having wondered "in the matrimonial cases (remembering Dora) how it was that married people could ever be otherwise than happy" (458; ch. 26). (Like his author, he has only to try it to see.)

Besides providing a good story with the advantages of self-chiding hindsight, all of these encounters combine to offer a picture of love, passion, sexuality, and marriage that, reasonably enough, gravitates from youthful, innocent abandon, including the delightful intoxication of courtship, to a more staid, settled reality, a transformation that is as grievous as it may be inexorable. As Uriah's infiltration of the social world and his horrifying—to David—pretensions to Agnes illustrate, a serpent in the garden of love symbolizes the threatening side of eroticism. The sea is beguiling; it also forebodes death by drowning. Emily is adorable, as, in her way, is Dora; both are flawed and inadequate. Something, David increasingly senses, is missing in his storybook marriage.

Part of what John Lucas seizes upon as the core of David's story, "the Growth of a Disciplined Heart" (170), asserts the need to constrain or discipline erotic impulses. One manifestation of this constraint is, as Rachel Ablow discerns, David's inclination to bifurcate people he loves, disregarding the flawed portion and emotionally attaching himself to the idealized remnant. Only with the angelic Agnes can he transcend the mundane human drives and realities (Ablow, 33-36). Probably no critic goes so far as Robert Garnett in arguing that because David experiences sexual love as "dangerously destabilizing," he ultimately turns to Agnes, whose erotic nature he frustrates by a lack of real sexual response to her (220-21). A "capacity for intense feeling, a certain heightened response to life," which Robin Gilmour finds no longer possible for David (38), recalls Wordsworth's pansy, which "Doth the same tale repeat" ("Intimations," ll. 54-5).

Adam and Eve were exiled from Eden for transgressions commonly imagined to be sexual—that fruitful knowledge about which we persist in being so ambivalent. David witnesses, experiences, and seems to feel that eroticism is a threatening and unprofitable venture. His renaming by Betsey and his marriage at twenty-one are only precursors to his return to England and Agnes. That his second marriage is so briefly glossed (what more is there to say!) highlights the attitude of the book's concluding paragraph: "O Agnes, O my soul, so may thy face be by me when I close my life indeed; so may I, when realities are melting from me, like the shadows which I now dismiss, still find thee near me, pointing upward!" David has transformed the exciting, ludic sensuality associated with youth into a quasi-religious gazing upward with Agnes. In a world where love, youth, and homes prove as ephemeral as innocence, the unearthly, exceptional Agnes alone can keep everything as it was when they were children: "Nothing seemed to have survived that time [his happy youth] but Agnes" (914; ch. 60), David concludes. He has, in his exile and return, introjected and successfully mourned the fading of this innocent world and even its sensuality. Still, the transaction does not seem entirely satisfactory, and the words of Hopkins in "Spring and Fall" seem wistfully apposite: "It is Margaret that you mourn for," where Margaret's "goldengroves unleaving" poetically captures the exilic experiences and disappointments awaiting Young Copperfield.

The concern with innocence, the apprehension of its evanescence, and the consequent grief or tribulation are not limited to the protagonist; they reverberate around him. The most immediate example is that of Emily; more pronouncedly than David's, her crisis is sexual and her journey is tortuous, accompanied by betrayal and despair. Shadowing Emily is the figure of Martha Endell, the melodramatic incarnation of a fallen woman, with clear remorse for her fall from innocence. Mr. Dick, who rejects the more stately name of Richard Badger, is the epitome or Dickensian caricature of stymied innocence. Though he retained his childlike faculties, the cost was high: being cast out and then becoming a dependent. His patron, Betsey, is yet another incidental victim of a youthful indiscretion (a highly disadvantageous marriage) that costs and costs. No surprise, she is fanatical about chasing the intruding donkeys from the private garden she has willfully cultivated.

Annie Strong embodies an interesting, complementary narrative. The world, including David, appeared convinced of her duplicitous meanderings with the scalawag Jack Maldon. Because of this suspect connection, David was disillusioned and uneasy that Agnes's relationship with Annie was inappropriate. He reports his discomfort: "The innocent beauty of her face was not as innocent to me as it had been. . . . It was as if the tranquil sanctuary of my boyhood [he was seventeen] had been sacked before my face, and its peace and honour given to the winds" (339; ch. 19). Even the equable Mr. Wickfield was ready to abide Uriah's vigilante prosecution of Annie to Dr. Strong. Dramatically, Annie's sturdy self-vindication chastened her doubters. It also set her apart from the pervasively vulnerable surrounding society. Along with Agnes, she stands as a fixed, instructive figure of rectitude—even more obviously at the cost of her sexuality. The rush to judgment, especially David's, since we are primarily attuned to his retrospections, makes clear the fragility of innocence.

Annie's speech pushes David to reconsider his judgment and to recognize the virtues of "a disciplined heart." This becomes a personal reference for him throughout the remainder of the novel, one not without its awkwardnesses. In accepting the need for emotional discipline, David forsakes his youthful ebullience and openness. Eerily, however, the notion of discipline uncomfortably echoes Murdstone's demand for firmness of character. And the ogreish stepfather's insistence upon *firm*ness sounds alarmingly akin to the young husband's desire to *form* his bride's mind and character. David's intention disconcertingly mirrors the "satisfaction" Murdstone anticipated "in the thought of marrying an inexperienced and artless person, and forming her character" (100; ch. 4). In this, though, Dora is wiser than David and realizes the futility of his attempts; she will never achieve maturity and reason and practicality. Rather, she passes him on to Agnes. We again become aware that the successfully disciplined heart, successfully mended, exacts the price of ecstasy. David simply cannot respond to Agnes the way he did to Emily or to Dora, but he and his family will presumably prosper.

To round out the canvas, David witnesses instances of unsuccessful mourning—approximating the pathological alternative that Freud identified as melancholia. Mrs. Steerforth and Rosa Dartle in their different manners loved Steerforth and were immoderately invested in his prospects. When his unguided waywardness led to his destruction, both were devastated. Likewise, Ham may declare his enduring love for Emily and hold himself to blame, but there is no life for him beyond the loss of her. He, like Steerforth (and along with him), is overwhelmed by the turbulence of the seductive passions the sea represents. The climactic chapter, "The Tempest," as Tolstoy for one recognized it, makes driftwood and spume of those who do not manage to clip their adolescent wings. David was duly sobered; immediately after delivering her son's remains to Mrs. Steerforth, he undertakes his Wordsworthian, Byronic, Ruskinian, and even Arnoldian pilgrimage to the Alps.

The comprehensively remembered, lucidly and artfully retold journey of David, then, revolves around his painful—though hardly unique—loss of innocence and the concomitant grief and mourning. The story is replete with allusions to fairy tales, to nineteenth-century literature, and to the profession of writing (rooted in observing, remembering, and reading)—all of which contribute to this core emotional process. The Victorians garnered a reputation for valuing the hearth, marriage and the family; but the novels, those tell-all middle-class domestic mirrors, whether they be by Eliot, Meredith, Hardy, or even Thackeray or Dickens, expose an uneasy, compromised reality. David, as a writer, is peculiarly implicated in and aware of the compromise. As the artist-hero, he—unlike Dora, Mr. Dick, and others—must outgrow his innocence, if he is to succeed and be effective. This involves an unavoidable loss, one that he records and that he and Dickens acknowledge.

Works Cited

Ablow, Rachel. "Labors of Love: The Sympathetic Subjects of *David Copperfield*." *Dickens Studies Annual* 31 (2002): 23-46.

Buckley, Jerome. "The Identity of David Copperfield." *Victorian Literature and Society: Essays Presented to Richard Altick*. Eds., James R. Kincaid and Albert J. Kuhn. Columbus: Ohio State UP, 1984. Pp. 225-39.

Clewell, Tammy. "Mourning Beyond Melancholia: Freud's Psychoanalysis of Loss." *J. American Psychoanalytic Assoc.* 52 (2004): 443-77.

Dawson, Carl. *Victorian Noon*. Baltimore: Johns Hopkins UP, 1979.

Dickens, Charles. *David Copperfield*. London: Penguin, 1966. Rpt. 1988.

Freud, Sigmund. "Mourning and Melancholia." *Standard Edition of the Complete Psychological Works of Sigmund Freud*. Vol. 14. London: Hogarth Press. Pp. 243-58.

Garnett, Robert. "Why Not Sophy? Desire and Agnes in *David Copperfield*." *Dickens Quarterly* 14 (1997): 213-31.

Gilmour, Robin. "Memory in *David Copperfield*." *Dickensian* 71 (1975): 30-42.

Homas, Peter. Ed. *Symbolic Loss: The Ambiguity of Meaning and Memory at Century's End*. Charlottesville: U of Virginia P, 2000.

Hornback, Bert G. *Noah's Arkitecture: A Study of Dickens's Mythology*. Athens: Ohio UP, 1972.

Kellogg, David. "'My Most Unwilling Hand': The Mixed Motivation of David Copperfield." *Dickens Studies Annual* 20 (1991): 57-73.

Lucas, John. *The Melancholy Man: A Study of Dickens's Novels*. London: Methuen, 1970.

McMaster, Juliet. "Dickens and David Copperfield on the Art of Reading." *English Studies in Canada* 15 (1989): 288-304.

Eccentricity as Englishness
in *David Copperfield*

> In this age, the mere example of nonconformity, the mere refusal to bend
> the knee to custom, is itself a service. Precisely because the tyranny of
> opinion is such as to make eccentricity a reproach, it is desirable, in order to
> break through that tyranny, that people should be eccentric. Eccentricity
> has always abounded when and where strength of character has abounded;
> and the amount of eccentricity in a society has generally been propor-
> tional to the amount of genius, mental vigour, and moral courage it con-
> tained. That so few now dare to be eccentric marks the chief danger of the
> time.
>
> —John Stuart Mill, *On Liberty* (1859)[1]

Today, at the turn of the twenty-first century, the association of eccentricity with Englishness might seem an age-old commonplace—a
form of comic global cliché perpetuated by rollicking songs such as
Noël Coward's "Mad Dogs and Englishmen." The English, we are led
to believe, take pride in being wacky or harmlessly bloody-minded,
going "out in the midday sun" when others more sensible choose to
stay indoors.[2] But in this paper I want to argue that the association of
eccentricity with Englishness is a relatively recent phenomenon and
that its provenance lies in the rise of nationalism in the eighteenth and
nineteenth centuries. Although in retrospect it seems valid to apply the
term "eccentric" to numerous pre-Victorian literary texts—Laurence
Sterne's *Tristram Shandy* (1760-67) comes immediately to mind—I argue here that the coupling of eccentricity with Englishness is only cultivated consciously in the early-to-mid-Victorian period (1830s to
1860s), through figures such as Charles Dickens and Mill. What is
more, as the epigraph above will confirm, eccentricity is not treated
flippantly at this time. On the contrary, it has a range of ideological
possibility and moral substance much richer than it has today.

The earliest usages of "eccentricity" recorded in the OED refer to the field of astronomy, to planetary orbits with decentered axes, or to a lack of concentricity in the celestial sphere. Occasionally, with an archaic spelling, "excentric" is used figuratively to refer to odd human behavior. Only in the late eighteenth century do figurative usages begin to predominate. Frequently, the astronomical nuances linger in the coupling of the term "eccentric" with the idea of an excursion away from the beaten track of humdrum living. Eccentricity thus becomes an assertion of individual liberty that will not capitulate to containment but instead celebrates excess, an implication particularly evident in the titles of works about eccentrics.[3]

Recent explorations of English history and culture suggest that the notion of character played an intriguing role at a time when the national identity of Englishness was being forged. Character was frequently the articulating term that integrated the distinctiveness of the individual with the coherence of the nation. John Lucas and Linda Colley have both argued that liberty was one of the predominant cultural claims on which an Enlightenment sense of Englishness was founded in the early years of the eighteenth century.[4] Since character stood as a manifestation of individual freedom within a nation that prided itself on the liberty of its citizens, to be *a character* in the sense of feeling free to assert one's individuality was simultaneously to participate in defining the *national character* as free. Gerald Newman also notices this dual function, arguing that the distinguishing feature of the English claimed by myth makers of national identity in the mid-eighteenth century was sincerity. Through his sincerity a middle-class man of character could distinguish himself from rivals such as the aristocracy or, at an international level, the French. Like liberty, sincerity of character was the term through which individual and communal obligations could be negotiated.[5]

This dual imperative to balance the kind of difference that defines the individual as a character or discrete unit with the need for a degree of conformity that allows characters to function together toward social cohesiveness became particularly pressing in the early decades of the Victorian period. It played out in the expanding middle classes as the need to reconcile upward mobility and the drive toward personal betterment with the obligation to maintain the equilibrium of the family unit on which democratic politics and a capitalist industrial economy depend.

Dickens is an author unusually attentive to this dual imperative. His earliest works reflect his recognition that individualism could be readily available to the economically successful but beyond the range of the laboring poor and women in particular. Yet, if individualism were sacrificed to the interests of a broader common good, there would be little to prevent a middle-class world from devolving into dreary homogeneity. In *Sketches by Boz*, Dickens contemplates the resigned anonymity of numerous Londoners and invents the peripatetic Boz to roam at will and transform homogeneity into character through his powers of observation. In *The Pickwick Papers*, the colorful individualism of Sam Weller works as a foil to the staunch good sense of his employer, Pickwick; their relationship prefigures the way Dickensian eccentricity will link individual difference to common welfare in the later novels.

In its Dickensian form, eccentricity emerges as a nostalgic return to novelistic character of the preceding century, prompted and shaped by retrospective literary debates of the early nineteenth century. One of the most influential and memorable voices in these debates was William Hazlitt. In the sixth of his eight *Lectures on the English Comic Writers*, first published in 1819, he declares Henry Fielding, Tobias Smollett, Samuel Richardson, and Sterne to be "our four best novelwriters," attributing their greatness to the relative political stability and economic prosperity of George II's reign, a period when, in Hazlitt's words, "there was a general spirit of sturdiness and independence, which made the English character more truly English than perhaps at any other period."[6] There is an echo here of both the liberty noted by Lucas and Colley and the sincerity or capacity to be true to oneself identified by Newman.

The coding of such distinct character as specifically English, as opposed to French, is well illustrated by a passage from Sterne's novel *A Sentimental Journey*, in the episode in which Yorick uses "a few king William's shillings" to demonstrate to the Count de B**** at Versailles the "distinct variety and originality of character, which distinguishes [the English], not only from each other, but from all the world besides."[7] It is an argument that can also be found in Hazlitt's fourth essay on the drama written for the *London Magazine* in April 1820, where he argues that it is precisely the loss of this capacity to represent individual difference that has weakened early-nineteenth-century English drama.[8] Character needs to be preserved as part of a celebrated past heritage on the verge of becoming lost, but also reinvented to accommodate shifting cultural tensions. This, Dickens undertakes by reinventing character as eccentricity.

Even to mention eccentricity in relation to Dickens is surely to invoke his entire oeuvre, for all the characters in his novels—with the exceptions of the hero and heroine—seem to some degree eccentric. A number of features set *David Copperfield* apart from the rest of Dickens's work, however, as an interesting example for study. First, David himself as a nascent author is represented as an apprentice to the eighteenth-century genius for character invention when he reads the cache of novels left by his deceased father in a secluded upstairs room at Blunderstone Rookery. Among his mentors, Smollett and Fielding predominate.[9] David's autobiography is therefore both a *Bildungsroman* documenting his development as an inventor of characters, and an account of his own training to be himself a man of character.

A second feature distinguishing this novel is that, as the personal history of a novelist, it draws on Dickens's own autobiography in its first fourteen chapters and ironically provides material on which Dickens's intimate friend and biographer, John Forster, draws to constitute Dickens as "Dickens." As we shall see, *David Copperfield* thus illustrates Dickens's use of eccentricity to reconcile individualism with communal responsibility and at the same time shows self-reflectively the role eccentricity plays in articulating what it means to Dickens to be the pre-eminent English novelist of the period.

In fashioning this role of English novelist for himself, Dickens implicitly declares his own nationalist sentiments while distancing himself from nationalism of the cruder, more aggressive variety popular after the end of the Napoleonic wars and prefigurative of late 1870s jingoism. As George Orwell has declared, "never anywhere does he indulge in the typical English boasting, the 'island race,' 'bulldog breed,' 'right little, tight little island' style of talk."[10] Dickens's nationalism takes the form of a moral rather than a political concern about the condition of England. He parodies boastful nationalism as a brand of complacency that works against the country's best moral interests. It is embodied, for instance, in Mr. Podsnap of *Our Mutual Friend* as he blusters to "the foreign [French] gentleman," that "[T]here is in the Englishman a combination of qualities, a modesty, an independence, a responsibility, a repose, combined with an absence of everything calculated to call a blush into the cheek of a young person, which one would seek in vain among the Nations of the Earth."[11]

What is it, we may ask, that makes Podsnap so repugnant in his nationalism while Sterne's Yorick is endearing and a character? I suggest it is the former's lack of self-awareness, made apparent through authorial irony, as opposed to the self-irony practiced by the latter through first person narration. In the passage cited, Podsnap not only embodies precisely the opposite of the Englishness he touts—modesty, repose, and discretion are anathema to Podsnappery—but he also fails to see that what he says does not coincide with what he is. Self-awareness is the trademark of Dickensian eccentricity, making it the ally and guarantor of sincerity or sincerity's Victorian counterpart, earnestness.

Eccentricity's self-reflexive quality allows Dickens both to create a gallery of eccentrics and to define himself as the master eccentric, the "inimitable B [Boz]," as he calls himself in his correspondence with Forster.[12] From this it might seem that inimitability—an essential selfhood or ontological uniqueness that refuses to be curtailed by convention—is the defining feature of the eccentric. Yet this is not the case in Dickens's reinvention of the concept. As *David Copperfield* shows, the oddity of the most striking eccentrics in Dickens's novels is ironically less that "originality" for which Mill will subsequently yearn than the capacity to masquerade, the power to don and remove masks that does not *depend* on some original essence but rather brings that essence into being.

One of the problems inherent in claiming sincerity or earnestness as a national characteristic is the difficulty of distinguishing it from its counterparts, hypocrisy and cant. The great symbolic advantage of the mask as a vehicle for establishing moral value is that it can produce the effect of a bedrock of previously concealed truth. It is up to the author to choose whether the truths revealed are ultimately values that appear to be unquestionable (such as earnestness and decency), or the threat to those values (hypocrisy and cant), which are thankfully exposed. Dickens exploits both possibilities in *David Copperfield*. Eccentrics in this novel do not simply wear masks or assume poses; they do so self-consciously. In memorable scenes of revelation or self-exposure, eccentrics repeatedly acknowledge their oddity to be a guise, thereby implying that behind it lies a bedrock of moral value. This is one way in which eccentricity operates as the site of negotiation between individual and communal imperatives. For repeatedly the unveiled eccentric's core of moral values proves to be the generalized, implicitly Christian but class- and gender-neutral qualities of decency and earnestness that themselves echo eighteenth-century English sincerity. The political, economic, or psychic costs of these values—whether, for instance, it is easier for a financially secure member of the landed gentry to be decent than it is for an impoverished factory hand—are not a primary concern in Dickens's novels. Instead, the operations of eccentricity establish a supposedly shared core of cultural values. For once eccentrics put aside the mask of oddity, they cease to appear as outsiders or creatures of extremes, and become recognizable as part of a moderate, humane commonalty.

Through the performance of masking and unmasking, the eccentric earns the moral right to displace the masks of hypocrites, those enemies of earnestness and decency who hide humbug and cant under the veneer of respectability. In fact, one might go so far as to say that Dickensian eccentricity is the moral antidote to self-serving hypocrisy, which is itself perceived to be a specifically English vice. Forster interprets hypocrisy in nationalistic terms when he reminisces about the reception of *Martin Chuzzlewit* (1843). Focusing on the inveterate cant of Mr. Pecksniff, he remarks, "The confession is not encouraging to national pride, but this character is so far English, that though our countrymen as a rule are by no means Pecksniffs the ruling weakness is to countenance and encourage the race."[13] Forster goes on to declare that such hypocrisy is not to be found in either of the neighboring societies of America or France; for the former is an "Eden" too newly established to harbor such deception, while the latter—in the view of French critic and Dickens enthusiast, Hippolyte Taine—no longer knows the kind of respect for morality that could encourage a hypocritical pretense to virtue.[14] Pecksniff's hypocrisy and Tom Pinch's pliancy before it are therefore *English* vices, and by exposing them in his novels, Dickens implicitly defines himself as the national conscience and moral guide, even a Carlylean "Hero as Man of Letters," who follows the gospel preached by Samuel Johnson to "Clear your mind of Cant!"[15]

The operations of eccentricity—both as a mask and agent of unmasking—working against the pressures of respectability to promote earnestness and decency, are everywhere apparent in *David Copperfield*. Let me consider four of the novel's most obvious eccentrics. Aunt Betsey Trotwood, Mr. Dick, Miss Mowcher, and Wilkins Micawber all overtly participate in shaping David as a man of character: a "Man of Letters" hero, or national spokesman and celebrity. As Jerome H. Buckley argues, David himself, if not quite colorless, is certainly "at pains to establish his psychological 'normalcy.'"[16] He has the quality of gentlemanly blandness, the capacity to stand in for everybody and nobody in particular that characterizes the hero in novels of the mid-eighteenth century. This genteel moderation, of which Pickwick is an early embodiment, depends for both its stability and its charm on the mediating activities of the more colorful eccentrics that surround him.[17]

To begin with Aunt Betsey: her imposing demeanor is apparently the effect of her stubborn refusal to conform to the behavior expected of a middle-class Victorian woman. Far from being gently compliant or willing to effect change by the discreet exercise of influence—of the kind recommended in the late 1830s by Sarah Stickney Ellis—Aunt Betsey "seldom conduct[s] herself like any ordinary Christian," but bears herself with "a fell rigidity of figure" (p. 11). She is variously described as "pretty stiff in the back" (p. 165), having an "inflexibility in her face," and features that are "unbending and austere" (p. 170). In these respects, she seems to mirror Jane Murdstone; yet, where the latter's rigidity is directed toward upholding conventions and ensuring conformity and compliance, Aunt Betsey's is directed toward resisting conventions and celebrating her individuality through unorthodox conduct. If initially David fears Aunt Betsey for her unpredictability, later he finds her eccentricity reassuring, especially when she uses it to resist the grim resolution of the Murdstones.

Gradually it becomes clear that Aunt Betsey's eccentricity works in the interests of a new moral order in which the tyranny of humbug and cant is replaced by decency and earnestness. In David's education and upbringing, the guardianship of the Murdstones is supplanted by that of Aunt Betsey and Mr. Dick, while Mr. Creakle is displaced by Dr. Strong. It is the eccentric Aunt Betsey who encourages David to train himself never to be false, and to find a partner who will foster in him a "deep, downright, faithful earnestness" (p. 425). Her worthiness to be the champion of these virtues is guaranteed when she reveals her eccentricity to be a façade assumed to counter the emotional and financial devastation she experiences at the hands of her dissolute husband. The moment when she tells her "grumpy, frumpy story" (p. 579) to David is the moment when Aunt Betsey reveals her eccentricity to be not a unique self expressing itself in earnest, but instead the mask behind which the self, conscious of its own failing, works for a more moral society. Many critics have justifiably emphasized Aunt Betsey's outlandish qualities, but if, like A. O. J. Cockshut, we go so far as to argue that, being in the tradition of the fairy godmother, "she has no human need to conform herself to reality," we run the risk of overlooking the way in which her eccentricity determines the moral stability of David's world.[18] She is a reformer, not in any material sense of political, economic, or class reform, but in the moral sense of making the world better, where "better" has the ring of genteel, middle-class, Christian humanism.

Mr. Dick, perhaps the nonpareil of eccentrics in *David Copperfield*, is also otherworldly and conscious of being so. He declares to David that this world is "Mad as Bedlam, boy!" (p. 177), and in a variety of ways he declines to be a part of it. By refusing to use his proper name (Richard Babley), Mr. Dick refuses the place he has been assigned in this symbolic disorder. He is most at ease when transported vicariously above the world by his kite. If he seems mad, Aunt Betsey treats his insanity as a pose. Repeatedly she urges him to drop what she regards as a pretense of idiocy, and when David asks her if Mr. Dick is "at all out of his mind," she flatly responds, "Not a morsel" (p. 178).

Like Aunt Betsey's, Mr. Dick's eccentricity is a mask that he consciously dons to protect himself from the injustice of the world as he works to remedy that injustice. Eccentricity thus allows him to act as the agent of moral order when the world's madness has reached an intolerable level. When, for instance, he intervenes to reconcile Annie Strong with her husband, Mr. Dick declares himself able to do so because his eccentricity—which he explicitly acknowledges—earns him immunity from the constraints imposed on ordinary people. He is so eccentric that he no longer signifies—he is a "nobody" (p. 551). While neither Dr. Strong nor Annie dares to initiate a conversation that would explain Jack Maldon's standing in relation to Annie, Mr. Dick may do so without fear of indelicacy. The effect of Mr. Dick's intervention is to correct an earlier unveiling scene when Uriah Heep, in a fit of righteous respectability, supposedly for Dr. Strong's benefit, coerces Mr. Wickfield and David into admitting their suspicions that Annie Strong has been dallying with Jack Maldon. The subsequent revelation engineered by Mr. Dick reveals in turn Uriah's hypocrisy and Annie's virtue. More importantly, though, it reveals to David that his own marriage to Dora Spenlow is not "founded on a rock," as the Strongs' marriage is. From the earnestness of Annie's confession, David recognizes his marriage as the product of "the first mistaken impulse of [an] undisciplined heart," reflecting that worst disparity in marriage, "unsuitability of mind and purpose" (pp. 558, 560). Only after this revelation can David appreciate the role played by an angelic wife in shaping a "Man of Letters" hero into a man of moral character.

Notably, Mr. Dick's eccentricity is combined with a childlike ability to dispense with the ceremony and propriety that the Murdstones advocate and get directly to the point of social well-being. When Aunt Betsey asks his advice on what to do with the destitute David, Mr. Dick focuses directly on the creature comforts the child so badly needs: "I should wash him!" (p. 170); "I should put him to bed" (p. 174); and "Have him measured for a suit of clothes directly" (p. 186). This capacity is also linked to a creativity and ingenuity that has the freshness of youth, and a special charm for children: at Dr. Strong's school, Mr. Dick is a "universal favorite" (p. 218). More than a harmless wackiness, ingenuity of Mr. Dick's kind is repeatedly represented in the novel as part of a national creativity and initiative, the kind of spirit of enterprise that in Hazlitt's view flourished in George II's reign but now, in Carlyle's "Mechanical Age,"[19] threatens to disappear into the mindless bureaucracy of the "Circumlocution Office" (*Little Dorrit*), endless legal obfuscation (*Bleak House* and *David Copperfield*), rote learning in the cruel schools of hard fact (*Nicholas Nickleby, David Copperfield*, and *Hard Times*) and the dehumanization of workers into factory "hands" (*Hard Times*).

The third instance of striking eccentricity, that of Miss Mowcher, bears many similarities to the cases of both Aunt Betsey and Mr. Dick, except that here it is attributed to a working-class woman. Mowcher's volatility—her delight in the arts of transformation and disguise—is a masquerade, enabling her to dislodge the masks of humbug that guarantee power to the aristocratic and genteel. Thus, where Steerforth flaunts David's naïveté and vulnerability by referring to him as "Daisy" (p. 248), Mowcher exposes Steerforth's self-serving dandyism by addressing him as "My flower!" (p. 279). While she lets it be known that she is privy to the domestic secrets of the nobility, she simultaneously exposes them as ineffectual and impotent. A feature of her volatility is her ability to be omnipresent, to move effortlessly across economic, class, and geographic boundaries, making "little darts into the provinces . . . to pick up customers everywhere, and to know everybody" (p. 287), so that her potential for disruption seems limitless. Her chief function in the plot is to undermine Littimer's coercive propriety, which he uses to subdue communal resourcefulness and ingenuity of the kind displayed in the mutton-grilling scene at David's London dinner party (chap. 28). Mowcher abandons her volatility when she discovers that she has been unwittingly complicit in the deception of the Peggotty family and the seduction of Little Em'ly and has thereby been working against decency and earnestness.[20] Like Aunt Betsey's, Mowcher's eccentricity is revealed as a disguise that has hidden a closet sentimentalist. While initially it has the disruptive qualities of satire, it eventually gives way to the morality of the new social order in which humbugs and hypocrites such as the Murdstones, Littimer, and Uriah Heep are not tolerated.

The last eccentric I want to consider, Wilkins Micawber, shares some characteristics with the preceding examples but perhaps in his differences contributes the most interesting dimension of my argument. Like Aunt Betsey, Mr. Dick, and Miss Mowcher, Micawber acts as an agent of demystification and exposure, and he also expands the scope of David's *Bildung*. Micawber's utter inability to support himself and his family illustrates for David the ineffectiveness of a gentlemanly upbringing. As Chris Vanden Bossche observes, the Micawbers are a comic version of the upper-class Steerforth family David idealizes.[21] Through Micawber, David is forced to learn lessons he might otherwise have managed to evade; for instance, he learns the skills of barter and pawn that enable him to survive his journey to Dover. And through Micawber's eccentric sociability, David comes into contact with the host of paupers inhabiting the King's Bench Prison who will later become the material of the novels he writes, not for a restricted genteel readership, but for all inhabitants of the British Empire. Micawber's random eruptions into the course of David's life serve as a recurrent reminder to the young author of the abject impoverishment that he has managed to escape, but which is nevertheless endured by so many of the English public for whom, as the contributor to a truly national literature, he must write.

Yet if Micawber appears to encourage David's training in upper-middle-class gentility, there is also, as Alexander Welsh has remarked, a dimension of his behavior that is severely threatening to the bourgeois morality that underpins the novel.[22] Micawber resolutely refuses to view his financial difficulties as shameful. Rather, to David's chagrin, he boasts of them (p. 224), and this, in the 1830s and '40s, would have been decidedly un-English if we are to believe Edward Bulwer-Lytton, who declares that "In other countries poverty is a misfortune,—with us it is a crime," a view borne out repeatedly in Dickens's novels.[23] Characters such as Mr. Toots of *Dombey and Son* and Richard Carstone of *Bleak House* are driven to self-disgust by their own genteel incompetence. Not so Micawber; his personal peculiarity is to transform sordid financial deficiency into the stuff of high melodrama and histrionics, immersing himself in an endless carnival of threats by debtors, transports of mortification, epistolary and rhetorical flights, and consoling punchbowls.

Repeatedly Micawber gathers himself up to deliver to David solemn axioms for the attainment of social success—"Procrastination is the thief of time. Collar him!" (p. 154). At such moments Micawber seems poised to participate in the ideology of economic enterprise; but without fail, his apparent conformity transforms into a celebration of his own immunity to such social imperatives. Responsibility vanishes as he drinks "a glass of punch with an air of great enjoyment and satisfaction, and whistle[s] the College Hornpipe" (p. 154). Mrs. Micawber's declarations of domestic loyalty to her husband similarly verge on participation in middle-class propriety. Her emphatic announcement, "I never will desert Mr. Micawber" (p. 151), is of a kind with Agnes Wickfield's devotion to her father and David, or Sophy Traddles's loyalty to Tommy. Yet in Mrs. Micawber's case, steadfast earnestness collapses into hysteria, provoking a riotous scene in which the chorus "Gee up Dobbin" (p. 152), the heads and tails of shrimps, and the tears of both Micawbers and David mingle in a melodramatic chaos.

This transformation of the principles of earnestness and decency into the material of riotous comedy suggests the potential in Dickens's eccentricity to be radically unsettling; however, Dickens does not often exploit that capacity. More often he constrains his eccentrics to work in the interests of social and national cohesion. As the site of a reforming individualism, eccentricity disrupts the status quo only to guarantee a new social order that may be more morally decent but is not necessarily more politically or economically just than its predecessor. If we look back again, for instance, at Aunt Betsey, we find that, for all its vigor, her eccentricity persistently works to support a domestic order that rewards middle-class enterprise, which the working classes are encouraged to emulate but certainly not to challenge. For instance, although she herself is represented as a participant in a very unorthodox romantic misalliance, generating its own riotous black comedy, she readily recognizes the dangers of her nephew's marriage to the "wax doll" (p. 11) Clara, a woman incapable of acting in the best economic and moral interests of her husband, her family, or herself.

The discovery that Aunt Betsey's eccentricity is a guise behind which lies a closet sentimentalist compromises the reforming force of that eccentricity. Similarly, Miss Mowcher's volatility has the potential to disrupt the status quo radically, but in her final appearance in the novel, when she apprehends Littimer in the streets of Southampton, she proves herself a worthy vigilante, earning accolades from the public and the forces of the law for ensuring the arrest of one whose villainy lies chiefly in his wish to rise above his social station.

Only in Micawber's eccentricity do we see elements of a more subversive potential. On the surface, his genteel resistance to middle-class expectations of a family man might be read as simply the counterpart to Uriah Heep's seemingly "umble" (p. 203), but intently aggressive, self-help. There are many points of contrast between the two men. Uriah, on the one hand, is strongly associated with death: he is repeatedly referred to as "cadaverous," is dressed in black, and has "a long, lank skeleton hand" (p. 191). His father was a sexton, and his mother, extending the customary Victorian mourning period of two years, continues to wear widow's weeds although her husband has been dead for nearly five years (p. 203). Micawber, on the other hand, incarnates vitality. Through his sheer lust for life he manages to transform financial difficulties into the ritual consumption of luxury foods and beverages. Recurring references to his expanding family, underscored by descriptions of Mrs. Micawber's perpetual feeding of the twins from "Nature's founts" (p. 222), associate the Micawbers with an irrepressible fecundity.

Just as Aunt Betsey explodes the pretensions of the Murdstones, and Miss Mowcher unveils Littimer, Micawber's definitive role in the plot of *David Copperfield* is, of course, to expose the opportunistic machinations of Uriah Heep. His eccentric delight in melodrama and histrionics is at its most flamboyant when he exposes Heep's charity-school humility as an elaborate charade. What is peculiar about Micawber, however, is that his own histrionics are never clearly identified as an act. His delight in striking poses is so thoroughgoing that it is impossible to be sure whether his ability to be extraordinarily "elastic," to use David's term (p. 141), will ever be identifiable as the mask of eccentricity. The nearest we come to a scene of unmasking is in chapter 49, when Micawber's investigations into Heep's fraud are reaching a crisis point, and he meets with David and Tommy Traddles outside the King's Bench Prison. Earlier, when Micawber starts to work for Heep, he dons a suit of legal black in what appears to be a gesture of conformity. For several chapters it is difficult for the reader to tell whether his conformity has not developed into that worst of English vices—complicity with hypocrisy and deception. When at last Micawber meets with David and Tommy Traddles, however, he has relinquished the suit of black and returned to his old garb, only slightly lacking his former panache. Unlike Miss Betsey's rigidity, Mr. Dick's insanity, or Miss Mowcher's volatility, Micawber's eccentricity does not fall away here to produce a core of decency. Rather, in resuming his old outfit, he turns away from hypocrisy and respectability back to eccentricity, as if eccentricity were indeed no mask but an ontological uniqueness struggling to reassert itself.

In his original dress Micawber is able to resume his peculiar role in the novel as the embodiment of a comical, but potentially threatening contrariness. As an eccentric, he has the power to unmask hypocrisy, but he may even go so far as to refuse to participate in the "thorough-going, ardent, and sincere earnestness" (p. 512) that should be the effect of the new social order. Where Heep may represent the hypocrisy that pervades Dickens's England and is condoned by the morally ineffectual (the Mr. Wickfields, Tom Pinches, and Twemlows), Micawber embodies an eccentricity that is too extreme to inhabit a society that hallows moderation.

It is perhaps for this reason that Micawber must meet a fate parallel to Heep's. If the latter is ultimately to be transported, Micawber too must go "down under"; for as Stanley Tick points out, Micawber represents an expression of otherness that serves to test and modify David's autobiographical discourse.[24] In the mother country Micawber's eccentricity is unsettling, immoderate, and therefore potentially un-English. Only in another country, at a safe distance from England, can he be convincingly recuperated as a pillar of symbolic order and decency, learning fiscal responsibility, becoming a district magistrate, and in a final epistolary flourish sent to David via old Daniel Peggotty, standing witness to the novelist's moral influence on the farthest reaches of the British Empire.

As I have already remarked, because of the self-reflexive structure of this novel and of eccentricity as a trait, any observations about the relations between Micawber and David inevitably prompt one to extend the connection to include Dickens himself. From the time of the novel's first publication in parts, readers have remarked on the fatherly behavior of Micawber to David and surmised the original of Micawber to have been the author's father, John Dickens. To this we could add the possibility that Micawber represents a spirit of rebellion Dickens recognizes in himself. It is after all remarkable how many instances there are, both in Dickens's collected letters and in Forster's biography, of Dickens assuming the character of Micawber.

On 30 September 1849, as he is about to leave Bonchurch on the Isle of Wight for his favorite resort of Broadstairs in Kent, Dickens writes to Forster describing himself as "under the depressing and discomforting influence of paying off the tribe of bills that pour in upon an unfortunate family-young-man on the eve of a residence like this."[25] In subsequent letters he identifies both his compulsion to be constantly on the move and his oppression by the expenses of this itinerant lifestyle with Micawber. On 5 October 1849, he says in a letter to his friend John Leech, "I write, as my friend Mr. Micawber says, 'with a sickly mask of mirth,' but I am rather behind time."[26] Shortly after this, he writes to Forster "speaking dolefully of some family matters" and subscribes the letter "each word forming a separate line, 'Yours Despondently, And Disgustedly, Wilkins Micawber.'"[27] Then, in 1850, the day before the birth of his third daughter, Dora Annie, he writes of his wife Kate, "'Mrs. Micawber is still' (15 August) . . . 'I regret to say, *in statu quo*. Ever yours, WILKINS MICAWBER.'"[28] It is as if assuming the position of Micawber enables Dickens to defuse his anxieties about precisely those demands of decent, middle-class living that Micawber's eccentricity resists: the imperative for a family man to remain solvent; the necessity of his working indefatigably; and the questionable wisdom of keeping his wife interminably pregnant. In two later letters, Dickens's anxiety about his ability to be a constantly productive and effective writer emerges in reiterations of Micawber's memorable hope that "something will turn up."[29] Even a recipe for punch, reminiscent of Micawber's brew, in chapter 28 of *David Copperfield*, appears in Dickens's correspondence, replete with instructions about the peeling of lemons, the burning of rum, and the addition of boiling water.[30] In each of these cases, Micawber seems to return as the embodiment of a rogue impulse in Dickens—an impulse to escape and, by sheer excess, to unsettle the very decency, earnestness, and moderation on which his authorial eminence is based.

Once relegated to another country, the unsettling quality of Micawber's eccentricity is neutralized by distance and can become a difference that both distinguishes the Englishman from other colonists and, presumably, from the indigenous inhabitants of colonized countries, while at the same time clarifying David's, and by extension Dickens's, specifically English excellence. It is the hyperbolic difference that confirms the pre-eminent English author as reliably moderate—a man of genius in his capacity to champion moral decency without fanaticism. In this regard, Micawber's open letter in the *Port Middlebay Times*, brought from Australia by Daniel Peggotty, reassures David "You are not unknown here, you are not unappreciated. . . . Go on, my dear sir, in your Eagle course!" (p. 733). This letter, written on behalf of the inhabitants of Port Middlebay, is testimony of David's status as the pre-eminent English novelist. His influence is worthy to be felt throughout the empire, even among those territories that use literature as a forum for resisting English cultural sovereignty. Micawber's message is also reminiscent of an effusive letter received by Dickens toward the end of 1849 from the self-appointed Russian translator of *Dombey and Son*: "'For the last eleven years your name has enjoyed a wide celebrity in

Russia, and from the banks of the Neva to the remotest parts of Siberia you are read with avidity. Your *Dombey* continues to inspire with enthusiasm the whole of the literary Russia.'"[31] If David's reputation extends across the British Empire, the "inimitable Boz" is known and admired internationally.

Thus it is that eccentricity plays its double function. From within English society it is the mask of oddity that unmasks hypocrisy, constituting earnestness and decency as the bedrock of a moral society. Beyond the borders of England, within the broader empire, it takes the form of a rhetorical and affective excess that parades the Englishman's cultural difference even as it helps to stabilize and disseminate English moral values. Because these values are so broadly defined, they are easy to identify with and readily create a sense of like-mindedness among readers. It is Dickens's canny ability to indulge difference in the eccentrics of his novels while cultivating the sameness of apparently shared values that establishes his reputation as a master eccentric, preeminent Victorian novelist, and embodiment of the "genius, mental vigour, and moral courage" that Mill subsequently identified as the correlatives of eccentricity.

From *SEL: Studies in English Literature 1500-1900* 4 (Autumn 2002): 781-797. Copyright © 2002 by *SEL: Studies in English Literature 1500-1900*. Reprinted by permission of *SEL: Studies in English Literature 1500-1900*.

Notes

This essay was initially conceived for a panel on "Dickens and Eccentricity" at the 1995 MLA Convention in Chicago. I thank the organizer, Hilary Schor, for the idea, and Ian Duncan, Elizabeth Heckendorn Cook, and Deidre Lynch for invaluable readings of later drafts.

1. John Stuart Mill, *"On Liberty"* in *"Utilitarianism," "On Liberty," and "Considerations on Representative Government,"* ed. H. B. Acton (London: Dent, 1972), pp. 124-5.

2. *The Lyrics of Noël Coward* (London: Heinemann, 1965), pp. 122-3.

3. See, for instance, G. M. Woodward, *Eccentric Excursions; or, Literary and Pic-*

torial Sketches of Countenance, Character and Country in Different Parts of England and South Wales. Interspersed with Curious Anecdotes. Embellished with Upwards of One Hundred Characteristic and Illustrative Prints (London: Allen and West, 1797).

4. John Lucas, *England and Englishness: Ideas of Nationhood in English Poetry, 1688-1900* (Iowa City: Univ. of Iowa Press, 1990), pp. 24-5, 41-2; Linda Colley, *Britons: Forging the Nation, 1707-1837* (New Haven: Yale Univ. Press, 1992), pp. 42-3.

5. Gerald Newman, *The Rise of English Nationalism: A Cultural History, 1740-1830* (New York: St. Martin's Press, 1987), p. 155.

6. *Collected Works of William Hazlitt in Twelve Volumes*, ed. A. R. Waller and Arnold Glover, 12 vols. (London: J. M. Dent, 1903), 8:121-2. I thank Deidre Lynch for drawing my attention to this passage. For references to other early-nineteenth-century discussions of profuse character in the eighteenth-century novel see Lynch's *The Economy of Character: Novels, Market Culture, and the Business of Inner Meaning* (Chicago: Univ. of Chicago Press, 1998), pp. 18, 269-70.

7. Laurence Sterne, *A Sentimental Journey through France and Italy*, ed. Graham Petrie (New York: Penguin, 1986), p. 114. Lynch cites this episode at greater length, discussing the subtle intersection of economic and numismatic implications with the nuances of narrative and interpretative investments and returns (p. 115).

8. Hazlitt, "Essays on the Drama from the *London Magazine* 1820," in *Collected Works*, 8:417.

9. Charles Dickens, *David Copperfield*, ed. Jerome H. Buckley (New York: Norton, 1990), pp. 53-4. All subsequent references to the novel appear in the text parenthetically by page number.

10. George Orwell, "Charles Dickens," in *Inside the Whale and Other Essays* (London: Victor Gollancz, 1940), pp. 9-85, 40.

11. Dickens, *Our Mutual Friend* (Portsmouth, NH: Heinemann, 1991), p. 152.

12. *Letters of Charles Dickens*, ed. Madeline House, Graham Storey, and Kathleen Tillotson, 12 vols. (Oxford: Clarendon Press, 1965-2002), 5:605, 5:615, 5:619. I elaborate here on Duncan's argument in *Modern Romance and Transformations of the Novel: The Gothic, Scott, Dickens* (Cambridge: Cambridge Univ. Press, 1992), p. 181.

13. John Forster, *The Life of Charles Dickens*, 2 vols. (1872-74; rprt. Philadelphia: Lippincott, 1925), 1:308.

14. Forster, 1:309.

15. Thomas Carlyle, *On Heroes, Hero-Worship, and the Heroic in History*, ed. Michael K. Goldberg, Joel J. Brattin, and Mark Engel (1841; rprt. Berkeley: Univ. of California Press, 1993), p. 156.

16. Buckley, "The Identity of David Copperfield," in *Victorian Literature and Society: Essays Presented to Richard D. Altick*, ed. James R. Kincaid and Albert J. Kuhn (Columbus: Ohio State Univ. Press, 1984), pp. 225-39, 230-1.

17. For further discussion of the function of the bland gentleman-hero in eighteenth-century novels, see Lynch, pp. 80-94.

18. A. O. J. Cockshut, *The Imagination of Charles Dickens* (London: Collins, 1961), p. 121. See also Edwin Eigner, "*David Copperfield* and the Benevolent Spirit," *DSA* 14 (1985): 1-15, 1-2.

19. Thomas Carlyle, "Signs of the Times," in *Thomas Carlyle: Selected Writings*, ed. Alan Shelston (Harmondsworth, England: Penguin, 1971; rprt. 1986), p. 64.

20. According to Forster, Dickens received a distressed letter from a female acquaintance who recognized herself in Miss Mowcher. Shocked at the hurt he had caused, he altered the character so that she would appear less grotesque and more sympathetic (*Life*, 2:108-9).

21. Chris Vanden Bossche, "Cookery, Not Rookery: Family and Class in *David Copperfield*," *DSA* 15 (1986): 87-109, 91.

22. Alexander Welsh, *From Copyright to Copperfield: The Identity of Dickens* (Cambridge, MA: Harvard Univ. Press, 1987), p. 153.

23. Edward Bulwer-Lytton, *England and the English*, ed. Standish Meacham (1833; rprt. Chicago: Univ. of Chicago Press, 1970), p. 34.

24. Stanley Tick, "Dickens, Dickens, Micawber . . . and Bakhtin," *VN* 79 (Spring 1991): 34-7, 35.

25. Dickens, *Letters*, 5:619.

26. Dickens, *Letters*, 5:620.

27. Forster, 2:64.

28. Forster, 2:101.

29. Dickens, *Letters*, 6:157, 6:269.

30. Dickens, *Letters*, 5:10.

31. Forster, 2:70.

Expectations Well Lost:
Dickens' Fable for His Time _____

G. Robert Stange

Great Expectations is a peculiarly satisfying and impressive novel. It is unusual to find in Dickens' work so rigorous a control of detail, so simple and organic a pattern. In this very late novel the usual features of his art—proliferating sub-plots, legions of minor grotesques—are almost entirely absent. The simplicity is that of an art form that belongs to an ancient type and concentrates on permanently significant issues. *Great Expectations* is conceived as a moral fable; it is the story of a young man's development from the moment of his first self-awareness, to that of his mature acceptance of the human condition.

So natural a theme imposes an elemental form on the novel: the over-all pattern is defined by the process of growth, and Dickens employs many of the motifs of folklore. The story of Pip falls into three phases which clearly display a dialectic progression. We see the boy first in his natural condition in the country, responding and acting instinctively and therefore virtuously. The second stage of his career involves a negation of child-like simplicity; Pip acquires his "expectations," renounces his origins, and moves to the city. He rises in society, but since he acts through calculation rather than through instinctive charity, his moral values deteriorate as his social graces improve. This middle phase of his career culminates in a sudden fall, the beginning of a redemptive suffering which is dramatically concluded by an attack of brain fever leading to a long coma. It is not too fanciful to regard this illness as a symbolic death; Pip rises from it regenerate and percipient. In the final stage of growth he returns to his birthplace, abandons his false expectations, accepts the limitations of his condition, and achieves a partial synthesis of the virtue of his innocent youth and the melancholy insight of his later experience.

Variants of such a narrative are found in the myths of many heroes. In Dickens' novel the legend has the advantage of providing an action which appeals to the great primary human affections and serves as unifying center for the richly conceived minor themes and images which form the body of the novel. It is a signal virtue of this simple structure that it saves *Great Expectations* from some of the startling weaknesses of such excellent but inconsistently developed novels as *Martin Chuzzlewit* or *Our Mutual Friend*.

The particular fable that Dickens elaborates is as interesting for its historical as for its timeless aspects. In its particulars the story of Pip is the classic legend of the nineteenth century: *Great Expectations* belongs to that class of education or development-novels which describe the young man of talents who progresses from the country to the city, ascends in the social hierarchy, and moves from innocence to experience. Stendhal in *Le Rouge et le Noir*, Balzac in *Le Père Goriot* and *Les Illusions perdues*, use the plot as a means of dissecting the post-Napoleonic world and exposing its moral poverty. This novelistic form reflects the lives of the successful children of the century, and usually expresses the mixed attitudes of its artists. Dickens, Stendhal, Balzac communicate their horror of a materialist society, but they are not without admiration for the possibilities of the new social mobility; *la carrière ouverte aux talents* had a personal meaning for all three of these energetic men.

Pip, then, must be considered in the highly competitive company of Julien Sorel, Rubempré, and Eugène de Rastignac. Dickens' tale of lost illusions, however, is very different from the French novelists'; *Great Expectations* is not more profound than other development-novels, but it is more mysterious. The recurrent themes of the genre are all there: city is posed against country, experience against innocence; there is a search for the true father; there is the exposure to crime and the acceptance of guilt and expiation. What Dickens' novel lacks is the clarity and, one is tempted to say, the essential tolerance of the French. He could not command either the saving ironic vision of Stendhal or the disenchanted practicality and secure Catholicism of Balzac. For Dickens, always the Victorian protestant, the issues of a young man's rise or fall are conceived as a drama of the individual conscience; enlightenment (partial at best) is to be found only in the agony of personal guilt.

With these considerations and possible comparisons in mind I should like to comment on some of the conspicuous features of *Great Expectations*. The novel is interesting for many reasons: it demonstrates the subtlety of Dickens' art; it displays a consistent control of narrative, imagery, and theme which gives meaning to the stark outline of the fable, and symbolic weight to every character and detail. It proves Dickens' ability (which has frequently been denied) to combine his genius for comedy with his fictional presentation of some of the most serious and permanently interesting of human concerns.

* * *

The principal themes are announced and the mood of the whole novel established in the opening pages of *Great Expectations*. The first scene with the boy Pip in the graveyard is one of the best of the superbly energetic beginnings found in almost all Dickens' mature novels. In less than a page we are given a character, his background, and his setting; within a few paragraphs more we are immersed in a decisive action. Young Pip is first seen against the background of his parents' gravestones—monuments which communicate to him no clear knowledge either of his parentage or of his position in the world. He is an orphan who must search for a father and define his own condition. The moment of this opening scene, we learn, is that at which the hero has first realized his individuality and gained his "first most vivid and broad impression of the identity of things." This information given the reader, the violent meeting between Pip and the escaped convict abruptly takes place.

The impression of the identity of things that Pip is supposed to have received is highly equivocal. The convict rises up like a ghost from among the graves, seizes the boy suddenly, threatens to kill him, holds him upside down through most of their conversation, and ends by forcing the boy to steal food for him. The children of Dickens' novels always receive rather strange impressions of things, but Pip's epiphany is the oddest of all, and in some ways the most ingenious. This encounter in the graveyard is the germinal scene of the novel. While he is held by the convict, Pip sees his world upside down; in the course of Dickens' fable the reader is invited to try the same view. This particular change of viewpoint is an ancient device of irony, but an excellent one: Dickens' satire asks us to try reversing the accepted senses of innocence and guilt, success and failure, to think of the world's goods as the world's evils.

A number of ironic reversals and ambiguous situations develop out of the first scene. The convict, Magwitch, is permanently grateful to Pip for having brought him food and a file with which to take off his leg-iron. Years later he expresses his gratitude by assuming in secrecy an economic parenthood; with the money he has made in Australia he will, unbeknownst to Pip, make "his boy" a gentleman. But the money the convict furnishes him makes Pip not a true gentleman, but a cad. He lives as a *flâneur* in London, and when he later discovers the disreputable source of his income is snobbishly horrified.

Pip's career is a parable which illustrates several religious paradoxes: he can gain only by losing all he has; only by being defiled can he be cleansed. Magwitch returns to claim his gentleman, and finally the convict's devotion and suffering arouse Pip's charity; by the time Magwitch has been captured and is dying Pip has accepted him and come to love him as a true father. The relationship is the most important one in the novel: in sympathizing with Magwitch Pip assumes the criminal's guilt; in suffering with and finally loving the despised and rejected man he finds his own real self.

Magwitch did not have to learn to love Pip. He was naturally devoted to "the small bundle of shivers," the outcast boy who brought him the stolen food and the file in the misty graveyard. There is a natural bond, Dickens suggests, between the child and the criminal; they are alike in their helplessness; both are repressed and tortured by established society, and both rebel against its incomprehensible authority. In the first scene Magwitch forces Pip to commit his first "criminal" act, to steal the file and food from his sister's house. Though this theft produces agonies of guilt in Pip, we are led to see it not as a sin but as an instinctive act of mercy. Magwitch, much later, tells Pip: "I first become aware of myself, down in Essex, a thieving turnips for my living." Dickens would have us, in some obscure way, conceive the illicit act as the means of self-realization.

In the opening section of the novel the view moves back and forth between the escaped criminal on the marshes and the harsh life in the house of Pip's sister, Mrs. Joe Gargery. The "criminality" of Pip and the convict is contrasted with the socially approved cruelty and injustice of Mrs. Joe and her respectable friends. The elders who come to the Christmas feast at the Gargerys' are pleased to describe Pip as a criminal: the young are, according to Mr. Hubble, "naterally wicious." During this most bleak of Christmas dinners the child is treated not only as outlaw, but as animal. In Mrs. Joe's first speech Pip is called a "young monkey"; then, as the spirits of the revellers rise, more and more comparisons are made between boys and animals. Uncle Pumblechook, devouring his pork, toys with the notion of Pip's having been born a "Squeaker":

> "If you had been born such, would you have been here now? Not you. . . ."
>
> "Unless in that form," said Mr. Wopsle, nodding towards the dish.
>
> "But I don't mean in that form, sir," returned Mr. Pumblechook, who had an objection to being interrupted; "I mean, enjoying himself with his elders and betters, and improving himself with their conversation, and rolling in the lap of luxury. Would he have been doing that? No, he wouldn't. And what would have been your destination?" turning on me again. "You would have been disposed of for so many shillings according to the market price of the article, and Dunstable the butcher would have come up to you as you lay in your straw, and he would have whipped you under his left arm, and with his right he would have tucked up his frock to get a penknife from out of his waistcoat-pocket, and he would have shed your blood and had your life. No bringing up by hand then. Not a bit of it!"

This identification of animal and human is continually repeated in the opening chapters of the novel, and we catch its resonance throughout the book. When the two convicts—Pip's "friend" and the other fugitive, Magwitch's ancient enemy—are captured, we experience the horror of official justice, which treats the prisoners as if they were less than human: "No one seemed surprised to see him, or interested in seeing him, or glad to see him, or sorry to see him, or spoke a word, except that somebody in the boat growled as if to dogs, 'Give way, you!'" And the prison ship, lying beyond the mud of the shore, looked to Pip "like a wicked Noah's ark."

The theme of this first section of the novel—which concludes with the capture of Magwitch and his return to the prison ship—might be called "the several meanings of humanity." Only the three characters who are in some way social outcasts—Pip, Magwitch, and Joe Gargery the child-like blacksmith—act in charity and respect the humanity of others. To Magwitch Pip is distinctly not an animal, and not capable of adult wickedness: "You'd be but a fierce young hound indeed, if at your time of life you could help to hunt a wretched warmint." And when, after he is taken, the convict shields Pip by confessing to have stolen the Gargerys' pork pie, Joe's absolution affirms the dignity of man:

> "God knows you're welcome to it—so far as it was ever mine," returned Joe, with a saving remembrance of Mrs. Joe. "We don't know what you have done, but we wouldn't have you starved to death for it, poor miserable fellow-creatur.—Would us, Pip?"

The next section of the narrative is less tightly conceived than the introductory action. Time is handled loosely; Pip goes to school, and becomes acquainted with Miss Havisham of Satis House and the beautiful Estella. The section concludes when Pip has reached early manhood, been told of his expectations, and has prepared to leave for London. These episodes develop, with variations, the theme of childhood betrayed. Pip himself renounces his childhood by coming to accept the false social values of middle-class society. His perverse development is expressed by persistent images of the opposition between the human and the non-human, the living and the dead.

On his way to visit Miss Havisham for the first time, Pip spends the night with Mr. Pumblechook, the corn-chandler, in his lodgings behind his shop. The contrast between the aridity of this old hypocrite's spirit and the viability of his wares is a type of the conflict between natural growth and social form. Pip looks at all the shop-keeper's little drawers filled with bulbs and seed packets and wonders "whether the flower-seeds and bulbs ever wanted of a fine day to break out of those jails and bloom." The imagery of life repressed is developed further in the descriptions of Miss Havisham and Satis House. The first detail Pip notices is the abandoned brewery where the once active ferment has ceased; no germ of life is to be found in Satis House or in its occupants:

> . . . there were no pigeons in the dove-cot, no horses in the stable, no pigs in the sty, no malt in the storehouse, no smells of grains and beer in the copper or the vat. All the uses and scents of the brewery might have evaporated with its last reek of smoke. In a by-yard, there was a wilderness of empty casks. . . .

On top of these casks Estella dances with solitary concentration, and behind her, in a dark corner of the building, Pip fancies that he sees a figure hanging by the neck from a wooden beam, "a figure all in yellow white, with but one shoe to the feet; and it hung so, that I could see that the faded trimmings of the dress were like earthy paper, and that the face was Miss Havisham's."

Miss Havisham *is* death. From his visits to Satis House Pip acquires his false admiration for the genteel; he falls in love with Estella and fails to see that she is the cold instrument of Miss Havisham's revenge on human passion and on life itself. When Pip learns he may expect a large inheritance from an unknown source he immediately assumes (incorrectly) that Miss Havisham is his benefactor; she does not undeceive him. Money, which is also death, is appropriately connected with the old lady rotting away in her darkened room.

Conflicting values in Pip's life are also expressed by the opposed imagery of stars and fire. Estella is by name a star, and throughout the novel stars are conceived as pitiless: "And then I looked at the stars, and considered how awful it would be for a man to turn his face up to them as he froze to death, and see no help or pity in all the glittering multitude." Estella and her light are described as coming down the dark passage of Satis House "like a star," and when she has become a woman she is constantly surrounded by the bright glitter of jewelry.

Joe Gargery, on the other hand, is associated with the warm fire of the hearth or forge. It was his habit to sit and rake the fire between the lower bars of the kitchen grate, and his workday was spent at the forge. The extent to which Dickens intended the contrast between the warm and the cold lights—the vitality of Joe and the frigid glitter of Estella— is indicated in a passage that describes the beginnings of Pip's disillusionment with his expectations:

> When I woke up in the night . . . I used to think, with a weariness on my spirits, that I should have been happier and better if I had never seen Miss Havisham's face, and had risen to manhood content to be partners with Joe in the honest old forge. Many a time of an evening, when I sat alone looking at the fire, I thought, after all, there was no fire like the forge fire and the kitchen fire at home.
>
> Yet Estella was so inseparable from all my restlessness and disquiet of mind, that I really fell into confusion as to the limits of my own part in its production.

At the end of the novel Pip finds the true light on the homely hearth, and in a last twist of the father-son theme, Joe emerges as a true parent—the only kind of parent that Dickens could ever fully approve, one that remains a child. The moral of this return to Joe sharply contradicts the accepted picture of Dickens as a radical critic of society: Joe is a humble countryman who is content with the place in the social order he has been appointed to fulfill. He fills it "well and with respect"; Pip learns that he can do no better than to emulate him.

* * *

The second stage of Pip's three-phased story is set in London, and the moral issues of the fiction are modulated accordingly. Instead of the opposition between custom and the instinctive life, the novelist treats the conflict between man and his social institutions. The topics and themes are specific, and the satire, some of it wonderfully deft, is more social than moral. Not all Dickens' social message is presented by means that seem adequate. By satirizing Pip and his leisure class friends (The Finches of the Grove, they call themselves) the novelist would have us realize that idle young men will come to a bad end. Dickens is here expressing the Victorian Doctrine of Work—a pervasive notion that both inspired and reassured his industrious contemporaries.

The difficulty for the modern reader, who is unmoved by the objects of Victorian piety, is that the doctrine appears to be the result, not of moral insight, but of didactic intent; it is presented as statement, rather than as experience or dramatized perception, and consequently it never modifies the course of fictional action or the formation of character. The distinction is crucial: it is between the Dickens who *sees* and the Dickens who *professes*; often between the good and the bad sides of his art.

The novelist is on surer ground when he comes to define the nature of wealth in a mercantile society. Instead of moralistic condemnation we have a technique that resembles parable. Pip eventually learns that his ornamental life is supported, not by Miss Havisham, but by the labor and suffering of the convict Magwitch:

"I swore arterwards, sure as ever I spec'lated and got rich, you should get rich. I lived rough, that you should live smooth; I worked hard that you should be above work. What odds, dear boy? Do I tell it fur you to feel a obligation? Not a bit. I tell it, fur you to know as that there dung-hill dog wot you kep like in, got his head so high that he could make a gentleman—and, Pip, you're him!"

The convict would not only make a gentleman but own him. The blood horses of the colonists might fling up the dust over him as he was walking, but, "I says to myself, 'If I ain't a gentleman, nor yet ain't got no learning, I'm the owner of such. All on you owns stock and land; which on you owns a brought-up London gentleman?'"

In this action Dickens has subtly led us to speculate on the connections between a gentleman and his money, on the dark origins of even the most respectable fortunes. We find Magwitch guilty of trying to own another human being, but we ask whether his actions are any more sinful than those of the wealthy *bourgeois*. There is a deeper moral in the fact that Magwitch's fortune at first destroyed the natural gentleman in Pip, but that after it was lost (it had to be forfeited to the state when Magwitch was finally captured) the "dung-hill dog" did actually make Pip a gentleman by evoking his finer feelings. This ironic distinction between "gentility" and what the father of English poetry meant by "gentilesse" is traditional in our literature and our mythology. In *Great Expectations* it arises out of the action and language of the fiction; consequently it moves and persuades us as literal statement never can.

The middle sections of the novel are dominated by the solid yet mysterious figure of Mr. Jaggers, Pip's legal guardian. Though Jaggers is not one of Dickens' greatest characters he is heavy with implication; he is so much at the center of this fable that we are challenged to interpret him—only to find that his meaning is ambiguous. On his first appearance Jaggers strikes a characteristic note of sinister authority:

He was a burly man of an exceedingly dark complexion, with an exceedingly large head and a correspondingly large hand. He took my chin in his large hand and turned up my face to have a look at me by the light of the candle. . . . His eyes were set very deep in his head, and were disagreeably sharp and suspicious. . . .

"How do *you* come here?"

"Miss Havisham sent for me, sir," I explained.

"Well! Behave yourself. I have a pretty large experience of boys, and you're a bad set of fellows. Now mind!" said he, biting the side of his great forefinger, as he frowned at me, "you behave yourself."

Pip wonders at first if Jaggers is a doctor. It is soon explained that he is a lawyer—what we now ambiguously call a *criminal* lawyer—but he is like a physician who treats moral malignancy, with the doctor's necessary detachment from individual suffering. Jaggers is interested not in the social operations of the law, but in the varieties of criminality. He exudes an antiseptic smell of soap and is described as washing his clients off as if he were a surgeon or a dentist.

Pip finds that Jaggers has "an air of authority not to be disputed . . . with a manner expressive of knowing something secret about every one of us that would effectually do for each individual if he chose to disclose it." When Pip and his friends go to dinner at Jaggers' house Pip observes that he "wrenched the weakest parts of our dispositions out of us." After the party his guardian tells Pip that he particularly liked the sullen young man they called Spider: "'Keep as clear of him as you can. But I like the fellow, Pip; he is one of the true sort. Why if I was a fortune-teller. . . . But I am not a fortune-teller,' he said. . . . 'You know what I am don't you?'" This question is repeated when Pip is being shown through Newgate Prison by Jaggers' assistant, Wemmick. The turnkey says of Pip: "Why then . . . he knows what Mr. Jaggers is."

But neither Pip nor the reader ever fully knows what Mr. Jaggers is. We learn, along with Pip, that Jaggers has manipulated the events which have shaped the lives of most of the characters in the novel; he has, in the case of Estella and her mother, dispensed a merciful but entirely personal justice; he is the only character who knows the web of secret relationships that are finally revealed to Pip. He dominates by the strength of his knowledge the world of guilt and sin—called *Little Britain*—of which his office is the center. He has, in brief, the powers that an artist exerts over the creatures of his fictional world, and that a god exerts over his creation.

As surrogate of the artist, Jaggers displays qualities of mind—complete impassibility, all-seeing unfeelingness—which are the opposite of Dickens', but, of a sort that Dickens may at times have desired. Jaggers can be considered a fantasy figure created by a novelist who is forced by his intense sensibility to re-live the sufferings of his fellow men and who feels their agonies too deeply.

In both the poetry and fiction of the nineteenth century there are examples of a persistent desire of the artist *not to care*. The mood, which is perhaps an inevitable concomitant of Romanticism, is expressed in Balzac's ambivalence toward his great character Vautrin. As arch-criminal and Rousseauistic man, Vautrin represents all the attitudes that Balzac the churchman and monarchist ostensibly rejects, yet is presented as a kind of artist-hero, above the law, who sees through the social system with an almost noble cynicism.

Related attitudes are expressed in the theories of art developed by such different writers as Flaubert and Yeats. While—perhaps because—Flaubert himself suffered from hyperaesthesia, he conceived the ideal novelist as coldly detached, performing his examination with the deft impassivity of the surgeon. Yeats, the "last Romantic," found the construction of a mask or anti-self necessary to poetic creation, and insisted that the anti-self be cold and hard—all that he as poet and feeling man was not.

Dickens' evocation of this complex of attitudes is less political than Balzac's, less philosophical than Flaubert's or Yeats'. Jaggers has a complete understanding of human evil but, unlike the living artist, can wash his hands of it. He is above ordinary institutions; like a god he dispenses justice, and like a god displays infinite mercy through unrelenting severity:

> "Mind you, Mr. Pip," said Wemmick, gravely in my ear, as he took my arm to be more confidential; "I don't know that Mr. Jaggers does a better thing than the way in which he keeps himself so high. He's always so high. His constant height is of a piece with his immense abilities. That Colonel durst no more take leave of *him*, than that turnkey durst ask him his intentions respecting a case. Then between his height and them, he slips in his subordinate—don't you see?—and so he has 'em soul and body."

Pip merely wishes that he had "some other guardian of minor abilities."

* * *

The final moral vision of *Great Expectations* has to do with the nature of sin and guilt. After visiting Newgate, Pip, still complacent and self-deceived, thinks how strange it was that he should be encompassed by the taint of prison and crime. He tries to beat the prison dust off his feet and to exhale its air from his lungs; he is going to meet Estella, who must not be contaminated by the smell of crime. Later it is revealed that Estella, the pure, is the bastard child of Magwitch and a murderess. Newgate is figuratively described as a greenhouse, and the prisoners as plants carefully tended by Wemmick, assistant to Mr. Jaggers. These disturbing metaphors suggest that criminality is the condition of life. Dickens would distinguish between the native, inherent sinfulness from which men can be redeemed, and that evil which destroys life: the sin of the hypocrite or oppressor, the smothering wickedness of corrupt institutions. The last stage of Pip's progression is reached when he learns to love the criminal and to accept his own implication in the common guilt.

Though Dickens' interpretation is theologically heterodox, he deals conventionally with the ancient question of free will and predestination. In one dramatic paragraph Pip's "fall" is compared with the descent of the rock slab on the sleeping victim in the Arabian Nights tale: Slowly, slowly, "all the work, near and afar, that tended to the end, had been accomplished; and in an instant the blow was struck, and the roof of my stronghold dropped upon me." Pip's fall was the result of a chain of predetermined events but he was, nevertheless, responsible for his own actions; toward the end of the novel Miss Havisham gravely informs him: "You have made your own snares. *I* never made them."

The patterns of culpability in *Great Expectations* are so intricate that the whole world of the novel is eventually caught in a single web of awful responsibility. The leg-iron, for example, which the convict removed with the file Pip stole for him is found by Orlick and used as a weapon to brain Mrs. Joe. By this fearsome chain of circumstance Pip shares the guilt for his sister's death.

Profound and suggestive as is Dickens' treatment of guilt and expiation in this novel, to trace its remoter implications is to find something excessive and idiosyncratic. A few years after he wrote *Great Expectations* Dickens remarked to a friend that he felt always as if he were wanted by the police—"irretrievably tainted." Compared to most of the writers of his time the Dickens of the later novels seems to be obsessed with guilt. The way in which his development-novel differs from those of his French compeers emphasizes an important quality of Dickens' art. The young heroes of *Le Rouge et le Noir* and *Le Père Goriot* proceed from innocence, through suffering to learning. They are surrounded by evil, and they can be destroyed by it. But Stendhal, writing in a rationalist tradition, and Balzac, displaying the worldliness that only a Catholic novelist can command, seem astonishingly cool, even callous, beside Dickens. *Great Expectations* is outside either Cartesian or Catholic rationalism; profound as only an elementally simple book can be, it finds its analogues not in the novels of Dickens' English or French contemporaries, but in the writings of that other irretrievably tainted artist, Fyodor Dostoevski.

From *College English* 16 (1954): 9-17. Originally published by the National Council of Teachers of English.

The Sense of Self_____

Monroe Engel

With no more than the first words of the novel on paper, Dickens wrote to Forster that *Great Expectations* would "be written in the first person throughout, and . . . you will find the hero to be a boy-child, like David . . . To be quite sure I had fallen into no unconscious repetitions, I read *David Copperfield* again the other day, and was affected by it to a degree you would hardly believe."[1] In his own mind, the two books, *David Copperfield* and *Great Expectations*, were a pair. Comparison reveals not only a number of precise parallels, large and small, between the two books, but much too about the change in perspective that makes the two books so different despite these parallels.

David Copperfield was written in 1849-50, *Great Expectations* in 1860-61. The crucial years for the hardening or darkening of Dickens' thinking are the middle fifties. The two autobiographical novels span this time almost symmetrically, and the difference in perspective and tone accurately represents the change in Dickens' view of himself in his world. *Great Expectations* is in a sense the mirror image of *Copperfield*.

The earlier and more explicitly autobiographical novel is a success story, its dominant mood pathetic. *Great Expectations* describes a movement away from success, and its dominant mood is ironic. When the materials of the two novels are most similar, the change in point of view is often clearest. For example, Australia, which is a Utopia for Mr. Peggotty and the Micawbers, is a place of hard exile for Magwitch. Betsey Trotwood is made eccentric but wise by her disappointments in love, but Miss Havisham is crazed by hers. In *David Copperfield*, the moral view of crime is simple, uncomplicated; in *Great Expectations*, the more realistic and complicated view of crime provides much of the richness of the book. The depravity of Steerforth is mitigated; that of Bentley Drummle is undisguised and is given purposeful social context. The incompetence of David's mother is treated affectionately, but Mrs. Pocket is vicious.

In other cases, however, the parallelism in material indicates little of the difference in quality of the books. Herbert is a foil for Pip much as Traddles is for David. Biddy is the Agnes of the later book. The wedding of Wemmick and Miss Skiffins is clearly reminiscent of the wedding of Barkis and Peggotty. Similarly, the scarring of Estella's mother recalls the scarring of Rosa Dartle. Pip's servant is much like David's page; the butcher boy becomes Trabb's boy. Pumblechook's examination of Pip in arithmetic recalls a similar examination of David by Mr. Murdstone.

The number of these parallels (and there are more), both simple and complicated, major and minor, shows how often the two novels are embarked on related pieces of fictional exploration. It affords, too, specific and detailed evidence of the change in Dickens' view between the time of *David Copperfield* and that of *Great Expectations*. Yet the continuity of his imagination, of which the comparison provides at least equal evidence, is more profound than the change in his view or construction of those facts and configurations of experience in which his imagination is founded.

David Copperfield

David Copperfield is a novel about worldly prudence; and conversely, about the dangers of imprudence and trust. Nearly every character in the novel, nearly every event of importance, nearly ever relationship can be regarded as an example or variation on the theme of prudence: in business, in money matters, in friendship, in love. This consideration precedes David's birth. Miss Trotwood talks of the unworldliness of her dead nephew, David's father, who "Calls a house a rookery when there's not a rook near it, and takes the birds on trust, because he sees the nests!" Miss Trotwood is full of compassionate contempt for her nephew's "trust," but she has herself been the victim of trust in love, and is to be a victim of financial trust also. David's father had shown his imprudence in other and graver ways too. He had married a child wife, a form of imprudence that is to be part of his son's inheritance; and though when he dies he leaves his wife with an adequate income, a fact that surprises Miss Trotwood, he leaves her, as she herself confesses, totally unprepared for "being quite alone and dependent on myself in this rough world." The money he has left her in fact only undoes her, bringing the Murdstones to prey on her.

The beginning of the novel suggests a shape for what is to come. Even David's minor misadventures as a boy are likely to be misadventures of imprudence or unfounded trust: with the waiter at the inn, for example, who eats his dinner, or the carter who runs away with his box. This is a story in which innocence may and does have ultimate rewards, but is first much abused and preyed on. Mr. Mell is betrayed by David, bullied by Steerforth, abused by Creakle. Tommy Traddles, too, is abused for his feeling heart and good nature—by Steerforth, by Creakle, by Micawber. It is Traddles' trusting unworldliness, not any particular failure of either industry or intelligence, that makes him the foil to that part of Copperfield's history that is an account of the way to fame and worldly success. Dr. Strong is a trusting innocent too, who is preyed on by his wife's relatives, and is saved from actual cuckoldry, though not from the onus of it, by little more than Dickens' inclination to respect propriety. Dora Spenlow and Clara Copperfield represent a kind of extreme of innocence and trust, and each of them, in the scheme of this world, has to die young.

Dickens' inclination to respect propriety is only this, not a rule, even as Victorian propriety itself is more a convention of public admission than a description of conduct. Sex has its place and force in this novel, even though it is treated guardedly, and is seen equally in terms of prudence and trust—trust in this case being the trust in passion itself, which leads to ruin. In addition to the unfortunate loves of David's father, and Clara Copperfield, and Betsey Trotwood—all examples of imprudent love and its ravages—there are other examples in which the sexual passion is more openly at issue: Emily's seduction by Steerforth; the psychotic passion of Rosa Dartle for Steerforth; the ruin of

Emily's friend, Martha; Murdstone's insane second wife; and Mrs. Strong's infatuation with her no-good cousin, Jack Maldon. In the last case, the infatuation itself has far more force than does its comfortable resolution.

Imprudence in love brings disaster; and prudence—sensible love, aware of advantage—brings happiness. Tommy Traddles, though he waits many years to earn his marriage, is at last blissfully happy, and Barkis, who marries Peggotty for her cooking and housewifery, is domestically blessed too. Barkis's caution in love is related to his caution with money. Both are funny, even a little pathetic, but both turn out well.

The history of David's loves is a history of the mistakes survived in the learning of prudence. His first love, for Emily, is an idyllic child's love, but without future. Miss Shepherd, "a boarder at the Misses Nettingall's establishment," is a less poetic version of the same kind of love. "The eldest Miss Larkins," who dances with officers, is the Victorian English equivalent for the convention of the young man's older first mistress. Dora Spenlow, who signifies David's congenital imprudence in matters of love, is a self-confessed child-wife, unable even to manage her account books or order her house. Her attractiveness is rather pre-sexual, and like Clara she is unfit for adult life, and must die. Finally, of course, David prudently marries Agnes Wickfield and lives happily ever after.

While other characters are more or less permanently committed to their early choices or accidents, David has a succession of chances and choices. Other people are vulnerable, and their humanity lies in good part in their vulnerability, but David becomes increasingly an invulnerable figure, destined for success no matter what happens to him. Though the child David exists as a seen and felt presence in the novel, the older David becomes more and more a seeing eye and recounting voice to whom things do not happen in the same way that they happen to other people, and who tends therefore to recede. This effect is anticipated in the very first sentence of the novel: "Whether I shall turn out to be the hero of my own life, or whether that station will be held by any-body else, these pages must show."

In part, this recession of the central character from the novel—a re-cession in intensity, if not in importance—can be attributed to the tech-nique of narration employed. The story is told in the first person, from the vantage of the adult David. He can see himself as a boy with some detachment, in the round. When the narrator approaches closer to the time of the telling of the story, however, he can no longer separate him-self sufficiently from the hero whose adventures he recounts. But the strategy of the novel, too, affects this progressive paling of David in the story. *David Copperfield* is really a rags-to-riches story, or, with more convolutions, a series of descents and ascents heading toward a final ascent. As early as the time of his employment at Murdstone and Grinby's, David says: "I knew from the first, that if I could not do my work as well as any of the rest, I could not hold myself above slight and contempt." Now though success may capture our interest because of its reference to our own aspirations, it is unlikely to capture our imagina-tion. The real resources of literary art are rather on the side of failure.

But if all this is so, it still remains that *David Copperfield* has cap-tured the imagination of readers for a century. Dickens himself spoke of it as his "favourite child" among all his books, and specifically of how the book grasped his imagination: "It would concern the reader lit-tle, perhaps, to know how sorrowfully the pen is laid down at the close of a two-years' imaginative task; or how an Author feels as if he were dismissing some portion of himself into the shadowy world, when a crowd of the creatures of his brain are going from him for ever . . . no one can ever believe this Narrative in the reading more than I believed it in the writing."

This statement in a late preface reflects and even duplicates part of an extraordinary letter Dickens wrote to Forster as he was finishing the writing of *David Copperfield*: "I am within three pages of the shore; and am strangely divided, as usual in such cases, between sorrow and joy. Oh, my dear Forster, if I were to say half of what *Copperfield* makes me feel to-night, how strangely, even to you, I should be turned inside out! I seem to be sending some part of myself into the Shadowy World."

That there is a power, as suggested, in this novel, few readers will contest. That this power is not directly related to the overt moral of the novel means quite simply that Dickens is still, in 1849-50, endeavoring to deny the tragic implications of life that he, in fact, sees with great clarity and responds to with greatest imaginative force. On the surface, *David Copperfield* asserts the need for prudence and the beauty of success. But the power of the novel comes from its vital rendering of the beauty of incaution and the poignancy of limitation and defeat. In its plot, *David Copperfield* is conventionally Victorian. But essentially and imaginatively, it subverts its own contentions.

The novel is autobiographical to varying extents in its different parts, but most when it recounts the dark London period of David's childhood. It is this period that informs all the rest of David's life, and of the novel, even when it is past:

> A remoteness had come upon the old Blunderstone life—which seemed to lie in the haze of an immeasurable distance; and . . . a curtain had for ever fallen on my life at Murdstone and Grinby's. No one has ever raised that curtain since. I have lifted it for a moment, even in this narrative, with a reluctant hand, and dropped it gladly. The remembrance of that life is fraught with so much pain to me, with so much mental suffering and want of hope, that I have never had the courage even to examine how long I was doomed to lead it. Whether it lasted for a year, or more, or less, I do not know. I only know that it was, and ceased to be; and that I have written, and there I leave it.

In the fragment of an autobiography that Dickens showed to Forster, there follows after the blacking factory account a strikingly similar passage, ending: "I have never, until I now impart it to this paper, in any burst of confidence with any one, my own wife not excepted, raised the curtain I then dropped, thank God." David shares with Dickens not only certain grim experiences of childhood, but also the will and inability to forget them.

Though the scheme of *David Copperfield* points to the desirability of social status, the sanctity and authority of status are often under attack. David's first distinction, or assertion of self, is an abortive revolt against authority, the biting of Mr. Murdstone's hand. He has come to recite his lessons for his mother, with the two Murdstones as audience. Mr. Murdstone, in the process of bending a "lithe and limber" cane when David comes in, warns the boy that he must do better this time with his lessons. Given this encouragement, David of course forgets everything. When he has failed completely, Murdstone leads him from the room to his own room and beats him cruelly. David first begs him to stop, then catches his hand in his teeth and bites "it through. It sets my teeth on edge to think of it." Murdstone then beats him "as if he would have beaten me to death," and locks him in his room alone, feverish and raging.

> How well I remember, when my smart and passion began to cool, how wicked I began to feel!
>
> I sat listening for a long while, but there was not a sound. I crawled up from the floor, and saw my face in the glass, so swollen, red, and ugly that it almost frightened me. My stripes were sore and stiff, and made me cry afresh, when I moved; but they were nothing to the guilt I felt. It lay heavier on my breast than if I had been a most atrocious criminal, I dare say.

More striking here than the cruelty and sadism of Murdstone's authority is the fact that David is corrupted by that authority. Though the reader rejoices in the biting of Murdstone's hand, David himself is appalled by what he has done, his guilt lies heavier on him than his pain, and he feels "a most atrocious criminal." George Orwell, a careful reader of Dickens, tells a similar story of his own boyhood: of how, beaten by the master of his school for bedwetting, he felt guilty not only for his weak bladder, but also for the loss of the master's cane, broken over his back in the course of the beating. The attack in *David Copperfield* on the sadism of authority continues with Creakle and Tungay, at David's first school, whose chief victim is Traddles, the best-hearted boy in the school, and who fear and fail to exercise any authority over Steerforth, who genuinely needs it.

There is subversive humor too in *David Copperfield*, at the expense of institutions and honored professions. The intrusive Chapter 61 is the most blatant example, in which Creakle's educational genius has finally been properly put to work managing a model prison, among whose prisoners the shining stars of conduct and piety are Uriah Heep and Littimer. The legal profession too, not reserved for derision in *Bleak House* alone, comes in for the usual treatment. Mr. Spenlow tells David of the "very pretty pickings" likely to come from a disputed will for a "neat little estate of thirty or forty thousand pounds"; but he denies the possibility that there could be a better way of handling such matters. After all, he argues, "when the price of wheat per bushel had been highest, the Commons had been busiest." Finally, David's occupation as a Parliamentary reporter provides full opportunity to disparage the House of Commons more directly.

The humor of British institutions is bitter humor, relating as it does to the dire life of the lower class, of which, however, there are really only brief glimpses in *David Copperfield* once David himself leaves the blacking factory: Mr. Mell's visit to his mother, for instance, or the view of the house and quarter in which the fallen girl Martha lives in London. The Micawbers' life provides a similar insight, though refracted by the disproportioning views of Mr. and Mrs. Micawber; and even Uriah Heep and his mother are seen, as, in some part, victims of poverty and the British system of providing for the poor in a degrading way that fosters hypocrisy.

Dickens' darker vision, though, is founded on more than the existence of bad character and bad institutions. In an unforgettable passage, David thinks of his mother, after her death, as the younger, unworn mother of his infancy, and of himself as the dead and untried baby buried with her, "hushed forever on her bosom." The sense of aging, of death, and of loss—the passage of the river of life into the sea—pervades the book and gives it weight: David's loss of Dora, and of a vision of the thoughtless beauty of youth; the loss of Steerforth to David, to Rosa Dartle, to Mrs. Steerforth, and the agony that comes to each when death spells the end of the possibility of reconciliation; the death of Dora's dog at the instant of his mistress's death; Martha's attempt to drown herself in the river, and the deaths of Ham and Steerforth in the sea, in which always the river of life loses its identity; Barkis's departure with the tide. Against all this, Steerforth's picture of life as a race to be won is a preposterous affront; and, indeed, any notion of success is an affront, given the pathetic insufficiency of prudence or wisdom to slow or change the current of man's life into death.

Great Expectations

The end of the first part of *Great Expectations* suggests a context for the entire novel:

> I walked away at a good pace, thinking it was easier to go than I had supposed it would be, and reflecting that it would never have done to have an old shoe thrown after the coach, in sight of all the High-Street. I whistled and made nothing of going. But the village was very peaceful and quiet, and the light mists were solemnly rising, as if to show me the world, and I had been so innocent and little there, and all beyond was so unknown and great, that in a moment with a strong heave and sob I broke into tears. . . .
>
> So subdued I was by those tears, and by their breaking out again in the course of the quiet walk, that when I was on the coach, and it was clear of the town, I deliberated with an aching heart whether I would not get down when we changed horses and walk back, and have another evening at home, and a better parting. We changed, and I had not made up my mind,

and still reflected for my comfort that it would be quite practicable to get down and walk back, when we changed again. . . .

We changed again, and yet again, and it was now too late and too far to go back, and I went on. And the mists had all solemnly risen now, and the world lay spread before me.

No over-subtlety is required at this point to remember the departure of Adam and Eve from Eden—behind them the cherubim on the ground looking, Milton tells us, like mist risen from the marshes, while the other way, "The World was all before them."

The usefulness of this suggestion depends on caution. The suggestion is slight, and *Great Expectations* is no formal allegory. It would not have occurred to Dickens that one book could or should stand upon another. Obviously, however, the departure from Eden belongs in no exclusive way to Milton, but has become one of those great general metaphors by which man explains his reasonably inexplicable condition. The slight verbal parallel between the end of the first part of *Great Expectations* and the end of *Paradise Lost* may only be happy chance, but it exercises an imaginative control nonetheless over this perhaps most controlled of Dickens' novels.

The Eden from which young Philip Pirrip departs does not conform much to our idea of the garden: the marshes extending from the river where the prison ships are perpetually anchored; the warning gibbet on the shore; the mists and fogs and damp, cold weather; the unpromising village with its merchant rulers of the High-Street, its rough inn and pub, its tight provincial society; and the uncomfortable house by the forge where Mrs. Gargery brings up not only her young brother but her husband too, "by hand." None of this is much to the point except that it has the quality of being a place apart, isolated largely, though not completely, from the world.

What figures most here is not the cosmography of place, but the innocence of Pip's soul and mind in this place, an innocence which leads him to infer the characters and appearances of his parents and brothers from their tombstones; to love Joe "because the dear fellow let me love him"; to pity the desolation of the escaped convict and be glad that he enjoys his stolen food; to believe that the exhortation of his catechism, "to walk in the same all the days of my life," binds him to take the same route without variation whenever he leaves his house to walk through the village. This innocence, too, enables him to discriminate justly between good and bad, and wisely among people as to those who are his friends and those who are not. Pip's innocence is fractured by expectation—planted by his sister and Pumblechook, encouraged by the secret plans of Magwitch and of Miss Havisham. The objects of his expectation are, conventionally enough, property and love, scarcely distinguishable in his thinking, but each considered in detailed variation in this novel.

The evil of property lies in its tendency to use its possessors instead of being used by them. The point is made unambiguously and with force. Pip's first genuine act in *Great Expectations*, and an act from which ensue the consequences that in good part make the novel, is to steal food and a file from his home for the starving escaped convict Magwitch. It is notable that the guilt that haunts his mind has nothing to do with the genuinely serious matter of aiding an escaped and dangerous convict. It is his own theft he worries about, and not so much the stolen file as the stolen food, the broken vittles. Joe Gargery, who remains in the Eden of innocence throughout the novel, and is the control or fixed point in relation to which Pip's wandering is measured, makes overt the moral significance of this theft, when the escaped convict, to protect Pip, says that it was he who stole the food from the Gargerys' house: "'God knows you're welcome to it—so far as it was ever mine,' returned Joe, with a saving remembrance of Mrs. Joe. 'We don't know what you have done, but we wouldn't have you starved to death for it, poor miserable fellow creature—Would us, Pip?'"

Joe tries to bolster Pip in his innocence, but Mrs. Joe is another matter. For her, property is sacred and uncomfortable, like some people's religion. Her preparations for Christmas dinner blight the holiday, and when she walks to town, she carries "a basket like the Great Seal of England in plaited straw, a pair of pattens, a spare shawl, and an umbrella, though it was a fine bright day." Pip was not clear whether "these articles were carried penitentially or ostentatiously," but he thought they were probably "displayed as articles of property—much as Cleopatra or any other sovereign lady on the Rampage might exhibit her wealth in a pageant or procession."

Pumblechook (a good example of Dickens' genius for fitting names) is far worse than Mrs. Gargery, and it is he who pushes Pip into the Havisham connection, bullies and maltreats him, flatters him when his fortunes are risen, and turns on him self-righteously and full of injury when they fall. But the real nightmare of property is provided by Miss Havisham in Satis House. A rough irony of names is used frequently in *Great Expectations*, starting with the title itself; of the name of the Havisham house, Estella says: "It meant when it was given, that whoever had this house, could want nothing else. They must have been easily satisfied in those days, I should think." In a ruin of old symbolic goods, Miss Havisham lives a living death, and plots her vicarious vengeance on victims who have only a token culpability for her tragedy. It is her goods, her wealth, that have ruined her in the first place by attracting Compeyson to her, and now she will have the goods work in reverse, by making Estella rich, impregnable, heart-breaking.

To Pip at first she seems, quite accurately, a waxwork or a skeleton amidst her goods, but this perception does not save him from becoming a victim to his expectations of property, and of property as a means of access to love. Miss Havisham encourages his delusion that she is his patroness, the cause and source of his expectations, and that, as she intends him to have fortune, she intends him to have Estella too, and to be prepared for her and made more worthy of her by this money. So he is least prepared for the ultimate revelation of the true source of his expectations. In fact, he thinks his bond of complicity with Magwitch to be reduced, almost written off by his fortune:

If I had often thought before, with something allied to shame, of my companionship with the fugitive whom I had once seen limping among those graves, what were my thoughts on this Sunday, when the place recalled the wretch, ragged and shivering, with his felon iron and badge! My comfort was, that it happened a long time ago, and that he had doubtless been transported a long way off, and that he was dead to me, and might be veritably dead into the bargain.

No more low wet grounds, no more dykes and sluices, no more of these grazing cattle—though they seemed, in their dull manner, to wear a more respectful air now, and to face round, in order that they might stare as long as possible at the possessor of such great expectations—farewell, monotonous acquaintances of my childhood, henceforth I was for London and greatness: not for smith's work in general and for you! I made my exultant way to the old Battery, and, lying down there to consider the question whether Miss Havisham intended me for Estella, fell asleep.

But it is the fortune that makes Pip's bond to Magwitch indissoluble. In the world of this novel, property is harmless only when it is allowed no false aura of dignity or pretense, when it is clearly useful, and bears clear and preferably comic marks of human contrivance and effort. Of such property Wemmick's little estate at Walworth is the chief example; and in this setting there is a happy, loving society.

Of Pip's second expectation, love, Dickens draws an equally forbidding and infrequently relieved picture. It is useful to remember Dickens' own life at this point, though not to elaborate on it tenuously. By 1860, his marriage had ended in a legal separation, but was still a source of unrest and bitterness to him; and his relationship with Ellen Ternan too, now well past its first flush, had settled into some sort of disappointing resolution of its own. At least two critics[2] have found verbal plays and echoings of Ellen Ternan's name in the names of a number of Dickens' late heroines, including the Estella of *Great Expectations*. These heroines reflect too, they think, Ellen Ternan's failing in her relationship with Dickens: coldness, frigidity. Be this as it may—and the evidence gives the speculation great weight—it is clear enough that Estella is as cold and distant, as removed, as the stars her name suggests. She warns Pip herself that she has "no heart"; and, unable to manage a normal response to love, she has the decency to reserve herself from anyone capable of better, and gives herself instead to Bentley Drummle, who is as unfeeling as she, but a sensual brute in addition.

In some really frightful way here, anything like normal sexuality always makes for terror and tragedy. Miss Havisham falls passionately in love with Compeyson and is victimized by her love. The love of Magwitch and his wife ends in violence. Orlick, who desires Biddy, kills Mrs. Gargery and tries to kill Pip too. Mr. Pocket is victimized by his early love for Mrs. Pocket, and Joe by his for Pip's sister. The only relationships between men and women that work out are reasonable, nonpassionate relationships: the middle-aged love of Wemmick and Miss Skiffins; Joe's fatherly love for Biddy, and her motherly love for him; the patient domestic attachment of Herbert and Clara; and the final rapprochement of Pip and Estella after their misspent youths are well behind them.

It is no wonder, then, that with his great expectations of property and love, Pip comes a cropper. There is no doubt that these bad expectations seem to make inevitable his disappointments. Yet again, here as in *David Copperfield*, fate is beyond good, or bad choice, beyond prudence or prodigality. Pip's profoundest fate works by indirection, in which good comes out of bad and bad out of good. The basic first action in the novel is the encounter with Magwitch in the cemetery. Out of a mixture of fear and compassion, Pip helps the escaped convict, bringing him food, and a file with which to remove his fetters. Initially, everything seems to condone Pip's actions as simple charity toward someone in distress.

But the situation is not this simple. Magwitch is an escaped convict, a man both capable and guilty of great violence. After his escapade, Pip is in fear of the police, and feels guilty for his failure of openness with

Joe. But these are comparatively minor matters, only the direct consequences of his complicity with Magwitch. The indirect consequences are more dire. When his sister is struck over the head with a heavy object, that object turns out to be "a convict's leg-iron . . . filed asunder." Pip is certain it is Magwitch's iron, filed off with the file with which he provided him. Still Pip temporizes and does not disclose what he knows to Joe. He contains it, even as he kept his counsel when the strange man in the pub stirred a drink with a file, and presented him with a shilling wrapped in two one-pound notes, and when he had bad dreams at night, and thought—rather insufficiently to the point—what a "guiltily coarse and common thing it was, to be on secret terms of conspiracy with convicts."

The richest morality and realism of *Great Expectations* depends on the figure of Magwitch. The convict is a dangerous, violent man, and unregenerate in his violence, as his final murder of Compeyson shows. His wife, Molly, too, with her strong scarred wrists, is a woman whose violence is kept down only by strong restraint, her own and Jaggers'. Yet the violence of these two (and of many others, it is suggested) is not spontaneous, or not always and entirely so. In part at least, they are the victims of poverty and of a class system that fosters and gives protection to weak or evil villains like Miss Havisham's brother or Compeyson. Official justice, the justice of the courts and prisons, is an unfeeling and corrupt justice whose drunken ministers sell good seats in court for half-a-crown, and buy second-hand clothes cheap from the executioner.

The nature of this justice is made clear in the account of Magwitch's trial:

> The trial was very short and very clear. Such things as could be said for him, were said—how he had taken to industrious habits, and had thriven lawfully and reputably. But, nothing could unsay the fact that he had returned, and was there in the presence of the Judge and Jury. It was impossible to try him for that, and do otherwise than find him guilty.

At that time it was the custom (as I learnt from my terrible experience of that Sessions) to devote a concluding day to the passing of Sentences, and to make a finishing effect with the Sentence of Death. But for the indelible picture that my remembrance now holds before me, I could scarcely believe, even as I write these words, that I saw two-and-thirty men and women put before the Judge to receive that sentence together. Foremost among the two-and-thirty was he; seated, that he might get breath enough to keep life in him.

The whole scene starts out again in the vivid colours of the moment, down to the drops of April rain on the windows of the court, glittering in the rays of April sun. Penned in the dock, as I again stood outside it at the corner with his hand in mine, were the two-and-thirty men and women; some defiant, some stricken with terror, some sobbing and weeping, some covering their faces, some staring gloomily about. There had been shrieks from among the women convicts, but they had been stilled, and a hush had succeeded. The sheriffs with their great chains and nosegays, other civic gewgaws and monsters, criers, ushers, a great gallery full of people— a large theatrical audience—looked on, as the two-and-thirty and the Judge were solemnly confronted. Then, the Judge addressed them. Among the wretched creatures before him whom he must single out for special address, was one who almost from infancy had been an offender against the laws. . . .

The sun was striking in at the great windows of the court, through the glittering drops of rain upon the glass, and it made a broad shaft of light between the two-and-thirty and the Judge, linking both together, and perhaps reminding some among the audience, how both were passing on, with absolute equality, to the greater judgment that knoweth all things and cannot err. Rising for a moment, a distinct speck of face in this way of light, the prisoner said, "My Lord, I have received my sentence of Death from the Almighty, but I bow to yours," and sat down again. There was some hushing, and the Judge went on with what he had to say to the rest. Then, they were all formally doomed, and some of them were supported out, and some of them sauntered out with a haggard look of bravery, and a few nodded to the gallery, and two or three shook hands, and others went out chewing the fragments of herb they had taken from the sweet herbs lying about. He went last of all, because of having to be helped from his chair and to go very slowly; and he held my hand while all the others were removed, and while the audience got up (putting their dresses right, as they might at church or elsewhere) and pointed down at this criminal or that, and most of all at him and me.

In contrast to this justice of mass reprisal and of brutalizing public spectacle, Magwitch's administration of a personal justice that rewards good and punishes evil and takes the consequences for its own acts has its splendor and dignity, even though it cannot be allowed.

Pip, after visiting Newgate with Wemmick, thinks how strange it is that the taint of prison and crime should pervade his fortune and advancement. He thinks, too, what a contrast all this is to "the beautiful young Estella." But what he must still learn, of course, is that Estella is in fact the daughter of Magwitch and Molly. Eventually, he not only knows but is also reconciled. He comes not only to be unashamed of the dying Magwitch, but genuinely to love him, and just before Magwitch dies, Pip is able to tell him that his daughter whom he thought dead is alive, that she is a lady and very beautiful, and that he loves her. As Miss Havisham's foster-daughter and her false heir, Estella and Pip cannot come together. As Magwitch's true daughter and his deprived heir, they will.

There are no triumphantly happy endings in Dickens' later novels. Instead, there is the second chance that comes after chastening and acceptance. In *David Copperfield* still, the happiness that comes after chastening seems almost able to disregard its own past—it is a virtually uninjured, full happiness. But in the later books, life is made more consequential, and people are what they are because of what they have been. Their happiness is a reconciliation to knowledge, and in these later books too, knowledge without reconciliation produces the riven mind, as in the case of Flora Finching. The alternatives Dickens offers, with increasing exclusiveness, are either madness, or the muted happiness that comes after acceptance.

The actual reconciliation of Pip and Estella at the end of *Great Expectations* was, as everyone knows, not in the original draft of the novel, but was added when Bulwer-Lytton objected to the unrelievedly somber tone of the original ending. But the limited optimism of the resolution of the novel does not depend on, and is not modified by, the changed ending. Pip has lost all his property, and has only such money as he earns by his own labors. Estella too has lost all her property. The Estella whom Pip had loved, and expected, really exists no longer, nor has he won the relatively romantic consolation of Biddy. And he is reconciled to his losses. Both he and Estella, we are told, have paled but grown better with age.

So after many years they meet again on a misty early evening on the grounds of Miss Havisham's old house—in the ruined garden, in fact, to return to the metaphor of the loss of Eden. Now Estella has a heart, and can confess to Pip's place in it. She, of course, has her place still in his heart, too. It is reasonable then to suggest that Pip has reentered the ruined Eden in order to leave again, as Adam had left, chastened and with his chastened Eve: "I took her hand in mine, and we went out of the ruined place; and, as the morning mists had risen long ago when I first left the forge, so, the evening mists were rising now, and in all the broad expanse of tranquil light they showed to me, I saw no shadow of another parting from her."

Great Expectations provides a correction to the conventional optimism of *David Copperfield*. Pip must learn that fortune is not the way to happiness. Perhaps, too, Dickens is celebrating the losses that accompanied his success and the consequences of his will to forget his past. Certainly, to the modern reader, *Great Expectations* seems the more adult book—in its view of love, of success, of society; and its tighter structure and allegorical overtones are likely to please the chaste and intellectual modern taste more than the loose structure and folk tale elements of *David Copperfield*.

Yet though opinions and views may change, the basic vision of the individual imagination is relatively constant, and the greater the work of art, the more it founds the changing appearances dictated in part by view and opinion on the obsessional configurations of the imagination. Both *David Copperfield* and *Great Expectations* bear the profound marks of Dickens' imagination, and despite the many important ways in which one denies the other, essentially they reveal the same vision of life. Each of these books—*David Copperfield* as well as *Great Expectations*—is subversive, and the power of each depends on a response to the rendering of loss, of the beauty of hazard, of the horror of social injustice, and of the preposterous comedy of hypocrisy and self-delusion.

From *The Maturity of Dickens* by Monroe Engel, pp. 146-168. Cambridge, Mass.: Harvard University Press. Copyright © 1959 by Monroe Engel. Copyright © renewed 1987 by Monroe Engel. Reprinted by permission of the publisher.

Notes

1. *Letters* III, 186, October 1860.

2. Edmund Wilson; and Ada Nisbet in *Dickens and Ellen Ternan* (Berkeley, California, 1952).

Structure and Idea in *Bleak House*_____
Robert A. Donovan

> I propose therefore that we enquire into the nature of justice and injustice,
> first as they appear in the State, and secondly in the individual, proceeding
> from the greater to the lesser and comparing them.
>
> —*The Republic*, tr. Jowett

> 'Tis the Last Judgment's fire must cure this place,
> Calcine its clods and set my prisoners free.
>
> —Browning, "Childe Roland to the Dark Tower Came"

If anything can supply an intelligible principle of Dickens's development as a novelist, it is the constant strengthening and focusing of his protest against social injustice. This pervasive concern with social justice is the link connecting the otherwise light-hearted and high-spirited meanderings of Pickwick in a world of coaching inns and manor farms to the sinister events which are preparing in the dark world of Chancery in *Bleak House* or of the Marshalsea in *Little Dorrit*. Speaking of this last novel, Shaw remarked in his often quoted preface to *Great Expectations* that it "is a more seditious book than *Das Kapital*. All over Europe men and women are in prison for pamphlets and speeches which are to *Little Dorrit* as red pepper to dynamite." Shaw had, like Macaulay, his own heightened and telling way of putting things, but to a world which persisted in regarding Dickens as the great impresario of soap opera, Shaw's comments needed to be made. The indifference of society to the suffering of its members; the venality, brutishness, or sheer ineptitude of its public servants; its perverse substitution of the virtues of the head for those of the heart; the hopeless inadequacy of its political and philanthropic institutions: these are the recurring motifs of Dickens's novels, from the scenes in the Fleet Prison in *Pickwick* to the symbolic dust heap in *Our Mutual Friend*.

Dickens's aroused social conscience has of course led some of his critics into seeing his work as more doctrinaire, more rigorously ordered than it is. Thus T. A. Jackson and Jack Lindsay have tried to assimilate Dickens's "line" to the orderly fabric of Marxism, an attempt which few other critics regard as admissible. And Shaw, of course, tended to exaggerate the explosive force of the novels as propaganda. Nevertheless, in spite of Dickens's reluctance to make common cause with any philosophically grounded reform movement, it is possible to abstract from the novels a more or less consistent point of view toward society and its ills. This ground has been covered so often, and there is such substantial agreement on the articles of Dickens's creed, that I shall limit myself to the briefest summary.

The first point to be observed is that Dickens is not a radical who wants to tear society apart and rebuild it according to first principles. With all its anomalies and incidental absurdities, Dickens never really questioned the basic class structure of English society. It is certainly sounder to align him with the "conservative" tradition exemplified by Carlyle and Ruskin, for he shares with them a kind of perpetual and indignant astonishment that human beings should so far surrender their own nature as to consign their most fundamental interest to machines. The machines, of course, are the literal ones which were reshaping England into something brutal and ugly, but they are also the ones, figuratively speaking, represented by such doctrinaire systems of thought as Benthamism or the political economy of the Manchester School, or by the social or political institutions which assumed that human beings could be administered to by systematic processes in which the basic fact of man's spirituality might be conveniently ignored. Democratic government, for example, or evangelical religion.

Dickens's distrust of institutions and of intellectual systems is not the product of experience, for this distrust is clearly evident in *Pickwick*, and though it accumulates emotional charge, it is not really deeper in the late novels. His anti-intellectualism, if I may give it a currently fashionable name, is a kind of instinctive response to any attempt to stifle or destroy the irrational part of man's nature, hence Dickens's affectionate regard for the weak-minded and the prominent symbolic role given to the non-rational entertainments of Sleary's Circus in *Hard Times* (the logical culmination of a series, beginning with Mr. Vincent Crummles and Mrs. Jarley). The only forces of social amelioration to which Dickens gives his unqualified assent are man's native impulses of benevolence and self-sacrifice. At first he is prepared to believe that these impulses are strong enough in normal human beings to combat the various evils of society. Pickwick's benevolence is irrepressible and unconquerable. But either because the evils have grown greater, or because Dickens's faith in the humanity of ordinary people has grown less, the early optimism fades and is replaced by a heavy and virtually impenetrable gloom, lightened only occasionally, and inadequately, by acts of private charity and self-sacrifice. The fierce indignation that breaks out in the early novels becomes a kind of brooding melancholy as Dickens looks at the world in the ripeness of his age.

Though Dickens's social criticism runs through all his novels, it gathers to its greatest clarity and intensity in the six novels which comprise the bulk of his later work: *Dombey and Son, Bleak House, Hard Times, Little Dorrit, Great Expectations*, and *Our Mutual Friend*. Of these *Bleak House* is the most comprehensive criticism of society and may fairly be taken to represent Dickens's mature diagnosis of, and prognosis for his age. *Bleak House* is also one of his most artful books, and unlike *Hard Times*, another very artful book, it is quintessentially Dickensian in spirit and technique. In the present essay I propose to examine *Bleak House*, both as an embodiment of Dickens's social protest and as a narrative structure, in an effort to see how structure and idea engage each other.

I

The main theme of *Bleak House* is responsibility. The content of the book may most succinctly be described as a series of studies in society's exercise (more often the evasion or abuse) of responsibility for its dependents. In his earlier novels Dickens characteristically locates the source of evil in specific human beings, the villains in his typically melodramatic plots. Sometimes he makes evil grow out of sheer malignity (Quilp), but even when the evil represented is of a predominantly social character it is generally personified, in the acquisitiveness of a Ralph Nickleby, for example, or the officious cruelty of a Bumble. But *Bleak House* has no villain. It offers a jungle without predators, only scavengers. Evil is as impersonal as the fog which is its main symbol. The Court of Chancery, the main focus of evil in the novel and the mundane equivalent of hell, harbors no devil, only a rather mild and benevolent gentleman who is sincerely desirous of doing the best he can for the people who require his aid. Esther describes the Lord Chancellor's manner as "both courtly and kind," and remarks at the conclusion of her interview, "He dismissed us pleasantly, and we all went out, very much obliged to him for being so affable and polite; by which he had certainly lost no dignity, but seemed to us to have gained some" (pp. 29-30).[1] This is not irony; by an inversion of the mephistophelian paradox, the Lord Chancellor is *"ein Teil von jener Kraft, die stets das Gute will und stets das Böse schafft."*

Dickens found in the Court of Chancery specifically, and in the law generally, the true embodiment of everything that was pernicious. The law touched Dickens often enough in his private life, and the actual cases of victims of legal proceedings always roused his indignation even when he was not personally involved. The result was a vein of legal satire beginning with the Bardell-Pickwick trial and running throughout the novels, but it is not Dickens's private grievance against the law that I am here concerned with. The law was to become for him a means by which as an artist he could most faithfully and effectively image a world gone wrong. Like Jeremy Bentham, Dickens was appalled by the chaos of the British law; its random accumulation of statute law, common law, and precedents in equity; its overlapping and conflicting jurisdictions; its antiquated and mysterious rituals and procedures. But

Bentham was only appalled by the lack of intelligible system, not by the law itself, and he accordingly set out to put things right. Dickens, on the other hand, who shared with such other Victorian writers as Browning, Trollope, and W. S. Gilbert a profound misunderstanding and distrust of the legal mind, was as much disturbed by legal system as the lack thereof. It is perhaps suggestive that Dickens's satire does not merely attack abuses of the law, it attacks the fundamental postulates of the British legal system. Dodson and Fogg are contemptible less because they are lawyers than because they are grasping, mean, and hypocritical human beings. Dickens aims a subtler shaft at Perker, Mr. Pickwick's solicitor, an amiable and seemingly harmless man who cannot restrain his admiration for the acuity of Dodson and Fogg, and it is Perker, not his opponents, who is the prototype of the lawyers of *Bleak House*: Tulkinghorn, Vholes, and Conversation Kenge. None of these proves to be guilty of anything approaching sharp practice; on the contrary, they are all offered as examples of capable and conscientious legal practitioners, and the evil they give rise to is not a consequence of their abusing their functions but of their performing them as well as they do. Conversation Kenge may be taken as expressing the opinion of the legal fraternity at large when he holds up for Esther's admiration that "monument of Chancery practice," Jarndyce and Jarndyce, the case in which "every difficulty, every contingency, every masterly fiction, every form of procedure known in that court, is represented over and over again" (p. 18). To Dickens this is a little like the surgeon who can describe a sutured incision as "beautiful." He despised lawyers (and here Vholes is his principal example) because they drew their living from human misery without contributing significantly to alleviate it. But Dickens's feeling toward the cannibalistic Vholes is only incidental to the main point, which is the concept of the law implied by Kenge's rhapsody.

The law, especially British law, is an instrument of justice which often seems to the layman to put a higher value on consistency and orderly procedure than on justice itself. That in any given instance the law is capable of doing manifest injustice, no one would deny, but that the elaborate body of procedures, fictions, and precedents is the safest guarantee against capricious or arbitrary judgment, and in the long run, in the majority of cases, the most efficient mechanism of seeing justice done is the common ground for the defence of systems of jurisprudence. Justice becomes a by-product of law, and the law itself, by a kind of natural descent from the primitive trial by combat, assumes the character of an intellectual contest in which attack and counterattack, the play of knowledge, ingenuity, and skill, are of transcendent interest, even when the result is a matter of indifference. It amounts to no paradox, then, to say that the lawyer cares nothing for justice; he cares only for the law. Of the justice, that is to say, of the social utility of his professional activity he is presumably convinced antecedently to his engaging in it, but he goes about his business secure in the knowledge that justice will best be served by his shrewdness in outwitting his adversary. To the lawyer the law is intellectual, abstract, and beautiful, like a game of chess, and it is just here that the fundamental ground of Dickens's quarrel with him lies. Justice for Dickens was generally open and palpable. He couldn't understand why man's natural emotional response to injustice wasn't a sufficient impetus to lead him to correct it if he could. With the abstract and intellectual approach to the evils of life Dickens had no sympathy and no patience at all, and the law, therefore, became for him a comprehensive symbol of an attitude toward life that seemed to him perverse and wrong. Dickens's anti-intellectualism is concentrated and brought to bear in his satire on the law.

But there is special point and relevance to the attack on Chancery in *Bleak House*. In the first place, Chancery exemplifies more perfectly than the law courts properly so-called the characteristically slow and circuitous processes of British jurisprudence. Its ritual was more intricate, its fictions more remote from actualities, its precedents more opaque, than those of the Queen's Bench, or the Exchequer, or the Court of Common Pleas. And of course the slowness of Chancery proceedings was legendary. Holdsworth emphasizes this point neatly by quoting Lord Bowen: "Whenever any death occurred, bills of review or supplemental suits became necessary to reconstitute the charmed circle of the litigants which had been broken. . . . It was satirically declared that a suit to which fifty defendants were necessary parties . . . could never hope to end at all, since the yearly average of deaths in England was one in fifty, and a death, as a rule, threw over the plaintiff's bill for at least a year."[2] The High Court of Chancery, then, provided a microcosm of the legal world of 19th century England, magnifying the law's essential features and reducing its flaws to absurdity. In the second place, Chancery is specially appropriate as an image of the kind of responsibility that *Bleak House* is really about. The Lord Chancellor's legal responsibility is of a curious and distinctive character. The law courts, with their various ramifications and subdivisions, civil, criminal, and ecclesiastical, exist to provide a bar where anyone who believes himself injured according to the common or statute law may plead his case. But the law has many loopholes, and it is desirable that some provision be made to redress wrongs which are not covered by any existing law. Moreover a considerable body of potential litigants— chiefly widows and orphans—being unable to plead in their own behalf, must be protected against injustice. The Lord Chancellor's Court was devised for just such a purpose, to provide relief where the ordinary channels of legal procedure offered none. The origin of the Lord Chancellor's judicial function is described by Blackstone:

> When the courts of law, proceeding merely upon the ground of the king's original writs, and confining themselves strictly to that bottom, gave a harsh or imperfect judgment, the application for redress used to be to the king in person assisted by his privy council . . . and they were wont to refer the matter either to the chancellor and a select committee, or by degrees to the chancellor only, who mitigated the severity or supplied the defects of the judgments pronounced in the courts of law, upon weighing the circumstances of the case.[3]

From a court of appeals the Chancellor's Court developed into an ordinary court of equity in which a plaintiff could sue for redress by the presentation of a bill, and it claimed, furthermore, exclusive jurisdiction in supervising the proper administration of trusts and wills. It must be remembered, too, that antecedent to his judicial responsibility the Lord Chancellor bore a responsibility which was ecclesiastical and eleemosynary. Let me quote Blackstone once more on the Chancellor's office:

> Being formerly usually an ecclesiastic, (for none else were then capable of an office so conversant in writings,) and presiding over the royal chapel, he became keeper of the king's conscience; visitor, in right of the king, of all hospitals and colleges of the king's foundation; and patron of all the king's livings under the value of twenty marks *per annum* in the king's books. He is the general guardian of all infants, idiots, and lunatics; and has the general superintendance of all charitable uses in the kingdom. (III, 48)

Incorporating in his single office all the "charitable uses in the kingdom," the Lord Chancellor furnishes Dickens with a compendious symbol of all the ways in which one human being can be charged with the care of another: he is a father to the orphan, a husband to the widow, a protector to the weak and infirm, and an almoner to the destitute. What better focus of attention in a book about human responsibility could Dickens find than a suit in Chancery?

At one end of the scale is the Lord Chancellor in Lincoln's Inn Hall, at the other is Jo, society's outcast, with no proper place of his own, "moving on" through the atrocious slum of Tom-All-Alone's, itself a "monument of Chancery practice," for its dismal and neglected appearance proclaims its connection with Chancery. Who will take responsibility for Jo? Not government, engaged in an endless wrangle over the proper emolument for the party faithful; not religion, in the person of Mr. Chadband sermonizing over Jo's invincible ignorance; not law, concerned only with Jo's "moving on"; not organized charity, which finds the natives of Borrioboola-Gha or the Tockahoopo Indians a great deal more interesting than the dirty home-grown heathen. Jo subsists entirely on the impulsive generosity of Snagsby, who relieves his own feelings by compulsively feeding half-crowns to Jo, or on the more selfless generosity of Nemo, who supplies Jo's only experience of human companionship until Esther, and George, and Allan Wood-court come to his aid. Jo's function as an instrument of Dickens's social protest is clear. In his life and in his death he is a shattering rebuke to all those agencies of church and state which are charged with the care of the weak and the helpless and the poor, from the Lord Chancellor's court down to the Society for the Propagation of the Gospel in Foreign Parts. And Jo's experience throws a strong glare on the causes of their inadequacy; they fail conspicuously and utterly because they are noth-ing more than machines, because they are illuminated from the head, never from the heart, because, ultimately, they fail to acknowledge Dickens's most important moral and social maxim, that human beings can live together only on terms of mutual trust and love.

Between the Lord Chancellor and Jo, Dickens illustrates every rela-tion of dependency which is possible in civilized society, in every one of which, as we have seen, the Lord Chancellor himself participates by a species of legal fiction. Consider, for example, the condition of par-enthood. Every child begets a responsibility in his parents; in *Bleak House* Dickens examines a wide range of cases in order to trace the ex-tent to which that responsibility is successfully discharged. Only a very few parents in the sick society of this novel manage to maintain a healthy and normal relation with their children; one must contrive to get as far from the shadow of Chancery as Elephant and Castle, to find a domestic happiness like the Bagnets's. The virtuous mean of parental devotion is the exception, more often we have the excess, like Mrs. Pardiggle's ferocious bullying of her children, or still oftener the defi-ciency, instanced by Mrs. Jellyby's total neglect of her family, or Har-old Skimpole's similar behavior toward his. But the real symptom of disease is the frequency with which we find the normal relation between parent and child inverted. Skimpole is, as he frequently avers, a child, but the engaging qualities which this pose brings to the surface are quickly submerged again in his reckless self-indulgence, and his avocations, harmless or even commendable in themselves, the pursuit of art and beauty, become like the flush of fever, a sign of decay when we recognize that they are indulged at the expense of his responsibilities as the head of a family, and that his existence is so thoroughly parasitical. But just as there are parents who turn into children, a few children turn into parents. Charley Neckett, for example, at the death of her father is rudely thrust into maturity at the age of thirteen with a brother of five or six and a sister of eighteen months to care for. Esther describes her as "a very little girl, childish in figure but shrewd and older-looking in the face—pretty-faced too—wearing a womanly sort of bonnet much too large for her, and drying her bare arms on a womanly sort of apron. Her fingers were white and wrinkled with washing, and the soap-suds were yet smoking which she wiped off her arms. But for this she might have been a child, playing at washing, and imitating a poor working-woman with a quick observation of the truth" (p. 192). Even Esther herself exhibits a kind of reversal of roles. Like Charley (and a good many other characters in the story) she is an orphan, and her relations with the other inmates of Bleak House are curiously ambiguous and ill-defined. She is ostensibly the companion of Ada Clare and the ward of Mr. Jarndyce, both of which offices confer upon her a dependent status, yet in this household she assumes the moral leadership, a leadership which is explicitly recognized by the others' use of such nicknames as Little Old Woman, Mrs. Shipton, Mother Hubbard, and Dame Durden. Esther's relation with Mr. Jarndyce (whom she calls "Guardian") is further complicated by their betrothal; for as long as this lasts she stands toward him simultaneously as mother, daughter, and fiancée. In the Smallweed family the children all appear unnaturally old; only the senile display the attributes of childhood: "There has been only one child in the Smallweed family for several generations. Little old men and women there have been, but no child, until Mr.

ous instances of the neglect of marital (as well as maternal) responsibility like Mrs. Jellyby's high-minded disregard of her family, and there are equally obvious instances of abuse of the obedience enjoined by the marriage sacrament, like the abject submission of the brickmakers' wives to their husbands' brutality. Esther and Ada find one of these women furtively bringing comfort to the bereaved mother of a dead child, but with one eye always on the door of the public house:

> 'It's you, young ladies, is it?' she said, in a whisper. 'I'm a-watching for my master. My heart's in my mouth. If he was to catch me away from home he'd pretty near murder me.'
> 'Do you mean your husband?' said I.
> 'Yes, miss, my master.' (pp. 101-102)

But setting these instances aside, we are confronted in *Bleak House* by a stereotype of marriage in which the normal economic and social functions of husband and wife are reversed. Mr. Snagsby's uxoriousness remains within the bounds of conventional Dickensian social comedy and by itself is neither morbid nor especially significant:

> Mr Snagsby refers everything not in the practical mysteries of the business to Mrs Snagsby. She manages the money, reproaches the Tax-gatherers, appoints the time and places of devotion on Sundays, licenses Mr Snagsby's entertainments, and acknowledges no responsibility as to what she thinks fit to provide for dinner; insomuch that she is the high standard of comparison among the neighboring wives, a long way down Chancery Lane on both sides, and even out in Holborn. (p. 119)

But, as in the case of Skimpole, what begins in the light-hearted vein of comedy quickly darkens, and the relation assumes an unhealthy taint. Mrs. Snagsby, who enters as the conventional loud-voiced shrew, becomes, before her final exit, a shrinking paranoiac, "a woman overwhelmed with injuries and wrongs, whom Mr Snagsby has habitually deceived, abandoned, and sought to keep in darkness. . . . Everybody, it appears . . . has plotted against Mrs Snagsby's peace" (pp. 673-74). And the Snagsby ménage is further significant in that it provides a pattern of the marriage relation that is disturbingly common. Mr. Bayham Badger's uxoriousness far surpasses Mr. Snagsby's. It extends so far, in fact, that he is willing to suffer total eclipse in favor of his predecessors, Mrs. Badger's former husbands. And even the happy and amiable Bagnets display a domestic arrangement which, in spite of Matthew's stoutly (though not very convincingly) maintained fiction that "discipline must be preserved," places Mrs. Bagnet firmly in command of the family fortunes and policy. There is special meaning and pathos, however, in the union of Rick Carstone and Ada Clare, perhaps the only truly romantic pairing in the whole story (for, it must be noted in passing, some of the most admirable characters either are denied or deliberately evade the responsibilities of marriage—Mr. Jarndyce, Captain Hawdon, Boythorn, and Trooper George). This couple, the epitome of youth and hope and beauty, is doomed to frustration and tragedy because they take the contagion of Chancery, but that infection is itself made possible by the fact that the moral resources in their marriage, the courage, strength, and devotion, all belong to Ada. The corruption that marks the society of *Bleak House* may find its center and aptest symbol in Lincoln's Inn Hall, but its true origin is in the decay of the most fundamental social institution, the family. When parents will not or cannot take care of their children, when husbands refuse to be masters in their own houses, above all when these relations are not illuminated and softened by love, it is useless to expect those public institutions in which the relations of the family are mirrored to supply their defects.

But Dickens does not limit himself to the family. His novel is an intricate, if not always very systematic study of the bonds which link human beings together. Here are masters and servants, landlords and tenants, employers and employees, professional men and clients, officers and men, all enforcing the inescapable truth that men and women share a common destiny.[4] I do not propose to examine these various relations in detail; examples will suggest themselves to every reader of *Bleak House*. I believe that the breadth and the closeness of Dickens's analysis of society imply both his conviction that man cannot evade the consequences of his brotherhood with every other man, and his belief that human brotherhood can never be adequately affirmed or practiced through agencies which are the product of the intellect alone.

II

Edmund Wilson called *Bleak House* a novel of the "social group"; E. K. Brown called it a "crowded" novel. Both statements are undeniable; neither one offers any particular help in understanding how Dickens brought artistic order to a novel as broad in scope as *Bleak House*. A number of astute critics have grappled with the problem of structure in this novel, and the general tendency of their labors, at least in recent years, has been to refer the problem, not to such an obvious structural principle as plot, but to the infinitely more complex and subtle principle of language. Thus Norman Friedman, J. Hillis Miller, and Louis Crompton all seek the novel's fullest and deepest statement of meaning in the patterns of diction, imagery, and symbolism.[5] The insights derived from this species of criticism may be valuable; all three of these critics have important contributions to make. But so narrow a critical perspective has its dangers as well as its attractions. The art of the novel, as Dickens conceived and practiced it, was still a story-telling art, and though it is certainly true that his language, at least in the mature works, is richly charged and implicative, I do not believe that any acceptable reading of *Bleak House* can be reached without reference to those ingredients which are constituted by its participation in a story-telling tradition—I mean specifically, plot and the closely related layers of character and point of view.

First the plot. "Plot" here means the record of events, organized according to some intelligible principle of selection and arrangement.

The narration of unrelated (even though sequential) events does not give rise to plot; time sequence alone does not organize experience in any meaningful way. The loosest kind of organization is supplied by character; events may be related in that they happen to the same person, whether or not they reveal any growth, either in the character himself, or in our understanding of him. A somewhat more complicated structure arises when events are related to each other by their common illustration of a single idea or of several related ideas. Finally, events may be organized according to a causal sequence in which each successive event is in some way caused by the one which precedes it. Now only in the last sense does plot function as the unifying element in a story, for though it is possible for a story to *have* a plot in either of the first two senses, we would, in those cases, probably refer the story's unity to, respectively, character or theme.

It is virtually impossible to subsume the events of *Bleak House* into a single causal sequence, or even into several, as long as we understand by "events" what that word normally signifies, that is, births, deaths, betrothals, marriages, whatever, in short, is likely to be entered in the family Bible, and perhaps also such other occurrences (of a less public and ceremonial nature) as quarreling, making love, eating, drinking, working, etc., which may have an interest of their own. *Bleak House* is full enough of "events" in this sense; I count nine deaths, four marriages, and four births. The difficulty is in assigning their causes or their consequences. What are we to make of the death of Krook for example? The question is not one of physiology; I don't propose to reopen the question of spontaneous combustion. The question is properly one of psychology: how is Krook's death related to the play of human motives and purposes? The answer, of course, is that it is not so related at all; it is a simple *deus ex machina* whose only artistic justification is to be sought at the level of symbolism. Rick Carstone's death, by contrast, is integrated with plot, for though its physiological causes may be as obscure as those of Krook's death, its psychological causes are palpable and satisfying. Or take Esther's marriage to Allan Woodcourt. Is it, like the marriage of Jane Austen's heroines, the inevitable culmination of a pattern of events, or is it merely a concession to popular sentiment, like the second ending of *Great Expectations*? A great many, perhaps most, of the "events" of *Bleak House* consist of such hard and stubborn facts—stubborn in that they are not amenable to the construction of any intelligible law; they exist virtually uncaused, and they beget effects which are quite disproportionate to their own nature or importance. Events have a way of taking us by surprise, for even though Dickens is careful to create an appropriate atmosphere whenever he is about to take someone off, the time and manner of death are generally unpredictable.

The artistic center of the novel is generally taken to be Chancery, but if so it seems to me that Chancery functions as a symbol, not as a device of plot. We are permitted glimpses from time to time of what "happens" in Chancery, but Jarndyce and Jarndyce obviously follows no intelligible law of development, and so it is meaningless to talk about a Chancery plot or sub-plot. Furthermore, though Chancery affects the lives of many, perhaps all, of the characters in *Bleak House*, it does not do so in the sense that significant events take place there. The only event in the Court of Chancery that proves to have significant consequences for the people outside is the cessation of Jarndyce and Jarndyce when the whole property in dispute has been consumed in legal costs. But this is itself a conclusion reached by the stern requirements of economics rather than by the arcane logic of the law. Chancery affects men's lives the way God does, not by direct intervention in human affairs, but by commanding belief or disbelief.

In a few instances events align themselves in something approaching a genuine causal sequence. The story of Rick Carstone, for example, who undergoes a slow moral deterioration because he is gradually seduced into believing in Chancery, provides an example of a meaningful pattern of events. But Rick's story is neither central, nor altogether satisfying, principally, I believe, because it is observed only at intervals, and from without.[6] It remains true that it is all but impossible to describe what happens in *Bleak House* by constructing a causal sequence of events.

The difficulty largely disappears, however, when we stop trying to discover a more or less systematic pattern of events, and try instead to define the organization of the book in terms of discovery, the Aristotelian anagnorisis. The plot, in this case, is still woven of "events," but the word now signifies some determinate stage in the growth of awareness of truths which are in existence, potentially knowable, before the novel opens. Events, in the original sense of that term, become important chiefly as the instrumentalities of discovery. Krook's death, for example, leads to the unearthing of an important document in Jarndyce and Jarndyce, and incidentally to the disclosure of a complex web of relations involving the Smallweed, Snagsby, and Chadband families. The murder of Tulkinghorn or the arrest of Trooper George are red herrings, designed to confuse the issue, but ultimately they make possible the complete unveiling of the pattern of human relations that it is the chief business of the novel to disclose. The progressive discovery of that pattern is, then, the "plot" of the novel, and it constitutes a causal sequence, not in that each discovery brings about the next, but in that each discovery presupposes the one before. We need to know that Lady Dedlock harbors a secret which she regards as shameful before we can discover the existence of some former connection between her and Nemo, and we need to be aware of that connection before we can add to it the more important discovery that Esther is the daughter of Nemo and Lady Dedlock. And so on, until the whole complicated web stands clearly revealed.

This kind of structure is, as everyone knows, the typical pattern of the detective story. Such fundamentally human concerns as crime and punishment lie outside the scope of detective fiction, in which the murder may take place before the story begins, and the retribution may finally catch up with the murderer after it ends. The plot of the detective story consists simply in the discovery—withheld, of course, as long as possible—of the one hypothesis which will account for all the disparate facts or "events" that make up the story. The interest is centered, in classical specimens of the genre, not in the events, but in the process by which the events are rendered meaningful, ordinarily in the activity of the detective as he proceeds toward a solution. *Bleak House*, of course, has many detectives. Not counting the unforgettable Inspector Bucket "of the Detective," a great many characters are at work throughout the novel at unravelling some private and vexing problem of their own: Mr. Tulkinghorn, stalking Lady Dedlock's secret with fearful persistency, or Mr. Guppy approaching the same mystery from Esther's side, or Mrs. Snagsby endeavoring to surprise her husband's guilty connections, or even Esther herself, troubled by the riddle of her own mysterious origin and still more mysterious participation in the guilt of her unknown mother. But the presence or activity of a detective is incidental to the main scheme of such fiction, from *Oedipus the King* onward, to present a mystery and then solve it. The beginning, middle, and end of such an action can be described only in terms of the reader's awareness; the beginning consists of the exposition in which the reader is made aware of the mystery, that is of the facts that require explanation; the end consists of his reaching a full understanding of the mystery which confronted him, for when all is known the story must come to an end. The middle, then, is comprised of his successive states of partial or incorrect knowledge.

The mystery presents itself, in the typical detective novel, with crystalline purity. Someone has been murdered; the problem is to discover, in the graphic but ungrammatical language of the usual cognomen, Who done it? In *Bleak House* the problem is somewhat different. It is true that there is a murder, and that the murderer must subsequently be picked out of three likely suspects, but the main mystery, the one that sustains the motion of the whole book and gives it a unity of plot, is not a question of determining the agent of some past action (though the mystery *may* be formulated in these terms) so much as it is a question of establishing the identity of all the characters involved, and in the world of *Bleak House* one's identity is defined according to his relations to other people. Two recent writers, James H. Broderick and John E. Grant, consider that the novel is given its shape by Esther's successful quest for identity, or place, in the society of the book,[7] and I see no reason why the establishment of identity, not merely for Esther, but for all or most of the characters may not provide a workable principle of structure. Esther's identity is secure when she discovers who her parents are, and this is certainly the heart of *Bleak House*'s mystery, but that discovery comes shortly after the middle of the book, when Lady Dedlock discloses herself to Esther. The novel is not complete until all the relations of its various characters are recognized and established (or re-established) on some stable footing. Sir Leicester Dedlock must adjust his whole view of the world to conform to the discovery he makes about his wife; harmony must be restored between Mr. Jarndyce and Rick; Esther must discover her true relation to Mr. Jarndyce—and to Allan Woodcourt. Even the minor characters must be accounted for: Trooper George must become once again the son of Sir Leicester's housekeeper and the brother of the ironmaster; Mr. and Mrs. Snagsby must be reconciled as man and wife; all misunderstandings, in short, must be cleared away.

One of the most curious features of *Bleak House*, one of the attributes which is most likely to obtrude itself and bring down the charge of staginess, is Dickens's careful husbandry of characters. That he disposes of so many may perhaps be worthy of remark, but still more remarkable is the fact that he makes them all, even the most obscure, serve double and triple functions. Mr. Boythorn, for example, the friend of Mr. Jarndyce who is always at law with his next-door neighbor, Sir Leicester Dedlock, doubles as the rejected suitor of Miss Barbary, Esther's aunt. And it is surely a curious coincidence which sends Rick, when he is in need of a fencing teacher, to Trooper George, who is not only related to the Chesney Wold household through his mother, but also deeply in debt to Grandfather Smallweed (Krook's brother-in-law), and of course he has served under Captain Hawdon, Esther's father. Mrs. Rachael, Miss Barbary's servant, turns up again as the wife of the oily Mr. Chadband, and even Jenny, the brickmaker's wife, appears fortuitously to change clothes with Lady Dedlock. These examples, which might easily be multiplied, irresistibly create the impression, not of a vast, chaotic, utterly disorganized world, but of a small, tightly ordered one. That the novel thus smacks of theatrical artifice constitutes a threat to the "bleakness" of *Bleak House*, for we are never confronted, in this world, by the blank and featureless faces of total strangers, the heart-rending indifference of the nameless mob; all the evils of this world are the work of men whose names and domestic habits we know, and for that reason, it would appear, are deprived of most of their terrors.

Perhaps the most serious charge that can be brought against the artistry of *Bleak House* grows out of some of the characteristic features which I have been discussing. How can the discerning reader avoid being offended, it will be argued, by a novel which obviously wants to say something serious and important about society, but at the same time contrives to say it in the most elaborately artificial way possible? How can we be serious about social criticisms which come to us through the medium of the most sensational literary genre, and are obscured by every artifice of melodrama? The objection seems to be a damaging one, but I wonder if Dickens's employment of the techniques of the detective story and of melodrama may not enforce, rather than weaken, his rhetorical strategy. The plot, as I conceive it, consists of the progressive and relentless revelation of an intricate web of relations uniting all the characters of the novel, by ties of blood or feeling or contract. And Dickens's assignment of multiple functions to the minor characters is merely a means of reinforcing and underscoring our sense that human beings are bound to each other in countless, often unpredictable ways. It is difficult to see how Dickens could have found a clearer, more emphatic way of drawing up his indictment against society for its failure to exercise responsibility than by his elaborate demonstration of human brotherhood.

The bleakness of *Bleak House* is the sense of hopelessness inspired by the knowledge that men and women, subjected to the common shocks of mortality, will nevertheless consistently repudiate the claims which other people have on them. The sense of hopelessness is intensified and made ironic by the closeness, figuratively speaking, of their relations to other people (sometimes, of course, the closeness is literal, as in the hermetic little community of Cook's Court, Cursitor Street). It is appropriate that the novel should be shaped by discoveries rather than by events, for the sense of hopelessness, or bleakness, can hardly be sustained in a world that can be shaped to human ends by human will. The events of this novel are accidental in a double sense; most of them are unplanned and unpredictable, and they are moreover non-essential to the view of human experience that Dickens is concerned to present. Human relations, the ones that are important, are not constituted by events (though they may be revealed by events—Esther's smallpox, for example), because events just *happen*, they follow no intelligible law either of God or man. Human relations are inherent in the nature of society, and the duty of man is therefore not something arbitrary and intrinsically meaningless which can be prescribed and handed down to him by some external authority (like law); it is discoverable in, and inferable from, his social condition and only needs to be seen to command allegiance. The tragedy of *Bleak House* is that awareness of human responsibility invariably comes too late for it to be of any use. Nemo's or Coavinses', or Jo's membership in the human race is discovered only after his death, and Sir Leicester Dedlock awakens to recognition of the true nature of the marriage bond only when his wife has gone forth to die. Still, it is important to *have* that awareness, and the most effective way to produce it, surely, is to make its slow growth the animating principle of the novel.

III

If we choose to talk about the plot of *Bleak House* as constituted by a growing awareness of human relations and human responsibilities, sooner or later we must raise the question: *Whose* awareness? The problem of point of view is so important in the detective story, in fact, that it is most often met by the creation of a special point-of-view character. The classical instance, of course, is Dr. Watson, but Dr. Watson has had countless avatars. *Bleak House* is enough of a detective story so that it must reckon with some, at least, of the problems that Dr. Watson was invented to solve. The mystery must be preserved, so the narrator's perspicacity must have rather clearly defined limits, but at the same time the mystery must take hold of the reader, so the narrator must possess lively human sympathies and be capable of moral insights which are as just and true as his practical judgments are absurd. Such considerations impose limits on the choice of a narrative perspective for *Bleak House*, but there are other considerations which affect that choice too. The mystery whose solution dominates the novel is not such a simple, or at any rate such a limited problem as identifying a particular character as the criminal; Dickens's villain is a whole society, and its guilt cannot be disclosed by a sudden dramatic unveiling. Furthermore Dickens is only partly concerned with the disclosure of the truth to the reader; a more fundamental matter is the discovery by the participants of the drama themselves of the relations in which they stand toward all the other members of society. It is the story of Oedipus on a large scale.

Because of the staggering breadth of Dickens's design the selection of a narrative point of view is extraordinarily difficult. If he chooses an omniscient, third person point of view a good deal of the emotional charge is lost, particularly if the narrator remains (as he must) sufficiently aloof from the actions and events he describes to avoid premature disclosures. On the other hand, a first person narrator suffers equally important disabilities. The most immediately obtrusive of these is physical and practical. How can a single character be expected to participate directly in all the relations the novel is about? How can one character contribute evidence (as opposed to hearsay) of events which take place in London, in Lincolnshire, and in Hertfordshire, sometimes simultaneously? The difficulty could be partly met by the selection of one of those numerous characters like Tulkinghorn or Mr. Guppy or young Bart Smallweed who seem to be always on the "inside," in control of events simply because they know about them, yet one difficulty yields only to be replaced by another. Characters like Tulkinghorn obviously lack the "lively human sympathies" which give to the first person point of view its special value, and as narrator Tulkinghorn (who is in any case disqualified on the more fundamental ground that he is killed) would offer no advantage over the omniscient point of view. The obvious solution to this dilemma is to have both points of view, alternating the narration between them.

The dual point of view in *Bleak House* has always served as a speck of grit, around which the commentators have secreted their critical pearls. E. M. Forster regards it as a blemish, though he thinks Dickens's talent can make us forget it: "Logically, *Bleak House* is all to pieces, but Dickens bounces us, so that we do not mind the shiftings of the view point."[8] Others defend the double point of view as artistically appropriate.[9] I regard the device as a concession to a necessity that I can see no other way of circumventing, but there are perhaps one or two things to be said about it.

Bleak House is a novel without a center. There is no single character to whom the events of the story happen, or with reference to whom those events are significant. It is not even possible (as I have already argued) to understand the novel as a unified system of co-ordinate plots or of plot and sub-plots. Except for this want of a center the novel might be compared to a spider web in which each intersection represents a character, connected by almost invisible but nonetheless tenacious filaments to a circle of characters immediately surrounding him, and ultimately, of course, to all the other characters. But the spider web has a center (and a villain), so a more appropriate comparison might be made to a continuous section of netting, or better still, to the system of galaxies which make up the universe. It appears to a terrestrial observer that all the other galaxies are receding from him at an unthinkable rate of speed, implying that his own post of observation constitutes the center of things. Yet the centrality of his own position is merely a function of his special point of view. So with *Bleak House.* Esther is, in this special sense, the "center" of the novel, not because she so regards herself, but because she supplies the central observation point, because relations are measured according to their nearness or farness from her just as astronomical distances are measured in parsecs—heliocentric parallax (in seconds of arc) as recorded for a terrestrial observer. To pass, for example, from Esther to Nemo (or some other intermediate character) to George to Matthew Bagnet is to move, so to speak, from the center outward. But Esther is not *really* the center of the novel. To think of her as such is to destroy or at least to do serious violence to Dickens's view of the world, and transform his indictment of society into a sentimental fable. To deprive the novel of its specious center, to provide it with a new perspective which, like stereoscopic vision, adds depth, is an important function of the omniscient point of view.

Dickens's handling of that portion of the narrative which is related by the omniscient observer (roughly half of the novel) is, on the whole, masterly. I do not know that any critic denies the full measure of praise for things like the opening paragraph or two of the novel, that magnificent evocation of the London fog which has been quoted so often that I may be excused from doing so here. The laconic, unemotional style, with its sentence fragments and present participles in place of finite verbs, the roving eye, which, like the movie camera mounted on an overhead crane, can follow the action at will, are brilliantly conceived and deftly executed. It is a descriptive style emancipated from the limitations of time and space, and accordingly well-suited to its special role in the novel. But Dickens's control of this narrator is uneven. Superbly fitted for the descriptive passages of the novel, his tight-lipped manner must give way to something else in passages of narration or, still more conspicuously, in those purple rhetorical passages that Dickens loves to indulge in. As a narrator, the omniscient persona (now speaking in finite verbs in the present tense) suffers somewhat from a hollow portentousness, a lack of flexibility, and a rather pointless reticence which can become annoying, as in the narration of Tulkinghorn's death (though here again the descriptive powers get full play). The requirements of consistency do not seem to trouble Dickens when it is time to step forward and point the finger at the object of his satire. The narrative persona is dropped completely when Dickens speaks of Buffy and company, or apostrophizes the "right" and "wrong" reverends whom he holds responsible for the death of Jo. But these passages win us by their obvious sincerity, and we need not trouble ourselves over the fact that the mask has been inadvertently dropped. To insist on a rigorous consistency here is to quibble over trifles, for generally speaking the third person narration is adroit and effective.

The focus of discontent with the manipulation of point of view in *Bleak House* is Esther Summerson. Fred W. Boege writes: "There is nothing necessarily wrong with the idea of alternating between the first and third persons. The fault lies rather with Dickens' choice of a medium for the first-person passages. David Copperfield demonstrates that the conventional Victorian hero is not a commanding figure in the center of a novel. Esther Summerson proves that the conventional heroine is worse; for the hero is hardly more than colorless, whereas she has positive bad qualities, such as the simpering affectation of innocence."[10] I think it is essential to distinguish carefully between Esther's qualities as "heroine" and Esther's qualities as narrator, for though the two functions are not wholly separate, it ought to be possible to have a bad heroine who is a good narrator and vice versa. As a heroine she clearly belongs to a tradition that we tend to regard as hopelessly sentimental and out of date. She is sweet-tempered and affectionate, and she is also capable and strong and self-denying. The first two qualities almost invariably (at least within the conventions of Victorian fiction) render their possessor both unsympathetic and unreal. One thinks of Amelia Sedley or Dinah Morris or Dickens's own Agnes Wickfield, and prefers, usually, the society of such demireps as Becky Sharp or

Lizzie Eustace. Still, Esther's strength of character ought to save her, and give her a genuine hold on our regard, except for the fact that as narrator she is faced with the necessity of talking about herself, and her modest disclaimers ring false. When she tells us that she is neither good, nor clever, nor beautiful she forfeits a good deal of the regard that her genuinely attractive and admirable qualities demand. Esther the heroine is in a sense betrayed by Esther the narrator into assuming a posture that cannot be honestly maintained.

Whatever one thinks of Esther as a person, the important question at the moment is her discharge of the narrator's responsibility. The sensibility which is revealed by her attributes as a character (the term "heroine" is somewhat misleading) is of course the same one which will determine the quality of her perceptions and insights as narrator, and it is here, I think, that some confusion arises, for it is generally assumed that Esther's simplicity, her want of what might be called "diffractive" vision, the power of subjecting every experience to the play of different lights and colors, is held to undermine or even destroy her value as narrator. We have become so used to accepting the Jamesian canons of art and experience that we refuse validity to any others. The attitude is unfortunate, not to say parochial. For James "experience" (the only kind of experience that concerned the artist) was constituted by the perception of it. "Experience," he writes in "The Art of Fiction," "is never limited, and it is never complete; it is an immense sensibility, a kind of huge spider web of the finest silken threads suspended in the chamber of consciousness, and catching every air-borne particle in its tissue. It is the very atmosphere of the mind; and when the mind is imaginative . . . it takes to itself the faintest hints of life, it converts the very pulses of the air into revelations." This conception of experience is at the root of James's conception of the art of the novel, for it prescribes that the simplest kind of happening may be converted to the stuff of art by a sufficiently vibrant and sensitive point of view character. To a Lambert Strether the relations of Chad Newsome and Mme. de Vionnet are subtle, complex, and beautiful, because he is; but to another observer the same liaison is common and vulgar. Strether possesses what I have chosen to call diffractive vision, the ability to see a whole spectrum where the vulgar can see only the light of common day.

How can poor little Esther Summerson manage to perform the same function as a character with the depth and resonance of Lambert Strether? The answer, obviously, is that she can't. But I must hasten to add that she doesn't have to. The ontological basis of James's fiction is radically different from that of Dickens's; for in James what seems is more important than what is, and he accordingly requires a perceiving intelligence of the highest order. In Dickens, on the other hand, though he too is concerned with the characters' awareness, the relations which they are to perceive have a "real" existence which is not contingent on their being seen in a certain way. For this reason Esther does not have to serve as the instrument of diffraction; the light is colored at its source. To the sensitive Jamesian observer a single human relation appears in almost an infinite number of lights, and a single act may be interpreted in many ways. But Dickens does not work that way, at least not in *Bleak House*. Here the richness and infinite variety of human experience are suggested by the sheer weight of example, by the incredible multiplication of instances, and the narrator's chief function is simply to record them.

When Socrates and his friends Glaucon and Adeimantus differed over the nature of justice and injustice, Socrates proposed to settle the dispute, in the passage of the *Republic* from which my first epigraph is taken, by constructing an imaginary and ideal state in order to see how justice originates. The method is not at all unlike that of Dickens, who proposes to investigate the abstraction "injustice" by seeing how it arises in an imaginary replica of the real world. Both methods assume that what is universal and abstract is rendered most readily intelligible by what is particular and concrete, and furthermore that the particular and concrete establish a firmer hold on our feelings than the universal and abstract. For both Plato and Dickens are concerned not only with making justice and injustice understood, but with making them loved and hated, respectively. The method is perhaps suggestive of allegory, but it differs in important ways from any technique of symbolic representation. It is a species of definition which proceeds by attempting to specify the complete denotation of the thing to be defined. To the question, "What is Justice?" Plato replies by showing us his republic, perfect in all its details, and saying, "Justice is here." To a similar question about injustice Dickens need only reply by unfolding the world of *Bleak House*.

Let me particularize briefly. One of the important ethical abstractions the novel deals with is charity (a useful check list of such abstractions might be derived from the names of Miss Flite's birds). Dickens nowhere provides a statement of the meaning of this concept except by supplying a wide range of instances from which the concept may be inferred. Mrs. Jellyby (for example), Mrs. Pardiggle, Mr. Quale, and Mr. Chadband demonstrate various specious modes of the principal Christian virtue, and Captain Hawdon, Mr. Snagsby, Mr. Jarndyce, and Esther provide glimpses of the genuine article. None of these characters, and none of the acts by which they reveal their nature can be said to *stand for* the general idea, charity; collectively they *are* charity, which is thus defined by representing, on as ample a scale as possible, its denotation. Similarly with the whole spectrum of moral ideas and human relations in *Bleak House*; Dickens offers his main commentary, not by names or labels, certainly not by analysis, and not even by symbolic analogues (though he uses them). His principal technique is the multiplication of instances. To say that in a novel which is as richly and palpably symbolic as *Bleak House* symbolism is unimportant would be in the nature of an extravagant paradox, and I have no intention of going so far. I wish only to direct attention toward a narrative method which seems to me to have been strangely neglected by comparison with the symbolism which has proved so fruitful of insight.

At any rate, I think Esther is vindicated as narrator. The narrative design of the novel really requires only two qualities of her, both of which she exemplifies perfectly. In the first place, she should be as transparent as glass. The complex sensibility which is a characteristic feature of the Jamesian observer would be in Esther not simply no advantage, it would interfere with the plain and limpid narration she is charged with. We must never be allowed to feel that the impressions of characters and events which we derive from her are significantly colored by her own personality, that the light from them (to revert to my optical figure) is diffracted by anything in her so as to distort the image she projects. One partial exception to this generalization implies the second of the two characteristics I have imputed to her. In the second place, then, we require of Esther sufficient integrity, in a literal sense, to draw together the manifold observations she sets down. The most complex and elaborate act of synthesis is reserved for the reader, but to Esther falls the important choric function of suggesting the lines along which that synthesis should take place by drawing her observations together under a simple, traditional, and predictable system of moral values. If Esther occasionally strikes us as a little goody-goody, we must recall her function to provide a sane and wholesome standard of morality in a topsy-turvy world.

No critic, surely, can remain unimpressed by the richness of *Bleak House*, a quality which is both admirable in itself and characteristically Dickensian. But the quality which raises the novel to a class by itself among Dickens's works is its integrity, a product of the perfect harmony of structure and idea. Edmund Wilson long ago saluted *Bleak House* as inaugurating a unique genre, "the detective story which is also a social fable," but he provided no real insight into the method by which these radically unlike forms were made to coalesce. The secret, I believe, is partly in that instinctive and unfathomable resourcefulness of the artist, which enables him to convert his liabilities into assets, to make, for example, out of such an unpromising figure as Esther Summerson, just the right point of view character for the first-person portion of the novel. But the real greatness of *Bleak House* lies in the happy accident of Dickens's hitting upon a form (the mystery story) and a system of symbols (Chancery) which could hold, for once, the richness of the Dickensian matter without allowing characters and incidents to distract the reader from the total design. The mysterious and sensational elements of the plot are not superimposed on the social fable; they are part of its substance. The slow but relentless disclosure of the web of human relations makes a superb mystery, but what makes it a monumental artistic achievement is that it is also and simultaneously one of the most powerful indictments of a heartless and irresponsible society ever written. *Bleak House* is the greatest of Dickens's novels because it represents the most fertile, as well as the most perfectly annealed, union of subject and technique he was ever to achieve.

From *ELH* 29, no. 2 (1962): 175-201. Copyright © 1962 by The Johns Hopkins University Press. Reprinted with permission of The Johns Hopkins University Press.

Notes

1. Page references are to the Everyman edition.

2. William S. Holdsworth, *Dickens as a Legal Historian* (New Haven, 1929), p. 91.

3. Sir William Blackstone, *Commentaries on the Laws of England* (London, 1800), III, 50-51.

4. I must take exception to two recently offered interpretations of *Bleak House*, the one maintaining that the only order to be found in the novel is supplied by the consciousness of the narrator(s) (J. Hillis Miller, *Charles Dickens: The World of His Novels* [Cambridge, Mass., 1958], pp. 160-224), the other that the order implied by the pat manipulation of events is a reflection of Dickens's own faith in a controlling providence (Harland S. Nelson, "Dickens' Plots: 'The Ways of Providence' or the Influence of Collins?" *Victorian Newsletter*, Spring, 1961, pp. 11-14).

5. Norman Friedman, "The Shadow and the Sun: Notes Toward a Reading of *Bleak House*," *Boston University Studies in English*, III (1957), 147-66; J. Hillis Miller, *op. cit.*; Louis Crompton, "Satire and Symbolism in *Bleak House*," *Nineteenth-Century Fiction*, XII (1957-58), 284-303.

6. As Edgar Johnson has argued, Dickens was not to do justice to this theme until *Great Expectations* (*Charles Dickens: His Tragedy and Triumph* [New York, 1952], p. 767).

7. "The Identity of Esther Summerson," *Modern Philology*, LV (1958), 252-58.

8. *Aspects of the Novel* (London, 1927), p. 108.

9. For example, M. E. Grenander, "The Mystery and the Moral: Point of View in Dickens's 'Bleak House,'" *Nineteenth-Century Fiction*, X (1955-56), 301-305.

10. "Point of View in Dickens," *PMLA*, LXV (1950), 94.

"True Legitimacy":
The Myth of the Foundling in *Bleak House*

Michele S. Ware

I

> Creative mythology . . . springs not, like theology, from the dicta of author-
> ity, but from the insights, sentiments, thought, and vision of an adequate in-
> dividual, loyal to his own experience of value. Thus it corrects the author-
> ity holding to the shells of forms produced and left behind by lives once
> lived.
>
> —Joseph Campbell[1]

It has become commonplace to speak of artists and writers of the
early twentieth century as myth-breakers and myth-makers, to accept
these men and women as the vanguard of modern culture. Certainly the
self-conscious foregrounding of myth in fiction is one of the hallmarks
of modernism. Yet we should not limit mythopoeia to a single artistic
or literary epoch. All writers and artists of stature participate in the
modification of their received mythologies, rejecting myths that no
longer have any meaning in their cultures, and replacing or adapting
existing myths according to their needs or to the needs of individuals
within the cultures. The measure, then, of an artist's success is not only
the extent to which his or her myth-making informs the generations to
follow; it is the artist's ability to express the self in harmony with the
self, the world, and God. Charles Dickens participates in this mytho-
poeic process from his earliest novels, adapting old myths (both literary and cultural) and creating new myths from the fragments of the
past. Specifically, however, Dickens exhibits a self-consciousness
about his myth-making in *Bleak House* that is artful and hopeful, and
strikingly "modern." Dickens presents, over the course of the novel,
his vision of a harmonious universe. But in spite of the power of his
mythologies, Dickens's vision in *Bleak House* ultimately fails him.

We have only to read the opening chapter of *Bleak House* to see Dickens's mythic impulse at work. Numerous critics have noted the impressive sweep of the novel. In *Bleak House*, Dickens takes on the whole of English society, and his condemnation is thorough and absolute. To begin his representation of society in mud and fog, in darkness and decay, is to create, in the body of the lumbering Megalosaurus, an anti-myth to progress and light.[2] The High Court of Chancery, a massive megalosaurus in its own right, wallowing in the center of the fog and mud, takes on mythic significance:

> This is the Court of Chancery; which has its decaying houses and its blighted lands in every shire; which has its worn-out lunatic in every madhouse, and its dead in every churchyard; which has its mined suitor, with his slipshod heels and threadbare dress, borrowing and begging through the round of every man's acquaintance; which gives to monied might the means abundantly of wearying out the right; which so exhausts finances, patience, courage, hope; so overthrows the brain and breaks the heart; that there is not an honourable man among its practitioners who would not give—who does not often give—the warning, "Suffer any wrong that can be done you, rather than come here!" (pp. 2-3)

This description and its attendant warning, so reminiscent of Dante's, illustrate the pervasive stain on society; the England of *Bleak House* has become hellish, and no aspect of life remains untainted. In the novel, Dickens uses a network of myths to investigate and expose the evils of a litigious and disordered world. Characteristically, the denunciation of society is the province of the objective narrator, while Dickens develops, in the narrative of Esther Summerson, an alternative myth, the myth of the foundling, as a solution to those evils.

The . . . most vital, most critical function of a mythology, then, is to foster the centering and unfolding of the individual in integrity, in accord with *d*) himself (the microcosm), *c*) his culture (the mesocosm), *b*) the universe (the macrocosm), and *a*) that awesome ultimate mystery which is both beyond and within himself and all things. (Campbell, p. 6)

Although Dickens drew freely from a number of stories of lost children that abound in western culture, he was most immediately influenced by the elaborate literary myth of the foundling that he inherited from the novels of the eighteenth century, most notably from Henry Fielding's *Tom Jones*, whose subject (and subtitle) was the history of a foundling.[3] Briefly, the portrayal of the myth is the complex working out and revelation of the main character's parentage, along with the concurrent restoration to his rightful place in society. The foundling moves through the novel (and this movement *is* the plot) from illegitimacy and exclusion to self-knowledge and inclusion. Such a myth presupposes the existence of an ordered, orderly society, one in which birth and parentage clearly determine social status and maintain social stability. The society in which the discovery of a foundling's parentage has meaning is a stable, systematic, and predictable society. Dickens was drawn to the myth as early as his second novel, when he adopts the myth to create the character of Oliver Twist. But although the novel borrows considerably from Fielding and Smollett, *Oliver Twist* is no wholesale adoption of the foundling myth; Dickens appropriates and alters the myth, destroying in the process some of the underlying assumptions about society and social status. Indeed, by the time *Bleak House* is published, Dickens has completely recreated the myth of the foundling. The history of Esther Summerson is the culmination of the power and authority of Dickens's own foundling myth, but the seeds of that myth are visible in *Oliver Twist*.

Angus Wilson notes in his introduction to *Oliver Twist* Dickens's debt to the eighteenth century, and compares the final product rather unfavorably with its forebears: "To novels like *Tom Jones* and *Humphrey Clinker* Dickens owes the disputed-inheritance-cum-illegitimate-son plot of *Oliver Twist*, though it would be unfair to either Fielding or Smollett to attribute to their influence any of the extreme ineptitude with which Dickens handles or botches his plot."[4] Dickens's "ineptitude" stemmed at least partly from his inability to reconcile his vision of society with that of the received mythology. There is an imbalance in *Oliver Twist* (as there is in *Bleak House*) between the restorative happy ending and the reality portrayed in the novel, which simply doesn't exist in Fielding or Smollett. But the plotting follows the pattern of the received myth of the foundling: Oliver Twist, orphaned at birth in the workhouse and stigmatized by illegitimacy, through a series of adventures and misadventures, solves the mystery of his parentage. Oliver's good looks and shining innocence mark him as somehow different, better than his surroundings, so that the revelation of his true parentage—as well as his relation to Rose Maylie and his subsequent adoption by Mr. Brownlow—is a means of correcting the stigma of his birth and the accident of his involvement with Fagin's gang. Revelation in Oliver's case means restoration, an aspect of the foundling myth he shares with Tom Jones. Yet there are subtle alterations in the myth as Dickens presents it in *Oliver Twist*, and problems in the construction of the novel and in the presentation of the author's world view that render the myth somehow less effective than it appears in *Tom Jones*.

The revelation of Oliver's parentage, his restored inheritance (smaller due to Monks's mismanagement), and his newfound family do not fix Oliver firmly within society. His circumstances at the close of the novel rather provide him with a retreat from society. Mr. Brownlow, Rose and Harry Maylie, Mr. Losberne and Oliver, with frequent visits by Mr. Grimwig, maintain their own "little society, whose condition approached as nearly to one of perfect happiness as can ever be known in this changing world."[5] Their happiness can he sustained only if they remove themselves from a society already irremediably tainted by evil.

Dickens begins quite early in his career to offer the myth of private domestic bliss as an alternative to a corrupt society. The problem, of course, with this myth, is that it provides only illusory happiness, and never quite reconciles the individual with the world. As Angus Wilson notes, the evil characters in *Oliver Twist* are far more compelling than the good, and the resulting ambiguity is disturbing: "In some curious way Fagin's court for all its squalor and meanness has a sort of ghastly gaiety and life that makes Mr. Brownlow's hot punch by the fire and Rose Maylie's country flower picking expeditions seem like the feeble stirrings of the moribund" (p. 19). Yet Dickens returns to ambiguity with renewed vigor in *Bleak House*, explicitly confronting it with his dual narrative, in a kind of battle of myths.

Esther Summerson becomes Dickens's fully realized foundling myth. "Found" alive by her aunt after her supposed death, Esther is spirited away from her mother, and raised in isolation and shame. Though she is not literally an orphan, Esther remains unaware of her mother's existence for the first half of the novel. She knows nothing of her parentage but the short, chilling lesson she learns from Miss Barbary on her birthday, that her birth was her mother's disgrace. Esther, like Oliver, is different from other children, but according to Miss Barbary, she's different because of the magnitude of the sin in whose shadow she was born. Like Oliver Twist, Esther Summerson suffers the stigma of illegitimacy; but unlike Oliver, she understands the implications of her illegitimacy from a very early age. In developing his version of the foundling myth, Dickens creates a character who assumes the guilt of her parents. In contrast to Oliver Twist, the foundling of *Bleak House* is never completely innocent in her own mind of the circumstances of her birth. When Miss Barbary reveals Esther's "disgrace," Esther tells the story to her only friend, her doll:

> Dear, dear, to think how much time we passed alone together afterwards, and how often I repeated to the doll the story of my birthday, and confided to her that I would try, as hard as ever I could, to repair the fault I had been

born with (of which I confessedly felt guilty and yet innocent), and would strive as I grew up to be industrious, contented, and kind-hearted, and to do some good to some one, and win some love to myself if I could. (p. 18)

Although Esther's easy assumption of guilt, her submissiveness, and her desire for love and approval often irritate critics of the novel, Q. D. Leavis shows that Dickens's characterization is a tribute to his realism. "The psychology of an illegitimate child of her time," Leavis writes, "can never have been caught with greater fidelity."[6] The success of Dickens's myth depends at least in part on this fidelity. Prepared for a life of "submission, self-denial, [and] diligent work" (p. 17), and bereft of parental love, Esther embodies Dickens's search for a mythology in which the knowledge of an individual's birth and parentage is not essential to his or her ultimate happiness.

In *Bleak House*, Dickens drops the plot device of the inherited myth. Esther's movement through the novel is not solely the discovery of her parentage. Once Esther knows the unfortunate general circumstances of her birth, she is no longer curious about who her parents are, and she resists such knowledge assiduously. At one point, she imagines that John Jarndyce is her father, secretly working behind the scenes to provide for her, but she dismisses that as an "idle dream" (p. 80). Later, when her guardian offers to answer any questions she has about her birth, Esther deliberately chooses not to know:

"I am quite sure that if there were anything I ought to know, or had any need to know, I should not have to ask you to tell it to me. If my whole reliance and confidence were not placed in you, I must have a hard heart indeed. I have nothing to ask you; nothing in the world." He drew my hand through his arm, and we went away to look for Ada. From that hour I felt quite easy with him, quite unreserved, quite content to know no more, quite happy. (p. 99)

Esther's resistance serves a dual function. While it shows that Dickens's portrayal of an illegitimate child who resists knowledge as pain is remarkably realistic, it also underscores Dickens's belief that such knowledge is not only painful, it is unnecessary. Esther's eventual discovery of her mother's identity does not bring a close to the narrative of *Bleak House*. Nor does it restore Esther to her proper place in society. In fact, it has almost no effect on the plot itself. When Lady Dedlock first approaches Esther in the wood near Chesney Wold, Esther sees "something in her face that [she] had pined for and dreamed of" as a child (p. 508). Lady Dedlock reveals herself to Esther as her "wicked and unhappy mother" (p. 509), and while the knowledge of her mother's love is a restorative to Esther, she realizes the pain and danger her presence is to Lady Dedlock. Esther is even grateful for the disfiguring illness, so that her existence will not disgrace her mother. There is no tidy resolution in Esther's discovery as there was in Oliver Twist's. Restored to a knowledge of her mother, Esther is forever barred from expressing the love and pity she feels for her. After she burns her mother's explanatory letter, Esther describes her feelings:

> I hope it may not appear very unnatural or bad in me, that I then became heavily sorrowful to think I had ever been reared. That I felt as if I knew it would have been better and happier for many people, if indeed I had never breathed. That I had a terror of myself, as the danger and the possible disgrace of my own mother, and of a proud family name. That I was so confused and shaken, as to be possessed by a belief that it was right, and had been intended, that I should die in my birth; and that it was wrong, and not intended, that I should be then alive. (pp. 513-14)

Although Esther later reconciles herself to her secret, she draws more pain than comfort from her knowledge. And the complex plot moves forward inexorably beyond the revelation of Esther's parentage.

To build his alternative myth, Dickens places Esther in a bewildering set of circumstances in which she must painstakingly build a place for herself in society. Her parentage literally has no bearing on the world's acceptance of her. Dickens purposely develops in the character of Esther a legitimacy based on goodness, kindness, service, and unselfishness, those individual strengths and sympathies that Dickens counts on to regenerate a blighted society. Jarndyce articulates Dickens's belief in the value of individual accomplishments, and in the importance of "the natural feelings of the heart" (p. 755), in his defense of Esther to Mrs. Woodcourt, when he urges her to accept Esther as a possible daughter-in-law:

> "Now, madam," said I, "come you . . . and live with us. Come you, and see my child from hour to hour; set what you see, against her pedigree, which is this and this"—for I scorned to mince it—"and tell me what is the true legitimacy, when you shall have quite made up your mind on the subject." (p. 858)

Jarndyce confidently presents Esther for Mrs. Woodcourt's scrutiny, knowing that her virtues supersede the disadvantages of her "pedigree." Dickens does not have to resort to the manipulation of plot to restore Esther as the daughter of a nobleman; he creates a different kind of nobility for her, based on personal virtue rather than birth.

Dickens supports and embellishes his myth-making with numerous references to familiar fairy tales and legends, and he alludes as well to biblical stories. It is impossible not to associate Esther Summerson with the biblical queen who saved her people; both are "orphaned and low born but beautiful."[7] Additionally, the names that Jarndyce, Ada, and Richard call Esther are names of women in legend or song who, as one critic notes, either "attend to others or foster them" or who have some "prophetic ability."[8] With the sheer weight of reference, Dickens makes sure we understand completely the type of character he has created in *Bleak House*.[9]

While Dickens develops his myth, he undertakes at the same time the systematic destruction of the old foundling myth of the eighteenth century. The inherited notions of legitimacy and parentage take on strange forms in *Bleak House*. When Harold Skimpole admires Ada, calling her "a child of the universe," John Jarndyce replies almost prophetically: "'The universe,' he observed, 'makes rather an indifferent parent, I am afraid'" (p. 72). Dickens proceeds to introduce his readers to a stunning array of bad parents. Mrs. Jellyby cares more for her mission work for the natives of "Borrioboola-Gha" than for her own children's welfare and safety. Mrs. Pardiggle robs her sons of their allowance to fill the coffers of her various charitable organizations. Mr. Turveydrop is so completely caught up in his own "Deportment" that he ignores the material needs of his son, Prince. And Harold Skimpole's children "have tumbled up somehow or other" (p. 68), suffering for the irresponsibility of their childlike father. In his introduction to *Bleak House*, J. Hillis Miller notes that the Court of Chancery, in its capacity as a parent to the wards of Jarndyce, neglects and betrays its children.[10] And worst of all is that indifferent parent, society, who allows children like Jo, the crossing sweeper, to suffer and die needlessly. In the mud and fog of English society, in the stagnant, blighted world that Dickens denounces, everyone becomes a foundling, adults as well as children. Dickens describes the destitute Nemo on his deathbed: "And all that night, the coffin stands ready by the old portmanteau; and the lonely figure on the bed, whose path in life has lain through five-and-forty years, lies there, with no more track behind him, that any one can trace, than a deserted infant" (p. 145). Dickens substantiates his foundling myth with an overpoweringly negative vision of a "natural" parenthood that is dangerous and destructive. And through that wreckage of neglect comes Esther Summerson, with love and order, to restore the world to itself.

III

> For those in whom a local mythology still works, there is an experience both of accord with the social order, and of harmony with the universe. For those, however, in whom the authorized signs no longer work—or, if working, produce deviant effects—there follows inevitably a sense both of dissociation from the local social nexus and of quest, within and without, for life, which the brain will take to be for "meaning." (Campbell, p. 5)

When Dickens recreated the myth of the foundling in Esther Summerson, he was attempting to articulate for his society that experience of accord with the social order and harmony with the universe that mythographer Joseph Campbell defines as a working mythology. In the virtues of an individual who was selfless, compassionate, modest, and good, Dickens placed his faith for the future of mankind. As his biographer Edgar Johnson puts it, "the resolute belief in life and in humanity that Dickens maintained was a banner that he held high in spite of all the evils he saw in society."[11] And his myth is an undeniably powerful creation. Dickens took what was best about humanity and offered it as a corrective to what was the worst. But in *Bleak House* the myth does not work; it fails to express the individual in harmony with herself, with God and with the world. Ultimately, in Dickens's scheme, the indifferent parent of the world cannot be reconciled with the child humanity.

Much of the failure of Dickens's myth rests on the infiltrated, adulterated narrative. Because Dickens created a kind of counterpoint with Esther's and the objective observer's narratives, readers may expect the combination to produce a complete vision of the world, authorized by Dickens. But there is no harmonic relationship between the two narrators. In fact, as J. Hillis Miller points out, it helps "if one recognizes the degree to which the other [objective] narrator is an ironic commentary on [Esther's] language, her personality, and her way of seeing things" (p. 31). More, however, than an ironic commentary, the observer's text overpowers Esther's narrative, and nullifies the myth of the foundling. The sheer force of the observer's indictment of society renders the remedy powerless. The observer exposes evils that no amount of individual goodness can redress. Accordingly, after Allan Woodcourt attempts to lead the dying Jo through the Lord's Prayer, the narrator points an accusing finger: "Dead, your Majesty. Dead, my lords and gentlemen. Dead, Right Reverends and Wrong Reverends of every order. Dead, men and women, born with Heavenly compassion in your hearts. And dying thus around us every day" (p. 649). Jo's plight is not an isolated case. And the objective narrator hammers home the truth about society, that it is brutally unconcerned about its less fortunate members, and that it is growing increasingly brutal and callous, truths that Esther's narrative cannot escape.

Another reason for the failure of Dickens's myth to restore the individual to the world is Esther's qualified happy ending. The place that Esther has created for herself is a re-creation of society, but it is a retreat from the world rather than an active engagement in it. Oddly enough, it is a mirror-image, if not in aspect, at least in name, of *Bleak House*. The name reflects an ambiguity about what kind of happiness the inhabitants will be able to achieve. And the name of Esther's husband, Woodcourt, though it is softened by the organic "wood" is marred by "court," which is (according to both narrators) quite possibly the single most destructive place in society. Indeed, the Court of Chancery, according to Lawrence Boythorn, is a system almost beyond reform: "Nothing but a mine below it on a busy day in term time, with all its records, rules, and precedents collected in it, and every functionary belonging to it also, high and low, upward and downward, from its son the Accountant-General to its father the Devil, and the whole blown to atoms with ten thousand hundredweight of gunpowder, would reform it in the least!" (p. 118). Mr. Boythorn's tendency to hyperbole notwithstanding, the word "court" carries with it some unfortunate connotations at the close of *Bleak House*. Esther and her little society seem somehow insubstantial compared to the weight of the narrator's world. There has been too much death and destruction, too much inhumanity and suffering, to accept the foundling myth as a power great enough to unseat the "system." Barbara Hardy describes this final imbalance of *Bleak House*: "It is understandable if depressing to find that the conclusion to the novel seems to expect so much congratulation. The reconciliation is too tiny, too unrepresentative, to act as an exit from our total experience of this novel."[12] The total experience of *Bleak House*, then, is one of cemented misery. When Conversation Kenge congratulates himself on the greatness of his "system," Dickens describes him as "gently moving his right hand as if it were a silver trowel, with which to spread the cement of his words on the structure of the system, and consolidate it for a thousand ages" (p. 844). The private domestic tranquility that Dickens envisions as an alternative is touching, but it's no match against the forces of a litigious, venal, and leech-like society that bleeds the men and women who come into contact with it.

In *Bleak House*, Dickens the myth-maker confronts his own extraordinary perception and portrayal of evil in man and the world. Out of that confrontation, the myth of the foundling was born and survives still; we continue to find the myth of individual virtue compelling. But it is an anti-myth in at least two ways: Dickens offers it as an alternative to an inherited myth, and it ultimately fails to successfully replace it. And the myth of the foundling pales in comparison to the magnitude of Dickens's accusation. *Bleak House* is a dark world indeed, an indictment of society that no myth can brighten.[13]

From *Studies in the Novel* 22 (1990): 1-9. Copyright © 1990 by University of North Texas Press. Reprinted with permission of University of North Texas Press.

Notes

1. Joseph Campbell, *The Masks of God: Creative Mythology* (New York: The Viking Press, 1968), pp. 6-7. All epigraphs in this essay come from this volume and refer-

ences will appear in the text. Much of Campbell's study concerns the self-conscious myth-making of James Joyce and Thomas Mann.

2. Charles Dickens, *Bleak House* (London: Oxford Univ. Press, 1948. Rpt. 1951), p. 1. Subsequent references to this edition will appear in the text.

3. Dickens so admired Fielding that he named his eighth child Henry Fielding Dickens, a decision that John Forster reported in *The Life of Charles Dickens* (Philadelphia: J. B. Lippincott Company, 1897) as "made in a kind of homage to the style of work he was now so bent on beginning" (vol. 2, p. 463).

4. Introduction to Charles Dickens, *Oliver Twist* (New York: Penguin Classics, 1986), p. 13. Subsequent references to Wilson's introduction will appear in the text.

5. Charles Dickens, *Oliver Twist* (London: Oxford Univ. Press, 1949. Rpt. 1974), pp. 412-13. Subsequent references will appear in the text.

6. F. R. and Q. D. Leavis, *Dickens the Novelist* (London: Chatto & Windus, 1973), p. 156.

7. Susan Shatto, *The Companion to Bleak House* (London: Unwin Hyman Ltd., 1988). p. 46.

8. Shatto, p. 83.

9. Dickens uses the fairy-tale motif frequently in his novels, yet it's different in *Bleak House*. For example, Dickens adopted the straightforward fairy-tale explicitly in *Dombey and Son*; Florence Dombey is the heroine of a story of enchantment imprisoned by the monstrous indifference of her father. But she's rescued by the handsome prince, Walter, and her happy ending (unlike Esther's) is unqualified. Esther, from the beginning of her story, distances herself from the easy association of her situation with a fairy tale when she says, "I was brought up, from my earliest remembrance—like some of the princesses in the fairy stories, *only I was not charming*—by my god-mother" (p. 63, emphasis mine). Dickens signals the reader that this is no ordinary fairy tale.

10. Introduction to Charles Dickens, *Bleak House* (New York: Penguin Books, 1971. Rpt. 1982), pp. 15-16. Subsequent references to Miller's introduction will appear in the text.

11. Edgar Johnson, *Charles Dickens: His Tragedy and Triumph* (Boston: Little, Brown and Co., 1952), p. 1140.

12. Barbara Hardy, *Dickens: The Later Novels* (London: Longmans, Green & Co., Ltd., 1968), p. 22.

13. I would like to thank my friend and colleague Helena Maragou for her invaluable suggestions.

Hard Times and the Structure of Industrialism:
The Novel as Factory_____

Patricia E. Johnson

Since F. R. Leavis's elevation of *Hard Times* into *The Great Tradition* in 1948, critics have had a tendency to see *Hard Times* as somehow distinct from Dickens's other novels. Some, following Leavis, have discovered in it a coherence and a high seriousness lacking in his other works; others have disliked its constraint and found it wanting in the very Fancy that it celebrates.[1] However it has been evaluated, it has been recognized as Dickens's distinctive attempt to come to grips with the phenomenon of the industrial city and with the more hidden economic and social structures which that city visibly represents. A curious contradiction emerges in the criticism of *Hard Times* as a social novel. On the one hand, as a realistic description of the industrial city and the industrial worker, it has been unfavorably compared to blue book reports, to the work of Friedrich Engels and other commentators on the emerging industrial society, and to Dickens's own journalistic description of the Preston strike.[2] Yet, on the other hand, the enduring power of *Hard Times* as a representation of conditions in industrial societies has been repeatedly affirmed, even by its harshest critics, though the source of that power is left largely unexplained.

Although it is now a commonplace of Dickens criticism that he denaturalizes and problematizes entire social structures in his later fiction—that he presents social problems, not as isolated pollutions, but as mere manifestations of the growing, increasingly corporate power of social and economic organizations—this insight has not been successfully applied to *Hard Times* which, because of its status as an industrial novel, has been seen as somehow inherently self-contradicting. I would like to suggest that *Hard Times* is much more coherent as a representation of industrialism than has been realized. The imaginative constraint of *Hard Times* is the symbolic expression of Dickens's critique of the interlocking structures—economic, social, and political—of industrial capitalism. As Terry Eagleton argues in *Criticism and Ideology*, "Dickens is forced in his later fiction to use as aesthetically unifying images the very social institutions (the Chancery Court of *Bleak House*, the Circumlocution Office of *Little Dorrit*) which are the object of his criticism."[3] Eagleton, however, like many other critics of the novel, goes on to name the "aesthetically unifying image" of *Hard Times* as the educational system.[4] But, as his Chapter 5 entitled "The Key-note" demonstrates, Dickens uses a much more pertinent and concretely realized representation of industrialism to shape his novel. Just as *Bleak House*, published the preceding year, uses the labyrinthine law courts surrounded by fog as the symbol of social malfeasance, so *Hard Times* uses the physical structure of the factory itself as both the metaphor for the destructive forces at work on its characters' lives and as the metaphor for its own aesthetic unity as a novel.

It has recently been suggested by critics such as Catherine Gallagher and Stephen Spector that there are slippages and inconsistencies in Dickens's use of metaphor and metonymy in *Hard Times*. In *The Industrial Reformation of English Fiction, 1832-1867*, Catherine Gallagher argues that Dickens uses the metaphor of the society as family to organize the novel, a metaphor which ultimately fails.[5] In his article, "Monsters of Metonymy: *Hard Times* and Knowing the Working Class," Stephen Spector argues that Dickens's use of metonymy turns the working-class characters into lifeless machines.[6] But, if the central metaphor of the factory itself is put in its proper place, it becomes clear that Dickens's uses of metaphor and metonymy do not conflict but, instead, interlock with one another and together reenact the consumption of fuel on which the factory system is based. Spector's argument, taken together with Gallagher's, implies that Dickens's use of figurative language is class-conscious, that metaphor is more applicable to the middle class, metonymy to the working class. Gallagher concludes her discussion with the judgment that "[u]p to its very last page, *Hard Times* is a book that simultaneously flaunts and discredits its metaphoricality, calling into question both the possibility of paternalist reform and the validity of its own narrative practice."[7] This is certainly true in a novel which metaphorically identifies the middle class with the buttressing, external wall of the factory while the working class and women are presented metonymically as being used as fuel. In fact, the shape of the novel recreates the dynamics of urban industrialism. In its firm outer framework—focused on the competing philosophies of Mr. Gradgrind's Utilitarianism and the circus's traditional humanism—which surrounds and contains an inner core of smoke and fire—represented by the stories of Stephen Blackpool, the industrial worker, and Louisa Gradgrind, the central female character—*Hard Times* imitates the closed economy of the factory system.

The setting and shape of the novel cohere strikingly. *Hard Times* takes place in Coketown, a mill town that is polarized between the industrialists on the one side and working-class men on the other. Within this framework and delimited by it, the lives of Stephen and Louisa unfold. Dickens provides a unique description of Coketown as a physical environment. Unlike Elizabeth Gaskell or Friedrich Engels, for example, two other Victorian recorders of England's "shock cities," Dickens does not emphasize the pollution, the labyrinthine slums, or the hustling, bustling streets of the industrial city. Instead, he abstracts its essential structure, rather than the superficial manifestations of that structure, what he calls its keynote, *fact*, which he metaphorically represents by the shape of the *factory* itself, a word that significantly repeats the sound of fact.[8]

Coketown, he tells us, is "a town of red brick," "a town of machinery and tall chimneys," filled with "vast piles of buildings full of windows where there was a rattling and a trembling all day long, and where the piston of the steam engine worked monotonously up and down."[9] Every church, hospital, and jail in the town is built on the same model, a "warehouse of red brick" (p. 17). Mr. M'Choakumchild's school is "a plain, bare, monotonous vault of a schoolroom," and even Mr. Gradgrind's face repeats this pattern with its "square wall of a forehead" (p. 1). This unique emphasis by Dickens on the repetition of the factory structure in every aspect of Coketown's life has often been read as Dickens's recognition of the deadening sameness of factory work and the alienated nature of its system of production. Yet the metaphor of the specific structure that Coketown repeats has additional resonance. The square red brick walls, the factory's most visible manifestation, are cemented and maintained by the upper- and middle-class professions of religion, medicine, law, education, and politics.[10] The churches, hospitals, jails, schools, and even Mr. Gradgrind's face reproduce the external wall of the factory structure. They contain the rattle of life, the action of the pistons, while the only visible symbols of internal activity are the "interminable serpents of smoke," revealing that fuel is being consumed (p. 17).[11]

Having once established this outer structure of seeming "fact" that the factory symbolizes, *Hard Times* questions and then penetrates that shell to reveal and describe the processes that the walls of the factory hide. Having established the metaphorical key-note, Dickens asks, "A town so sacred to fact, and so triumphant in its assertion, of course got on well?" and answers, "No. Coketown did not come out of its own furnaces, in all respects like gold that had stood the fire" (pp. 17-18). The name Coketown itself points to this conclusion. "Coke" suggests both the fuel that stokes the furnaces and the waste product that is left after the process has been completed. According to the *OED*, coke is a North-country word, probably derived from the word "colk," which means core. Coke is "the hard core of the coal left after other parts have been consumed" or "the solid substance left after mineral coal has been deprived by dry distillation of its volatile constituents." Coketown is a city that founds its outer structure on this core-process of fuel consumption. But what is the true nature of the fuel that is being consumed? Dickens's answer, as the core of his novel shows, is that the true coke, both fuel and waste product, of the factory system is human life.

The shape of *Hard Times* as a fiction reproduces the shape of the factory—its supporting framework and its core of fuel. The first seven and last three chapters of the novel focus on the social and political framework. This framework tells the story of Mr. Gradgrind, the Utilitarian Member of Parliament. Like the square red brick walls that surround the inner workings of the factory, this framework is the most immediately apparent feature of the novel and seems almost detachable from the novel's core. Thus many critics have read the novel solely through Gradgrind's story and argued over the effectiveness of Dickens's critique of Utilitarianism or the realism of Gradgrind's conversion to a more humanistic way of thinking.[12] Yet structurally the answers to such questions do not really matter. Regardless of what changes are made in the framework, as long as it still stands, the system itself is maintained. It is only in the framework of the novel, and by implication of society, that change is allowed to occur. The framework can contain, adapt, and even be strengthened by such changes as long as they are kept separate from the core of the novel and from the dynamics of production and reproduction. Neither Gradgrind nor the circus can restore the wasted lives of Louisa or Stephen Blackpool. Gradgrind only preserves and prolongs the life of his son Tom, and by implication of himself, by further withdrawing from the center of the system. Thus, despite, or even because of, humanistic conversion, the framework of the novel and of society remains in place, and the dynamics of capitalist industrial production are untouched.

The only point where systemic change and perhaps explosion are possible is at the core of the system and in the central stories in *Hard Times*. Yet here Dickens metonymically reproduces the system in its harnessing and control of energy, rather than the free release of it. *Hard Times* is organized into three books, named "Sowing," "Reaping," and "Garnering." These titles underline the significance of what I have called the core of the novel and Dickens's central theme. By using these references to natural production, Dickens implicitly criticizes the unnatural method of production that the factory system represents. The central portion of the novel, occupying 27 out of 37 chapters, focuses on the private lives and unhappy marriages of Stephen Blackpool, the novel's representative working-class man, and Louisa Gradgrind, the daughter of its central spokesman for Utilitarianism. *Hard Times* counterpoints the events of their lives, drawing a series of parallels between these two seemingly disparate characters. Superficially, there would seem to be little connection between this older working-class man and this young middle-class woman, but Stephen and Louisa follow the same metonymic pattern. Each begins the novel in a state of confusion, smoke. This is underlined by Stephen's oft repeated statement that everything is "in a muddle." The connection is strengthened by the fact that both characters' entrapment within the system is manifested primarily in their unhappy marriages. Each, in fact, comes to despise the mate that he or she is tied to for life. Each becomes increasingly isolated from his or her own class and gender, as Louisa seldom returns home after her marriage and Stephen is ostracized by other working-class men for his refusal to join the union. Finally, each appears to suffer a moral fall, which is followed by a literal, physical fall. Stephen appears to have broken the law by stealing, and he literally falls into an abandoned mine pit. Louisa is imagined by Mrs. Sparsit to be slowly descending a moral staircase that leads to adultery and the status of fallen woman, what the novel calls "a dark pit of shame and ruin" (p. 154). She, too, literally falls at the feet of her father at the climactic turning-point in her life. While each is in a sense rescued, and by the same agent, the circus girl Sissy Jupe, neither is brought back to a full life. Stephen survives for only a few minutes after his maimed body is pulled out of the mine, and Louisa's scarring past prevents her from marrying again or ever having children.

My argument is that these two lives, described in the central portion of *Hard Times*, are metonymically presented by Dickens as the "coke," the fuel and eventually the waste products, of the factory system. Dickens's use of metonymy encourages such a reading as he repeatedly connects Stephen and Louisa with images of smoke and fire. Stephen most obviously fits this reading as the representative factory hand. The system obviously measures him as fuel: "So many hundred Hands in this Mill; so many hundred horse Steam Power," Dickens tells us (p. 53). Stephen exists at the heart of the system, almost in the heat of the furnace as it were. His flat is described as being "in the hardest working part of Coketown; in the innermost fortifications of that ugly citadel, where Nature was as strongly bricked out as killing airs and gases were bricked in" (p. 48). Dickens stresses the factory-like shape of Coketown's working-class slums where the fuel for the system is housed: "in the last close nook of this great exhausted receiver, where the chimneys, for want of air to make a draught, were built in an immense variety of stunted and crooked shapes, as though every house put out a sign of the kind of people who might be expected to be born in it" (pp. 48-49). This is where the factory hands live, and, when they die, black ladders are raised to the windows to dispose of the dead, "the sliding away of all that was most precious in this world to a striving wife and a brood of hungry babies," like coal down a chute (p. 63).

It is no wonder that Stephen looks old for his age. Dickens describes him emerging from "the hot mill," "haggard and worn" (p. 53). His "volatile constituents" consumed by the factory, he is nearly a burnt-out cinder of a man even as the novel begins.[13] It is not that Stephen has internalized the factory, but that he is internal to it. In the first glimpse we have of him, he is "standing in the street, with the odd sensation upon him which the stoppage of the machinery always produced—the sensation of its having worked and stopped in his own head" (p. 49). Even his nightmares are shaped by this key-note: "He stood on a raised stage, under his own loom; and, looking up at the shape the loom took, and hearing the burial service distinctly read, he knew that he was there to suffer death" (p. 66). Here he dreams that his station in the factory is a scaffold where he will be punished for attempting to internally transform his life by making a second marriage. His dreams and nightmares, therefore, do not provide him with an imagined escape from his place within the system but instead reenact his physical and emotional entrapment.

At the novel's opening Stephen still hopes for transformation, hopes to salvage something from his life by divorcing his first wife and making a happier second marriage. Dickens tells us, "In the strength of his misfortune, and the energy of his distress, he *fired* for the moment like a proud man" (emphasis mine, p. 56). There is still a spark left in him, but the title of the chapter that contains this description, "No Way Out," indicates that the system will soon consume that spark. There is "no way out" of the system for the factory hand, an idea that Dickens ironically illustrates by having Stephen leave Coketown only to fall into an abandoned mine pit, called the Old Hell Shaft, just on the outskirts of town.[14] Stephen himself recognizes that his end is a metonym for the factory hand's life: just before he dies, he says,

> I ha' fell into th' pit, my dear, as have cost wi'in the knowledge o' old fok now livin', hundreds and hundreds o' men's lives—fathers, sons, brothers, dear to thousands an' thousands, an' keeping 'em fro' want and hunger. I ha' fell into a pit that ha' been wi' th' Fire-damp crueller than battle. (pp. 206-207)

The word "Fire-damp" again returns us to the idea of fuel and to the processes of combustion. It is a miner's term for the gas given off by coal which is liable to explode if mixed with air. Yet the explosion is fully contained within the pit, hurting only the miners themselves. Stephen underlines the separation between the outer social structure and the inner process of production when he goes on to say,

> I ha' read on 't in the public petition, as onny one may read, fro' the men that works in pits, in which they ha' pray'n and pray'n the lawmakers for Christ's sake not to let their work be murder to 'em, but to spare 'em for th' wives and children that they loves as well as gentlefok loves theirs. When it were in work, it killed wi'out need; when 'tis let alone, it kills wi'out need. See how we die an' no need, one way an' another—in a muddle—every day! (p. 207)

Here Stephen recognizes the daily destructiveness of the system. Though "in a muddle," he has experienced the interior of factory life and describes its nature in a way that the lawmakers and gentlefolk are incapable of doing. Yet, like the Old Hell Shaft, in work or out of work, Stephen's life is structured by the factory process. Like Stephen, the pit provided fuel for the system; having been stripped, it is abandoned. As fuel or as waste product, Stephen's life is fully contained and defined by the factory system.

As Stephen is shown to be fuel for the system of production, so Louisa is fuel for the system of marriage and reproduction. The most potentially explosive connection that Dickens makes in *Hard Times* is the structural parallel that he implicitly draws between the factory system and the patriarchal family. Though it is situated a mile or two outside of Coketown, Stone Lodge, the Gradgrind family home, is "a great square house," another repetition of the factory structure: "Not the least disguise toned down or shaded off that uncompromising fact in the landscape" (p. 8). Our first glimpse inside Stone Lodge gives us the other essential element of the factory structure. We see Mr. Bounderby, the novel's Captain of Industry and Louisa's future husband, significantly "warming himself before the fire" (p. 11). Both Tom and Louisa Gradgrind grow up within this structure: "Their shadows were defined upon the wall" (p. 40). But, because Tom will eventually move to the external structure of the Bank while Louisa will remain within, of the two, Louisa alone is persistently connected to the image of fire. She is first described as "a fire with nothing to burn" (p. 10). And her most frequently described activity in *Hard Times* is gazing into the fire. Tom remarks on this activity and connects it directly with gender: "'You seem to find more to look at in it than ever I could find,' said Tom. 'Another of the advantages, I suppose, of being a girl'" (pp. 40-41). Louisa's seemingly perverse insistence that the fire indicates something about her own position in life is emphasized when her mother reproves her for "wondering" what it means:

After I have heard you myself, when the whole of my right side has been benumbed, going on with your master about combustion, and calcination, and calorification, and I may say every kind of ation that could drive a poor invalid distracted, to hear you talking in this absurd way about sparks and ashes! (p. 42)

But Louisa is simply applying "combustion, and calcination, and calorification," all processes of fuel consumption, to herself and reaching the logical conclusion: "I was encouraged by nothing, mother, but by looking at the red sparks dropping out of the fire, and whitening and dying. It made me think, after all, how short my life would be, and how little I could hope to do in it" (pp. 41-42).

Thus Louisa early recognizes her function within the system, but, as with Stephen, this knowledge does not provide a way out. Instead, she allows herself to be used as an object of exchange by her father and her brother, Tom, in her marriage to Bounderby. She accepts her position because a part of her agrees with her family and her society's valuation of her as fuel. During the scene in which Tom indirectly suggests how useful she will be to him as Bounderby's wife, Louisa gazes persistently at the fire. When, after congratulating her on being "a *capital* girl" (emphasis mine), Tom leaves, Louisa shifts her gaze from the fire in the house to the fires of Coketown, instinctively connecting her personal position with that of the wider processes and effects of industrialism: "It seemed as if, first in her own fire within the house, and then in the fiery haze without, she tried to discover what kind of woof Old Time, that greatest and longest-established Spinner of all, would weave from the threads he had already spun into a woman" (p. 73). In the proposal scene which follows, Louisa continues to gaze not at the fire within but at the larger landscape, and the imagery of smoke and fire is even more insistent. Even her father is struck by the direction of her look: "Are you consulting the chimneys of the Coketown works, Louisa?" (p. 76). They lead her to conclude that she has been too shaped by the system to effectively change it: "While [my life] lasts, I would wish to do the little I can, and the little I am fit for. What does it matter?" (p. 77).

Yet the danger of an outbreak of fire, an explosion, is present. As Louisa gazes out of the window at the smoke pouring from the Coketown factories, she takes the scene as an emblem of her life, warning her father: "There seems to be nothing there but languid and monotonous smoke. Yet when the night comes, Fire bursts out, father!" (p. 76). Eventually, both Stephen and Louisa try to break out of their lives. With his wife in a drunken stupor, Stephen is filled with such hatred of her that he is tempted to poison her. Louisa comes close to disgracing her father and husband by eloping with James Harthouse. Finally, however, both Stephen and Louisa are unable to act out their terrible anger because they accept the framework for which they provide the fuel. They implode, rather than explode, ending their lives as burnt-out cinders: Stephen dies slowly and significantly at the bottom of a mine shaft while Louisa lives on, a barren woman, denied the only satisfactions—home and children—that her society allows women.

It could be argued that Dickens did not intend his novel to be read in this way. Certainly, he appears to control the radical implications of his own representation of the factory system, to provide a safety valve as it were, by placing much of the anger about the system in Louisa rather than in Stephen and by providing the floating circle of the circus as a possible, temporary release from the monotony of the square, immovable factory walls. Yet in its interlocking use of metaphor and metonymy, *Hard Times* does recreate the dynamics of capitalist production. Dickens pays a chilling tribute to the power of the factory system by allowing his own creative energy to be harnessed to it, by producing his novel as factory. At the end of Book 3, "Garnering," Dickens enumerates the goods that this system of production has stored up for itself: Stephen is dead; Tom will die exiled and alone; Louisa is living a life of self-sacrifice. The circus girl Sissy's happy children, outside the factory, are the only notes of hope. In his conclusion Dickens unrelentingly directs our gaze to the shape of the factory and its underlying significance. The last pages of the novel return us to Louisa, still looking into the fire. The last two paragraphs dwell on the metaphors of the wall and the fire. Dickens tells us that "national prosperity figures" will be "the Writing on the Wall," and asks us with what feelings we will watch while "the ashes of our fires turn grey and cold" (pp. 226-27). Fancy itself can do little more than decorate this enclosure. Thus Dickens's primary purpose goes beyond Fancy. He does not provide us with an escape from the system but instead holds us to a strict accounting of what it costs to maintain it. When we read *Hard Times*, the process we are put through leaves us enclosed, and at the conclusion we are left staring at the cinders of the fire and the stark contours of the factory walls.

Notes

1. See F. R. Leavis, *The Great Tradition* (New York: New York Univ. Press, 1960), pp. 227-48. Among the many critical rebuttals to Leavis are Peter Bracher's "Muddle and Wonderful No-Meaning: Verbal Irresponsibility and Verbal Failures in *Hard Times*," *Studies in the Novel* 10 (1978): 305-19; Joseph Butwin's "The Paradox of the Clown in Dickens," *Dickens Studies Annual* 5 (1976): 115-32; and David Sonstroem's "Fettered Fancy in *Hard Times*," *PMLA* 84 (1969): 520-29.

2. See Sheila M. Smith, *The Other Nation: The Poor in English Novels of the 1840s and 1850s* (Oxford: Clarendon Press, 1980); and Nicholas Coles, "The Politics of *Hard Times*: Dickens the Novelist versus Dickens the Reformer," *Dickens Studies Annual* 15 (1986): 145-79.

3. Terry Eagleton, *Criticism and Ideology: A Study in Marxist Literary Theory* (London: Redwood Burn, Ltd., 1976), p. 129.

4. Eagleton, p. 130.

5. Catherine Gallagher, *The Industrial Reformation of English Fiction, Social Discourse and Narrative Form, 1832-1867* (Chicago: Univ. of Chicago Press, 1985), pp. 149-66.

6. Stephen J. Spector, "Monsters of Metonymy: *Hard Times* and Knowing the Working Class," *ELH* 51 (1984): 365-84.

7. Gallagher, p 166.

8. John Lucas criticizes Dickens's representation of Coketown as "largely a com-

pilation of cliches based on an external and distanced acquaintance" and questions its "adequacy" and "relevance" (pp. 176, 179). See John Lucas, "Mrs. Gaskell and Brotherhood," in *Tradition and Tolerance in Nineteenth-Century Fiction*, eds. David Howard et al. (London: Routledge and Kegan Paul, 1966). I am arguing, on the other hand, that Dickens's Coketown is stripped of inessentials in order to lay bare the essence of industrialism inherent in the factory structure itself.

9. Charles Dickens, *Hard Times*, eds. George Ford and Sylvère Monod (New York: Norton Critical Edition, 1966), p. 17. Subsequent citations to the novel will be from this edition and will appear in the text.

10. In "Social Criticism in Dickens: Some Problems of Method and Approach," *Critical Quarterly* 6 (1964), Raymond Williams argues that Dickens shows that "Parliament, the trade unions, educational reform, public protective legislation of many kinds . . . could not operate, at that level, in the fiction itself" (p. 221). Dickens further underlines the irrelevance of these largely upper- and middle-class institutions and activities to the industrial process by pointing out that none of the factory workers attend the churches provided by the eighteen denominations.

11. Thomas M. Leitch also points out the importance of "the image of fire, which produces energy by reducing its fuel to ashes" in his commentary on the ending of *Hard Times*. See his article, "Closure and Teleology in Dickens." *Studies in the Novel* 18 (1986): 150.

12. This approach can be briefly represented by Fredric Jameson's schematic analysis of *Hard Times* in *The Prison-House of Language: A Critical Account of Structuralism and Russian Formalism* (Princeton, NJ: Princeton Univ. Press, 1972):

> In *Hard Times* we witness the confrontation of what amounts to two antagonistic intellectual systems: Mr. Gradgrind's utilitarianism ("Facts! Facts!") and that world of anti-facts symbolized by Sissy Jupe and the circus, or in other words, imagination. The novel is primarily the education of the educator, the conversion of Mr. Gradgrind from his inhuman system to the opposing one. (p. 167)

In this analysis the experiences of Louisa and Stephen are present as mere object lessons for Mr. Gradgrind. Catherine Gallagher, on the other hand, has pointed out that the true significance of *Hard Times* must also take into account the parallel lives of Louisa and Stephen. See her article, "*Hard Times* and *North and South*: The Family and Society in Two Industrial Novels," *Arizona Quarterly* 36 (1980): 70-96.

13. This metonymic presentation of Stephen, emphasizing his function as fuel for the system, provides an explanation to the critics who have questioned the "realism" of Dickens's representation of the industrial worker's "slowness." Stephen Spector states, "Dickens bestows hardly a single *spark* of his vitalizing genius" on Stephen Blackpool (emphasis mine, p. 365). But he interprets Stephen's lack of fire as a failure of metonymy which turns the working class into monsters whereas I am arguing that Dickens shows that it is the factory system, not the working class, that is monstrous.

14. Nicholas Coles points out that Stephen's death can be interpreted as "a form of industrial accident" (p. 148).

Little Dorrit

Lionel Trilling

Little Dorrit is one of the three great novels of Dickens' great last period, but of the three it is perhaps the least established with modern readers. When it first appeared—in monthly parts from December 1855 to June 1857—its success was even more decisive than that of *Bleak House*, but the suffrage of later audiences has gone the other way, and of all Dickens' later works it is *Bleak House* that has come to be the best known. As for *Our Mutual Friend*, after having for some time met with adverse critical opinion among the enlightened—one recalls that the youthful Henry James attacked it for standing in the way of art and truth—it has of recent years been regarded with ever-growing admiration. But *Little Dorrit* seems to have retired to the background and shadow of our consciousness of Dickens.

This does not make an occasion for concern or indignation. With a body of works as large and as enduring as that of Dickens, taste and opinion will never be done. They will shift and veer as they have shifted and veered with the canon of Shakespeare, and each generation will have its special favorites and make its surprised discoveries. *Little Dorrit*, one of the most profound of Dickens' novels and one of the most significant works of the nineteenth century, will not fail to be thought of as speaking with a peculiar and passionate intimacy to our own time.

Little Dorrit is about society, which certainly does not distinguish it from the rest of Dickens' novels unless we go on to say, as we must, that it is *more* about society than any other of the novels, that it is about society in its very essence. This essential quality of the book has become apparent as many of the particular social conditions to which it refers have passed into history. Some of these conditions were already of the past when Dickens wrote, for although imprisonment for debt was indeed not wholly given up until 1869, yet imprisonment for small debts had been done away with in 1844, the prison of the Marshalsea had been abolished in 1842 and the Court of the Marshalsea in 1849. Bernard Shaw said of *Little Dorrit* that it converted him to socialism; it is not likely that any contemporary English reader would feel it appropriate to respond to its social message in the same way. The dead hand of outworn tradition no longer supports special privilege in England. For good or bad, in scarcely any country in the world can the whole art of government be said to be How Not To Do It. Mrs. General cannot impose the genteel discipline of Prunes and Prisms, and no prestige whatever attaches to "the truly refined mind" of her definition—"one that will seem to be ignorant of the existence of anything that is not perfectly proper, placid, and pleasant." At no point, perhaps, do the particular abuses and absurdities upon which Dickens directed his terrible cold anger represent the problems of social life as we now conceive them.

Yet this makes *Little Dorrit* not less but more relevant to our sense of things. As the particulars seem less immediate to our case, the general force of the novel becomes greater, and *Little Dorrit* is seen to be about a problem which does not yield easily to time. It is about society in relation to the individual human will. This is certainly a matter general enough—general to the point of tautology, were it not for the bitterness with which the tautology is articulated, were it not for the specificity and the subtlety and the boldness with which the human will is anatomized.

The subject of *Little Dorrit* is borne in upon us by the symbol, or emblem, of the book, which is the prison. The story opens in a prison in Marseilles. It goes on to the Marshalsea, which in effect it never leaves. The second of the two parts of the novel begins in what we are urged to think of as a sort of prison, the monastery of the Great St. Bernard. The Circumlocution Office is the prison of the creative mind of England. Mr. Merdle is shown habitually holding himself by the wrist, taking himself into custody, and in a score of ways the theme of incarceration is carried out, persons and classes being imprisoned by their notions of their predestined fate or their religious duty, or by their occupations, their life schemes, their ideas of themselves, their very habits of language.

Symbolic or emblematic devices are used by Dickens to one degree or another in several of the novels of his late period, but nowhere to such good effects as in *Little Dorrit*. The fog of *Bleak House*, the dust heap and the river of *Our Mutual Friend* are very striking, but they scarcely equal in force the prison image which dominates *Little Dorrit*. This is because the prison is an actuality before it is ever a symbol;[1] its connection with the will is real, it is the practical instrument for the negation of man's will which the will of society has contrived. As such, the prison haunted the mind of the nineteenth century, which may be said to have had its birth at the fall of the Bastille. The genius of the age, conceiving itself as creative will, naturally thought of the prisons from which it must be freed, and the trumpet call of the "Leonore" overture sounds through the century, the signal for the opening of the gates, for a general deliverance, although it grows fainter as men come to think of the prison not as a political instrument merely but as the ineluctable condition of life in society. "Most men in a brazen prison live"—the line in which Matthew Arnold echoes Wordsworth's "shades of the prison-house begin to close/ Upon the growing boy," might have served as the epigraph of *Little Dorrit*. In the mind of Dickens himself the idea of the prison was obsessive, not merely because of his own boyhood experience of prison life through his father's three months in the Marshalsea (although this must be given great weight in our understanding of his intense preoccupation with the theme), but because of his own consciousness of the force and scope of his will.

If we speak of the place which the image of the prison occupied in the mind of the nineteenth century, we ought to recollect a certain German picture of the time, inconsiderable in itself but made significant by its use in a famous work of the early twentieth century. It represents a man lying in a medieval dungeon; he is asleep, his head pillowed on straw, and we know that he dreams of freedom because the bars on his window are shown being sawed by gnomes. This picture serves as the frontispiece of Freud's *Introductory Lectures on Psychoanalysis*—Freud uses it to make plain one of the more elementary ideas of his psychology, the idea of the fulfillment in dream or fantasy of impulses of the will that cannot be fulfilled in actuality. His choice of this particular picture is not fortuitous; other graphic representations of wish-fulfillment exist which might have served equally well his immediate didactic purpose, but Freud's general conception of the mind does indeed make the prison image peculiarly appropriate. And Freud is in point here because in a passage of *Little Dorrit* Dickens anticipates one of Freud's ideas, and not one of the simplest but nothing less bold and inclusive than the essential theory of the neurosis; and the quality of mind that makes this striking anticipation is at work everywhere in *Little Dorrit*.

The brief passage to which I make reference occurs in the course of Arthur Clennam's pursuit of the obsessive notion that his family is in some way guilty, that its fortune, although now greatly diminished, has been built on injury done to someone. And he conjectures that the injured person is William Dorrit, who has been confined for debt in the Marshalsea for twenty years. Clennam is not wholly wrong in his supposition—there is indeed guilt in the family, incurred by Arthur's mother, and it consists in part of an injury done to a member of the Dorrit family. But he is not wholly right, for Mr. Dorrit has not been imprisoned through the wish or agency of Mrs. Clennam. The reasoning by which Arthur reaches his partly mistaken conclusion is of the greatest interest. It is based upon the fact that his mother, although mentally very vigorous, has lived as an invalid for many years. She has been imprisoned in a single room of her house, confined to her chair, which she leaves only for her bed. And her son conjectures that her imprisoning illness is the price she pays for the guilty gratification of keeping William Dorrit in his prison—that is, in order to have the right to injure another, she must unconsciously injure herself in an equivalent way: "A swift thought shot into [Arthur Clennam's] mind. In that long imprisonment here [i.e., Mr. Dorrit's] and in her long confinement to her room, did his mother find a balance to be struck? I admit that I was accessory to that man's captivity. I have suffered it in kind. He has decayed in his prison; I in mine. I have paid the penalty."

I have dwelt on this detail because it suggests, even more than the naked fact of the prison itself, the nature of the vision of society of *Little Dorrit*. One way of describing Freud's conception of the mind is to say that it is based upon the primacy of the will, and that the organization of the internal life is in the form, often fantastically parodic, of a criminal process in which the mind is at once the criminal, the victim, the police, the judge, and the executioner. And this is a fair description of Dickens' own view of the mind, as, having received the social impress, it becomes in turn the matrix of society.

In emphasizing the psychological aspects of the representation of society of *Little Dorrit* I do not wish to slight those more immediate institutional aspects of which earlier readers of the novel were chiefly aware. These are of as great importance now as they ever were in Dickens' career. Dickens is far from having lost his sense of the cruelty and stupidity of institutions and functionaries, his sense of the general rightness of the people as a whole and of the general wrongness of those who are put in authority over them. He certainly has not moved to that specious position in which all injustice is laid at the door of the original Old Adam in each of us, not to be done away with until we shall all, at the same moment, become the new Adam. The Circumlocution Office is a constraint upon the life of England which nothing can justify. Mr. Dorrit's sufferings and the injustice done to him are not denied or mitigated by his passionate commitment to some of the worst aspects of the society which deals with him so badly.

Yet the emphasis on the internal life and on personal responsibility is very strong in *Little Dorrit*. Thus, to take but one example, in the matter of the Circumlocution Office Dickens is at pains to remind us that the responsibility for its existence lies even with so good a man as Mr. Meagles. In the alliance against the torpor of the Office which he has made with Daniel Doyce, the engineer and inventor, Mr. Meagles has been undeviatingly faithful. Yet Clennam finds occasion to wonder whether there might not be "in the breast of this honest, affectionate, and cordial Mr. Meagles, any microscopic portion of the mustard-seed that had sprung up into the great tree of the Circumlocution Office." He is led to this speculation by his awareness that Mr. Meagles feels "a general superiority to Daniel Doyce, which seemed to be founded, not so much on anything in Doyce's personal character, as on the mere fact of [Doyce's] being an originator and a man out of the beaten track of other men."

Perhaps the single best index of the degree of complexity with which Dickens views society in *Little Dorrit* is afforded by the character of Blandois and his place in the novel. Blandois is wholly wicked, the embodiment of evil; he is, indeed, a devil. One of the effects of his presence in *Little Dorrit* is to complicate our response to the theme of the prison, to deprive us of the comfortable, philanthropic thought that prisons are nothing but instruments of injustice. Because Blandois exists, prisons are necessary. The generation of readers that preceded our own was inclined, I think, to withhold credence from Blandois—they did not believe in his aesthetic actuality because they did not believe in his moral actuality, the less so because they could not account for his existence in specific terms of social causation. But events have required us to believe that there really are people who seem entirely wicked, and almost unaccountably so; the social causes of their badness lie so far back that they can scarcely be reached, and in any case causation pales into irrelevance before the effects of their actions; our effort to "understand" them becomes a mere form of thought.

In this novel about the will and society, the devilish nature of Blandois is confirmed by his maniac insistence upon his gentility, his mad reiteration that it is the right and necessity of his existence to be served by others. He is the exemplification of the line in *Lear*: "The prince of darkness is a gentleman." The influence of Dickens upon Dostoevski is perhaps nowhere exhibited in a more detailed way than in the similarities between Blandois and the shabby-genteel devil of

The Brothers Karamazov, and also between him and Smerdyakov of the same novel. It is of consequence to Dickens as to Dostoevski that the evil of the unmitigated social will should own no country, yet that the flavor of its cosmopolitanism should be "French"—that is, rationalistic and subversive of the very assumption of society. Blandois enfolds himself in the soiled tatters of the revolutionary pathos. So long as he can play the game in his chosen style, he is nature's gentleman dispossessed of his rightful place, he is the natural genius against whom the philistine world closes its dull ranks. And when the disguise, which deceives no one, is off, he makes use of the classic social rationalization: Society has made him what he is; he does in his own person only what society does in its corporate form and with its corporate self-justification. "Society sells itself and sells me: and I sell society."[2]

Around Blandois are grouped certain characters of the novel of whose manner of life he is the pure principle. In these people the social will, the will to status, is the ruling faculty. To be recognized, deferred to, and served—this is their master passion. Money is of course of great consequence in the exercise of this passion, yet in *Little Dorrit* the desire for money is subordinated to the desire for deference. The Midas figure of Mr. Merdle must not mislead us on this point—should, indeed, guide us aright, for Mr. Merdle, despite his destructive power, is an innocent and passive man among those who live by the social will. It is to be noted of all these people that they justify their insensate demand for status by some version of Blandois's pathos; they are confirmed in their lives by self-pity, they rely on the great modern strategy of being the insulted and injured. Mr. Dorrit is too soft a man for his gentility mania ever to be quite diabolical, but his younger daughter Fanny sells herself to the devil, damns herself entirely, in order to torture the woman who once questioned her social position. Henry Gowan, the cynical, incompetent gentleman-artist who associates himself with Blandois in order to *épater* society, is very nearly as diabolical as his companion. From his mother—who must dismiss once and for all any lingering doubt of Dickens' ability to portray what Chesterton calls the delicate or deadly in human character—he has learned to base his attack on society upon the unquestionable rightness of wronged gentility. Miss Wade lives a life of tortured self-commiseration which gives her license to turn her hatred and her hand against everyone, and she imposes her principle of judgment and conduct upon Tattycoram.

In short, it is part of the complexity of this novel which deals so bitterly with society that those of its characters who share its social bitterness are by that very fact condemned. And yet—so much further does the complexity extend—the subversive pathos of self-pity is by no means wholly dismissed, the devil has not wholly lied. No reader of *Little Dorrit* can possibly conclude that the rage of envy which Tattycoram feels is not justified in some degree, or that Miss Wade is wholly wrong in pointing out to her the insupportable ambiguity of her position as the daughter-servant of Mr. and Mrs. Meagles and the sister-servant of Pet Meagles. Nor is it possible to read Miss Wade's account of her life, "The History of a Self Tormentor," without an understanding that amounts to sympathy. We feel this the more—Dickens meant us to feel it the more—because the two young women have been orphaned from infancy, and are illegitimate. Their bitterness is seen to be the perversion of the desire for love. The self-torture of Miss Wade—who becomes the more interesting if we think of her as the exact inversion of Esther Summerson of *Bleak House*—is the classic maneuver of the child who is unloved, or believes herself to be unloved; she refuses to be lovable, she elects to be hateful. In all of us the sense of injustice precedes the sense of justice by many years. It haunts our infancy, and even the most dearly loved of children may conceive themselves to be oppressed. Such is the nature of the human will, so perplexed is it by the disparity between what it desires and what it is allowed to have. With Dickens as with Blake, the perfect image of injustice is the unhappy child, and, like the historian Burckhardt, he connects the fate of nations with the treatment of children. It is a commonplace of the biography and criticism of Dickens that this reflects his own sense of having been unjustly treated by his parents, specifically in ways which injured his own sense of social status, his own gentility; the general force of Dickens' social feelings derives from their being rooted in childhood experience, and something of the special force of *Little Dorrit* derives from Dickens' having discovered its matter in the depths of his own social will.

At this point we become aware of the remarkable number of false and inadequate parents in *Little Dorrit*. To what pains Dickens goes to represent delinquent parenthood, with what an elaboration of irony he sets it forth! "The Father of the Marshalsea"—this is the title borne by Mr. Dorrit, who, preoccupied by the gratification of being the First Gentleman of a prison, is unable to exercise the simplest paternal function; who corrupts two of his children by his dream of gentility; who will accept any sacrifice from his saintly daughter Amy, Little Dorrit to whom he is the beloved child to be cherished and forgiven. "The Patriarch"—this is the name bestowed upon Mr. Casby, who stands as a parody of all Dickens' benevolent old gentlemen from Mr. Pickwick through the Cheerybles to John Jarndyce, an astounding unreality of a man who, living only to grip and grind, has convinced the world by the iconography of his dress and mien that he is the repository of all benevolence. The primitive appropriateness of the strange—the un-English!—punishment which Mr. Pancks metes out to this hollow paternity, the cutting off of his long hair and the broad brim of his hat, will be understood by any reader with the least tincture of psychoanalytical knowledge. Then the Meagles, however solicitous of their own daughter, are, as we have seen, but indifferent parents to Tattycoram. Mrs. Gowan's rearing of her son is the root of his corruption. It is Fanny Dorrit's complaint of her enemy, Mrs. Merdle, that she refuses to surrender the appearance of youth, as a mother should. And at the very center of the novel is Mrs. Clennam, a false mother in more ways than one; she does not deny love but she perverts and prevents it by denying all that love feeds on—liberty, demonstrative tenderness, joy, and, what for Dickens is the guardian of love in society, art. It is her harsh rearing of her son that has given him cause to say in his fortieth year, "I have no will."

Some grace—it is, of course, the secret of his birth, of his being really a child of love and art—has kept Arthur Clennam from responding to the will of his mother with a bitter, clenched will of his own. The alternative he has chosen has not, contrary to his declaration, left him no will at all. He has by no means been robbed of his ethical will, he can exert energy to help others, and for the sake of Mr. Dorrit or Daniel Doyce's invention he can haunt the Circumlocution Office with his mild, stubborn, "I want to know. . . ." But the very accent of that phrase seems to forecast the terrible "I prefer not to" of Bartleby the Scrivener in Melville's great story of the will in its ultimate fatigue.

It is impossible, I think, not to find in Arthur Clennam the evidence of Dickens' deep personal involvement in *Little Dorrit*. If we ask what Charles Dickens has to do with poor Clennam, what The Inimitable has to do with this sad depleted failure, the answer must be: nothing, save what is implied by Clennam's consciousness that he has passed the summit of life and that the path from now on leads downward, by his belief that the pleasures of love are not for him, by his "I want to know . . . ," by his wish to negate the will in death. Arthur Clennam is that mode of Dickens' existence at the time of *Little Dorrit* which makes it possible for him to write to his friend Macready, "However strange it is never to be at rest, and never satisfied, and ever trying after something that is never reached, and to be always laden with plot and plan and care and worry, how clear it is that it must be, and that one is driven by an irresistible might until the journey is worked out." And somewhat earlier and with a yet more poignant relevance: "Why is it, that as with poor David, a sense always comes crushing upon me now, when I fall into low spirits, as of one happiness I have missed in life, and one friend and companion I have never made?"

If we become aware of an autobiographical element in *Little Dorrit*, we must of course take notice of the fact that the novel was conceived after the famous incident of Maria Beadnell, who, poor woman, was the original of Arthur Clennam's Flora Finching. She was the first love of Dickens' proud, unfledged youth; she had married what Dickens has taught us to call Another, and now, after twenty years, she had chosen to come back into his life. Familiarity with the story cannot diminish our amazement at it—Dickens was a subtle and worldly man, but his sophistication was not proof against his passionate sentimentality, and he fully expected the past to come back to him, borne in the little hands of the adorable Maria. The actuality had a quite extreme effect upon him, and Flora, fat and foolish, is his monument to the discovered discontinuity between youth and middle age; she is the nonsensical spirit of the anticlimax of the years. And if she is in some degree forgiven, being represented as the kindest of foolish women, yet it is not without meaning that she is everywhere attended by Mr. F's Aunt, one of Dickens' most astonishing ideas, the embodiment of senile rage and spite, flinging to the world the crusts of her buttered toast. "He has a proud stomach, this chap," she cries when poor Arthur hesitates over her dreadful gift. "Give him a meal of chaff!" It is the voice of one of the Parcae.

It did not, of course, need the sad comedy of Maria Beadnell for Dickens to conceive that something in his life had come to an end. It did not even need his growing certainty that, after so many years and so many children, his relations with his wife were insupportable—this realization was as much a consequence as it was a cause of the sense of termination. He was forty-three years old and at the pinnacle of a success unique in the history of letters. The wildest ambitions of his youth could not have comprehended the actuality of his fame. But the last infirmity of noble mind may lead to the first infirmity of noble will. Dickens, to be sure, never lost his love of fame, or of whatever of life's goods his miraculous powers might bring him, but there came a moment when the old primitive motive could no longer serve, when the joy of impressing his powers on the world no longer seemed delightful in itself, and when the first, simple, honest, vulgar energy of desire no longer seemed appropriate to his idea of himself.

We may say of Dickens that at the time of *Little Dorrit* he was at a crisis of the will which is expressed in the characters and forces of the novel, in the extremity of its bitterness against the social will, in its vision of peace and selflessness. This moral crisis is most immediately represented by the condition of Arthur Clennam's will, by his sense of guilt, by his belief that he is unloved and unlovable, by his retirement to the Marshalsea as by an act of choice, by his sickness unto death. We have here the analogy to the familiar elements of a religious crisis. This is not the place to raise the question of Dickens' relation to the Christian religion, which was a complicated one. But we cannot speak of *Little Dorrit* without taking notice of its reference to Christian feeling, if only because this is of considerable importance in its effect upon the aesthetic of the novel.

It has been observed of *Little Dorrit* that certain of Dickens' characteristic delights are not present in their usual force. Something of his gusto is diminished in at least one of its aspects. We do not have the amazing thickness of fact and incident that marks, say, *Bleak House* or *Our Mutual Friend*—not that we do not have sufficient thickness, but we do not have what Dickens usually gives us. We do not have the great population of characters from whom shines the freshness of their autonomous life. Mr. Pancks and Mrs. Plornish and Flora Finching and Flintwinch are interesting and amusing, but they seem to be the fruit of conscious intention rather than of free creation. This is sometimes explained by saying that Dickens was fatigued. Perhaps so, but if we are aware that Dickens is here expending less of one kind of creative energy, we must at the same time be aware that he is expending more than ever before of another kind. The imagination of *Little Dorrit* is marked not so much by its powers of particularization as by its powers of generalization and abstraction. It is an imagination under the dominion of a great articulated idea, a moral idea which tends to find its full development in a religious experience. It is an imagination akin to that which created *Piers Plowman* and *Pilgrim's Progress*. And, indeed, it is akin to the imagination of *The Divine Comedy*. Never before has

Dickens made so full, so Dantean, a claim for the virtue of the artist, and there is a Dantean pride and a Dantean reason in what he says of Daniel Doyce, who, although an engineer, stands for the creative mind in general and for its appropriate virtue: "His dismissal of himself [was] remarkable. He never said, I discovered this adaptation or invented that combination; but showed the whole thing as if the Divine Artificer had made it, and he had happened to find it. So modest was he about it, such a pleasant touch of respect was mingled with his quiet admiration of it, and so calmly convinced was he that it was established on irrefragable laws." Like much else that might be pointed to, this confirms us in the sense that the whole energy of the imagination of *Little Dorrit* is directed to the transcending of the personal will, to the search for the Will in which shall be our peace.

We must accept—and we easily do accept, if we do not permit critical cliché to interfere—the aesthetic of such an imagination, which will inevitably tend toward a certain formality of pattern and toward the generalization and the abstraction we have remarked. In a novel in which a house falls physically to ruins from the moral collapse of its inhabitants, in which the heavens open over London to show a crown of thorns, in which the devil has something like an actual existence, we quite easily accept characters named nothing else than Bar, Bishop, Physician. And we do not reject, despite our inevitable first impulse to do so, the character of Little Dorrit herself. Her untinctured goodness does not appall us or make us misdoubt her, as we expected it to do. This novel at its best is only incidentally realistic; its finest power of imagination appears in the great general images whose abstractness is their actuality, like Mr. Merdle's dinner parties, or the Circumlocution Office itself, and in such a context we understand Little Dorrit to be the Beatrice of the *Comedy*, the Paraclete in female form. Even the physical littleness of this grown woman, an attribute which is insisted on and which seems likely to repel us, does not do so, for we perceive it to be the sign that she is not only the Child of the Marshalsea, as she is called, but also the Child of the Parable, the negation of the social will.

Notes

1. Since writing this, I have had to revise my idea of the actuality of the symbols of *Our Mutual Friend*. Professor Johnson's biography of Dickens has taught me much about the nature of dust heaps, including their monetary value, which was very large, quite large enough to represent a considerable fortune: I had never quite believed that Dickens was telling the literal truth about this. From Professor Dodd's *The Age of Paradox* I have learned to what an extent the Thames was visibly the sewer of London, of how pressing was the problem of the sewage in the city as Dickens knew it, of how present to the mind was the sensible and even the tangible evidence that the problem was not being solved. The moral *disgust* of the book is thus seen to be quite adequately comprehended by the symbols which are used to represent it.

2. This is in effect the doctrine of Balzac's philosophical-anarchist criminal, Vautrin. But in all other respects the difference between Blandois and Vautrin is extreme. Vautrin is a "noble" and justified character; for all his cynicism, he is on the side of virtue and innocence. He is not corrupted by the social injustices he has suffered and perceived, by the self-pity to which they might have given rise; his wholesomeness may be said to be the result of his preference for power as against the status which Blandois desires. The development of Blandois from Vautrin—I do not know whether Dickens's creation was actually influenced by Balzac's—is a literary fact which has considerable social import.

Charles Dickens, James Joyce, and the Origins of Modernism

Matthew J. Bolton

"On or about December 1910," novelist Virginia Woolf famously declared, "human character changed." Woolf had seen the Post-Impressionist Exhibit that year, the first of a series of showings at London's Grafton Galleries that featured the works of Paul Cézanne, Paul Gauguin, and Vincent van Gogh. An emerging generation of artists and writers were creating work that would challenge how people thought and felt. In 1910 alone, for example, Pablo Picasso painted *Les Mademoiselles des Avignon*, Igor Stravinsky composed "The Firebird Suite," and T. S. Eliot wrote the drafts of what would become "The Love Song of J. Alfred Prufrock." In art, music, and literature, the rules of the game were being rewritten. The Victorian era had been over for a decade, and a new era was being defined by artists and writers who saw themselves as breaking with the past. By the time Woolf wrote her 1923 essay "Mr. Bennett and Mrs. Brown," Eliot had published *The Waste Land* and James Joyce had published *Ulysses*, and within a few years Ernest Hemingway, William Faulkner, and Woolf would publish their great early novels. According to the sort of narrative that Woolf and subsequent critics established, modernism consists of a series of radical departures from the conventionalities of nineteenth-century art and literature. Modernists experimented with form in a way their parents' and grandparents' generations had not. These bold innovations culminated in such monumental works as Eliot's *The Waste Land* (1922), Joyce's *Ulysses* (1922), and Woolf's *To the Lighthouse* (1927). Like Woolf, the other modernists knew that their work broke from the literary tradition they had inherited. Eliot told Woolf, for example, that Joyce's *Ulysses* "would be a landmark, because it destroyed the whole of the nineteenth century" (57). According to Eliot and Woolf, modernism was not just the inheritor of the Victorian literary tradition but its executioner.

Yet the narrative that Woolf and Eliot establish is inherently problematic, for by focusing exclusively on differences between the Victorians and the modernists, it ignores the very real continuities between the two periods. Two generations of English and American literary critics would operate under much the same set of assumptions, reading modernist literature as breaking decisively from nineteenth-century models of prose and poetry. In doing so, they have failed to see a fascinating counternarrative in which Victorian authors themselves experiment with form in a way that prefigures modernism. Or, to put it conversely, they have failed to acknowledge the degree to which twentieth-century authors found in their Victorian predecessors the raw materials and early experiments with the forms that we now think of as inherently modernist. Accordingly, one might think of there being a transitional period of "Victorian modernism," a period marked not by hard-and-fast dates but rather by the degree to which a given Victorian author experiments with modernist forms and devices. This is certainly the way the French view their nineteenth- and twentieth-century bodies of literature; poets such as the Symbolists are read as being transitional in a way that their English counterparts are not. Critic Ivan Kreilkamp asks a powerful question:

> Why do we have no English Charles Baudelaire, no mid-nineteenth-century poet whose work participates, explicitly and consciously, in the early theorization of modernity occurring at the time in France and Germany and America? Is it possible that this lack is at least in part a byproduct of the questions we ask of Victorian poetry? (605)

One need only substitute "Flaubert" for "Baudelaire" and "novelist" for "poet" to see that Kreilkamp's question is equally valid in the realm of prose. For some reason, Anglo-American readers and critics have tended to accept the modernists' own formulation of themselves as being radically different from their Victorian predecessors.

To construct a more nuanced relationship between the Victorian and the modernist novel, one might read two great authors of each period in light of each other. Perhaps no two novelists are considered more quintessentially of their time than Charles Dickens and James Joyce. Yet in comparing the novels of Dickens—particularly later works such as *Little Dorrit* (1855-1857) and *Our Mutual Friend* (1864-1865)—to Joyce's *Ulysses*, a number of striking parallels and continuities emerge. Evaluating Dickens in light of the modernist movement that will follow him, a reader may be struck by just how experimental a writer Dickens himself is. His later novels exhibit a mutability of form that seems to anticipate the work of the modernists. From his use of free indirect discourse to his inclusion of nonnaturalistic elements in his narrative, Dickens lays the groundwork for the innovations of the twentieth-century novel. Joyce, for his part, seems to have learned more from Dickens than most critics have acknowledged—and indeed, more than Joyce himself acknowledged. During the period in which he was beginning to write *Ulysses*, Joyce made a genuine study of Dickens's novels, and in his own great novel he puts a number of Dickensian techniques and devices to new use. Joyce's novel may owe something to Dickensian narration, for in Dickens the lines separating narrator, character, and author are often blurred in a way that prefigures the more radical experimentation of *Ulysses*. Joyce also learned from Dickens's dialogue: the great volubility of some of Dickens's characters may have provided Joyce with a model on which to construct his interior monologues. Dickensian mile-a-minute dialogue becomes Joycean stream-of-consciousness monologue. By identifying in Dickens some of the foundations of what are generally considered to be modernist techniques and preoccupations, one reformulates the relationship between Victorian and modernist literature, seeing not just the change and destruction that Woolf and Eliot described, but continuity and evolution. We might even hold Dickens up as Kreilkamp's "English Baudelaire," an author whose work is central both to nineteenth- and twentieth-century literature.

In reevaluating Dickens, one might begin by acknowledging that our vision of the author is mediated by a host of film, television, and stage adaptations of his work. Dickens is one of those authors whom many people feel they know well—even if they have not read one of his novels for years. Yet a critical element of Dickens's art is lost when his novels are adapted for stage or screen: narration. One need only compare Dickens's novel *Little Dorrit* with the 2008 British miniseries version of the story (aired in the United States on the Public Broadcasting Service's *Masterpiece* series in 2009) to see how much of the novel's language is omitted from the adaptation. Generally speaking, it is only the dialogue that makes it to the screen. The Dickensian narrator's rich and ironic descriptions are replaced by stock images: instead of hearing Dickens's words, we see an establishing shot of Victorian rowhouses or cobblestoned streets. Even in a production that uses voice-over narration or finds some other way of bringing description and exposition to the screen, the very length of Dickens's novels demands that a screenwriter make significant cuts and edits to the text. An adaptation of Dickens is therefore fundamentally different from, say, a stage or film production of a William Shakespeare play. In the latter case, all of Shakespeare's words are retained: the work was written to be acted, and there is no narrative element to the text that need be cut. With Dickens, on the other hand, adaptation always involves elimination.

The mediating presence of so many Dickens adaptations, as well as Dickens's status as the definitive Victorian novelist, can lull us into complacency regarding Dickens's artistry. The novels themselves, however, retain a capacity to surprise. Take, for example, this passage from *Our Mutual Friend* in which Eugene Wrayburn is struck from behind:

> He had sauntered far enough. Before turning to retrace his steps, he stopped upon the margin, to look down at the reflected night. In an instant, with a dreadful crash, the reflected night turned crooked, flames shot jaggedly across the air, and the moon and stars came bursting from the sky.

Was he struck by lightning? With some incoherent half-formed thought to that effect, he turned under the blows that were blinding him and mashing his life. (767)

In a film adaptation of this scene, Dickens's narration would be translated into physical action: we would watch someone strike Wrayburn and see the expression on his face as he realized that he was under attack. Yet Dickens's narration of the scene is a tremendously powerful example of how the author blurs the lines between narrator and character; Wrayburn is under assault and disoriented, and the narrative itself reflects this disorientation. Critic F. S. Schwarzbach cites this scene as one of "several remarkable passages of sustained stream of consciousness in the novel in a mode that looks forward to Henry James and James Joyce" (215). For a brief but critical moment, narrator and character become indistinguishable. Dickens's narrator relates not objective reality, but reality as perceived by one individual. Flames shoot jaggedly across the sky for only one man: Wrayburn. Couched as it is amidst an otherwise clearly narrated series of events, this moment of disorientation is easily reconciled with the rest of the story of the attack. Nevertheless, in the momentary disappearance of the objective narrator and the presenting of the phantasmagoric as objective reality ("the moon and stars came bursting from the sky") one may see the germs of modernism and of Joyce's narrative style. If we could linger over and extend the moment when Wrayburn is struck and his world becomes topsy-turvy, we would be entering the phantasmagoric domain of Joyce's "Circe" or "Nighttown" chapter.

Perhaps it was Dickens's narrative experimentations that caught and held Joyce's attention during the time that he was beginning *Ulysses*. Biographer Richard Ellmann's catalogue of Joyce's library reveals that the author owned five Dickens novels by 1920, at least four of which he purchased in or after 1912. This was the period that Joyce was revising *A Portrait of the Artist as a Young Man*, which would be published in 1914, and beginning to write the novel that would be published as *Ulysses*. The popular notion of modernism as decisively breaking from the Victorian tradition is undercut by the idea of Joyce's browsing continental bookshops for copies of *Barnaby Rudge*, *Bleak House*, *David Copperfield*, *Nicholas Nickleby*, and *Oliver Twist*. Even as Joyce was writing what would be considered the definitive expressions of literary modernism, he was learning from the Victorian novel. Joyce wrote about Dickens when he took a series of English and Italian proficiency tests at the University of Padua in 1912. Passing this battery of tests would qualify Joyce to teach English in Italy, and while he never followed through with teaching, his qualifying essays sat neatly filed away in a government office for several decades before scholars thought to look for them. In his essay on Dickens, Joyce identifies "exaggeration" as a hallmark of the author's style, writing, "It is precisely by this little exaggeration that Dickens has influenced the spoken language of the inhabitants of the British Empire as no other writer since Shakespeare's time" (Berrone 12).

If in his essay Joyce characterizes "exaggeration" as central to Dickens's art, in his novels he exaggerates Dickensian language to comic effect. *Ulysses* and *Finnegan's Wake* (1939) abound with references to Dickens. The "Oxen of the Sun" chapter of *Ulysses*, written so as to mimic the development of the English language, contains one of the most obvious of these parodies. A scene in a maternity ward is cast in the sentimental language of a Dickens novel:

> She had fought the good fight and now she was very very happy. Those who have passed on, who have gone before, are happy too as they gaze down and smile upon the touching scene. Reverently look at her as she reclines there with the motherlight in her eyes, that longing hunger for baby fingers (a pretty sight it is to see), in the first bloom of her new motherhood, breathing a silent prayer of thanksgiving to one above, the Universal Husband. (343)

Joyce's language here echoes that of several Dickens deathbed scenes, particularly the death of Little Nell. That Joyce is so readily able to parody Dickens speaks to his familiarity with the author.

Yet Joyce's interest in Dickens goes beyond the merely parodic; mimicry is only one facet of his relationship to Dickens' novels. In studying Dickens, Joyce found not only sentimentality that he could exaggerate to comic effect but also devices, techniques, and typographical conventions that he could redeploy in new dramatic contexts. Michael Patrick Gillespie asserts that Joyce's "brief but intense" interest in Dickens "does not reflect a nostalgia for conventional nineteenth-century narrative. Rather, it suggests the turning point in his own conception of fiction" (72, 76). Joyce adopted elements of Dickensian narration and dialogue and transformed them, putting them to new use in the context of *Ulysses*. Dickens may have served as a model for a narrating presence that expands and contracts according to the dictates of its subject matter and which is frequently colored or overridden by the language of the characters he describes.

Comparing representative passages from Dickens and Joyce suggests that the authors have more in common than has generally been admitted. Take, for example, this description of Arthur Clennam listening to a church bell ringing in *Little Dorrit*:

> Mr. Arthur Clennam sat in the window of the coffee-house on Ludgate Hill, counting one of the neigbouring bells, making sentences and burdens of songs out of it in spite of himself, and wondering how many sick people it might be the death of in the course of a year. As the hour approached, its changes of measure made it more and more exasperating. At the quarter, it went off into a condition of deadly lively importunity, urging the populace in a voluble manner to Come to Church, Come to Church, Come to Church! . . .
>
> "Thank Heaven" said Clennam when the hour struck and the bell stopped.
>
> But its sound had revived a long train of miserable Sundays, and the procession would not stop with the bell, but continued to march on. (41-42)

This is not the sort of language that would make it into a film adaptation of the novel; on the screen, we would simply hear a bell ringing rather than have that ringing described to us. Yet the passage is not mere exposition: instead, it explores the relationship between external stimuli and internal response. We hear not what a church bell sounds like, but what its sounds like to Arthur Clennam. As in the scene of Wrayburn being assaulted, Dickens here is experimenting with techniques that would eventually be termed the interior monologue, free indirect discourse, and stream-of-consciousness narration.

When Clennam hears the church bell ringing, he automatically and unconsciously responds to it by "making sentences and burdens of songs out of it in spite of himself." His distracted mind produces words and phrases to match the bell's measured soundings. The narrative is therefore filtered through Clennam's perceptions and sensibilities: it is he who assigns to the bell's pealing the words "Come to Church!" and who finds its tolling to be "exasperating" and "deadly." The line between the third-person narrator and Clennam becomes blurred, such that Clennam's consciousness colors the narrative. Finally, the bell calls to mind memories of his grim childhood Sundays, memories that persist after the external stimulus that elicited them—the ringing bell—has been removed. There is in this passage an intermeshing of external stimulus and internal response that we tend to think of as a modernist innovation. Here in the 1850s, Dickens is experimenting with narrative form to a degree that might surprise readers who have a fixed notion of Victorian literature.

Compare Dickens's representation of Clennam with a scene from Joyce's *Ulysses*. Here, Stephen Dedalus walks along the beach with his eyes closed:

> Am I walking into eternity along Sandymount strand? Crush, crack, crick, crick. Wild sea money. Dominie Deasy kens them a'.
>> *Won't you come to Sandymount,*
>> *Madeline the mare?*

Rhythm begins, you see. I hear. A catalectic tetrameter of iambs marching. No, agallop: *deline the mare.* (31)

Like Clennam, Stephen responds to rhythmic sound (the "crush, crack,
crick, crick" of his own feet tramping across the mast) by unconsciously calling up words to suit that rhythm. His conscious mind follows on the heels of his unconsciousness, analyzing the meter of the
song that has floated into his consciousness. He also takes note of the
very process by which his footfalls have established a rhythm that in
turn has called to mind these lines. His self-corrections (". . . you see. I
hear . . ." and ". . . marching. No, agallop . . .") further the impression of
internal dynamics, of a mind in dialogue with itself.

Both Clennam and Stephen are stimulated by sound, but in Stephen's case there is no narrator to explicate the relationship between
external stimulus and internal response. In his absence, the reader him-
or herself must construct the associative chain of logic that connects
the momentarily blind Stephen's question, the onomatopoeic "crush,
crack, crick, crick" of his boots on sea-shingle, the equating of shells
and currency, and the relentlessly rhythmic lines of poetry that invade
the text. The reader must determine what is thought, what is heard,
what is recalled. Moreover, the reader must decide how and why these
thoughts and perceptions suggest each other. The withdrawal of the
narrator has an effect on the text that is at once elliptical, in that it re-
moves the framework by which internal and external phenomena are
differentiated, and expansive, in that there is a concomitant loss of narrative structures that shape, summarize, and delimit a character's
thought processes. There is no mediating narratorial presence filtering
and shaping Stephen's thoughts. Where Dickens's narrative is only
colored by Clennam's consciousness, Joyce's narrative *is* Stephen's
consciousness.

There is a degree of continuity between Dickens's scene and
Joyce's, therefore, and it might be fair to think of the relationship between the two novelists as evolutionary rather than revolutionary. One

way to demonstrate this process of evolution is by triangulating the two scenes with a third literary representation of the return of memory. In his seminal work *Mimesis: The Representation of Reality in Western Literature* (1968), critic Erich Auerbach analyzes a scene from Homer's *Odyssey* in which Eurycleia, Odysseus's nurse, bathes her disguised master and sees his distinguishing scar:

> Bending closer
> she started to bathe her master . . . then
> In a flash, she knew the scar—
> that old wound
> made years ago by a white boar's tusk . . .
> (19.444-48)

Eurycleia recognizes the scar, and Homer's narrator then launches into the story of how Odysseus received the wound that would form this scar. The scar triggers not so much Eurycleia's personal and subjective memories, as the narrator's epic digression. Auerbach notes in the account of the boar hunt "a complete externalization of all the elements of the story" (4). The narrator's voice, in other words, is not affected by Eurycleia's sensibilities; she is left out of the narrative that her flash of insight has precipitated. Homer's narrator is sovereign and detached, and his presence is not modified by the characters whose stories he tells.

The Dickensian narrator, however, is fundamentally different from the Homeric one. The characters in *Little Dorrit* are, like Odysseus, scarred: Clennam by both his childhood and by some unspeakable experience overseas, his mother by her disastrous marriage, and the Dorrit family by their years in the Marshalsea prison. Events in the present reopen these wounds such that the consciousness is forever returning to a traumatic past. In both Dickens and Joyce, characters struggle to stave off their own memories. Mr. Dorrit, even when he is wealthy and free, cannot abide looking on the prison that was once his home:

[Mr. Dorrit] astonished the coachman by being very fierce with him for proposing to go over London Bridge, and recross the river by Waterloo Bridge—a course which would have taken him almost within sight of his old quarters. Still for all that, the question had raised a conflict in his breast. (566)

Dorrit is loath to pass the Marshalsea prison, for doing so would awake in him a string of bad memories. The coachman's proposed route serves not as an occasion for digressive, externalized narration but as a window into Dorrit's own traumatized soul.

In *Ulysses*, Stephen Dedalus is similarly tormented by memory. His mother's death, his tumultuous relationship with his father, and his fear of artistic failure return to haunt him. Like Mr. Dorrit, he goes out of his way to avoid sights and even words that will revive in him unhappy memories. In discussing Shakespeare's *Hamlet* with some friends, Stephen interrupts the conversation before they reach the ghost's line "If thou didst ever thy dear father love." In this passage, Joyce's italicized lines represent a character's recitation, and the plain text lines are Stephen's thoughts and words:

> *List! List! O List!*
> My flesh hears him: creeping, hears.
> *If thou didst ever . . .*
> —What is a ghost? Stephen said with tingling energy. (187-88)

Much as Dorrit redirected the course of a carriage, Stephen redirects the course of a conversation to avoid a mnemonic trigger. His flesh creeps as he hears the recitation of the ghost's lines, and he cannot bear to hear the words "thy father's ghost." He interrupts the recitation with the question, "What is a ghost?" Stephen, like Hamlet himself, is haunted.

The past may therefore be harder to escape in Joyce than in Dickens. For in Joyce, perception and memory interact in a far more freely associative, irrational, and unpredictable manner. Dorrit looks at the Marshalsea prison and remembers the time he spent there. Memory can be this logical in Joyce, as when Bloom sees a child's funeral and thinks of his own dead son: "a dwarf's face, mauve and wrinkled like little Rudy's was" (79). But more often than not memories are summoned up by less directly associative stimuli. Stephen, for example, looking at the ocean from atop the Martello Tower, remembers the bowl of bile that rested by his dying mother's bed (8). It is an image and a comparison that could only appear before Stephen's mind's eye, and speaks to the degree to which guilt and traumatic memories color everything he sees.

Comparing the relationship between narration and the individual consciousness in Homer, Dickens, and Joyce, one marks a progression from objectivity to subjectivity. For Homer's narrator, it does not matter who sees Odysseus' scar: the boar hunt will be presented in the same even light that the narrator casts on any event. In the case of Dickens, however, narrative content affects narrative form. The formal and technical properties of the text change in accordance with the events that it is describing. In summarizing a speech Mr. Dorrit has made to Amy, the narrator's own voice merges with that of Dorrit. Dorrit's characteristic nervous interjections, which should, logically speaking, be represented only in direct discourse, contaminate the narrative:

> But he had spoken to her alone, and had said that people—ha—people in an exalted position, my dear, must scrupulously exact respect from their dependants; and that for her, his daughter, Miss Amy Dorrit, of the sole remaining branch of the Dorrits of Dorsetshire, to be known to—hum—to occupy herself in fulfilling the functions of—ha, hum—a valet, would be incompatible with that respect. Therefore, my dear, he—ha—he laid his parental injunctions upon her. (417)

A passage that purports to summarize rather than directly represent Dorrit's speech to his daughter instead is filtered through the character's consciousness and voice. The Dickensian narrator has what Samuel Taylor Coleridge termed negative capability: he can empty himself of his own character in order to inhabit fully the character of another. This quality is alien to Homer, whose narrator remains ever whole and sovereign, but it is central to the radical form of *Ulysses*. While Joyce drew his title and the arc of his story from Homer, therefore, his mode of narration is far more indebted to the Victorian novel than to the classical epic.

Joyce may owe a debt not only to Dickens's narration but also to his dialogue; in fact, some aspects of Joyce's stream-of-consciousness narration seem to have evolved directly out of Dickensian dialogue. The critic Fred Kaplan and the novelist Anthony Burgess make compelling arguments for the influence of the unpunctuated prose of *Little Dorrit*'s Flora Finching on Molly Bloom's soliloquy in the "Penelope" chapter. Here is a brief excerpt from one of Flora's speeches, which flow from one topic to another in a process of free association: ". . . there I still am snoring I dare say if the truth was known and if you don't like either cold fowl or hot boiled ham which many people don't I dare say . . ." (276). Molly Bloom's chapter has become a *locus classicus* of modernism, yet in returning to it after *Little Dorrit* one is struck by the familiarity of Molly's voice. Here is the opening of her chapter:

> Yes because he never did a thing like that before as ask to get his breakfast in bed with a couple of eggs since the City Arms hotel when he used to be pretending to be laid up with a sick voice doing his highness to make himself more interesting for that old faggot Mrs. Riordan that he thought he had a great leg of and she never left us a farthing. (608)

The parallel is less typological than it is typographical: Flora and Molly are not necessarily similar women, but the speech of the one and the thoughts of the other are represented through a similar excision of punctuation and reliance on conjunctions. Kaplan sees Dickens's comic speech as a forerunner of stream-of-consciousness narration, arguing that Flora's "verbal responses correspond to her psychological responses in the stylistic form that we have come to call interior monologue" (344). Burgess draws the connection between Flora and Molly, and further argues that Joyce's portraits of Father Conmee, Mr. Kernan, and Paddy Dignam's son in the chapter "Wandering Rocks" represent "an intermediate stage between speech and thought and suggest what is so often found in Dickens—stream-of-consciousness language which becomes comic by being externalized" (61). Stream-of-consciousness narration may be a modernist development, but its spring and its headwaters are to be found in the Victorian novel.

Joyce may have seen in Dickens's dialogue a method for representing in print the mind's continuous, fluid, associative processes of thought. Flora Finching is silly and vapid precisely because she verbalizes her thoughts in their raw form rather than first ordering and delineating them. Properly punctuated and with her self-iterative tags ("I dare say") removed, Flora's dialogue would be just as expansive, but no longer funny. Dickens seems to understand that the speech act involves using language's structure to direct the mind's current. In short, Dickens has in Flora's torrent of speech anticipated modernism's stream-of-consciousness. When Joyce employs Dickens's technique in Molly Bloom's internal monologue, the effect is one of psychological verisimilitude rather than of comic loquacity. In Joyce's hands, the excision of punctuation creates a continuous flow of language that represents Molly's consciousness at work. Flora's florid speech blooms into Molly's fluid thoughts.

Nor is Flora the only Dickens character whose patterns of speech seem to prefigure stream-of-consciousness techniques. Mr. Jingle of *Pickwick Papers* habitually drops articles and subject pronouns, speaking in staccato fragments separated only by a long dash. Joyce's contemporary Wyndham Lewis noted the connection between Dickensian speech and Joycean thought in his 1926 article "Mr. Jingle and Mr. Bloom." Lewis shows himself to be a shrewd reader in recognizing—

even in the midst of the modernist decade itself—the importance of the Victorian novel to Joyce's *Ulysses*. Mrs. Gamp of *Martin Chuzzlewit* (1843-1844), Mrs. Nickleby of *Nicholas Nickleby*, as well as the narrators of several of Dickens's short stories all speak in breathless, continuous prose. In fact, Dickens's own description of how Mrs. Nickleby talks might be readily applied to stream-of-consciousness discourse as a whole: she speaks "in one unbroken monotonous flow, perfectly satisfied to be talking, and caring very little whether anybody listened or not" (204). Dickens's experimentation with how best to represent on the page such an "unbroken monotonous flow" may have laid some of the foundations of modernism. *Nicholas Nickleby* is among the books that Joyce purchased sometime between 1912 and 1920, and it may have been Dickens's blurring of the line between speech and thought that drew Joyce to his Victorian predecessor's work.

Reading Dickens and Joyce in relation to each other challenges the notion that modernism represents a radical departure from the conventions of Victorian literature. The point of such an exercise is not to diminish Joyce's status as a great experimental writer, but rather to see Dickens as one, too. Dickens's experiments with narration and dialogue alike provided an important model for Joyce. Like Charles Baudelaire or Gustave Flaubert, Dickens ought to be thought of as a central force not only in regard to the novels of his own era but also in regard to those of the modernist era that followed him.

Works Cited

Auerbach, Eric. *Mimesis: The Representation of Reality in Western Literature*. Trans. Willard R. Trask. Princeton, NJ: Princeton UP, 1968.

Berrone, Louis. "The James Joyce Essays Unveiled: 'The Centenary of Charles Dickens' and 'L'influence letteraria universale del rinascimento.'" *Journal of Modern Literature* 5 (Feb. 1976): 3-18.

Burgess, Anthony. *Joysprick: An Introduction to the Language of James Joyce*. New York: Harcourt Brace Jovanovich, 1973.

Dickens, Charles. *Little Dorrit*. 1855-1857. New York: Penguin, 1998.

_____. *Nicholas Nickleby*. 1838-1839. London: J. M. Dent (Everyman), 1994.

_____. *Our Mutual Friend*. 1864-1865. New York: Penguin, 1985.

Ellmann, Richard. *James Joyce*. New York: Oxford UP, 1959.

Gillespie, Michael Patrick. *Inverted Volumes Improperly Arranged: James Joyce and His Trieste Library*. Ann Arbor, MI: UMI Research Press, 1983.

Homer. *The Odyssey*. Trans. Robert Fagles. New York: Penguin, 1996.

Joyce, James. *Ulysses*. 1922. New York: Random House, 1986.

Kaplan, Fred. "Dickens' Flora Finching and Joyce's Molly Bloom." *Nineteenth-Century Fiction* 23.3 (Dec. 1968): 343-46.

Kreilkamp, Ivan. "Victorian Poetry's Modernity." *Victorian Poetry* 41 (2003): 603-11.

Lewis, Wyndham. "Mr. Jingle and Mr. Bloom." *The Art of Being Ruled*. London: Chatto & Windus, 1926.

Schwarzbach, F. S. *Dickens and the City*. London: Athlone Press, University of London, 1979.

Woolf, Virginia. "Mr. Bennett and Ms. Brown." *Collected Essays*. London: Hogarth Press, 1971.

RESOURCES

1812	Charles John Huffam Dickens, the second of eight children, is born on February 7 to John and Elizabeth Dickens.
1813	Alfred Allen Dickens (brother) is born.
1814	John Dickens, a clerk in the Navy Pay Office, is transferred from Portsea to London. During these early years, Dickens is schooled by his mother and takes a strong interest in reading the fiction classics found in his father's library. Alfred Allen Dickens dies.
1816	Letitia Mary Dickens (sister) is born.
1817	John Dickens moves the family to Chatham. Charles attends Dame School with his sister Fanny.
1819	Harriet Dickens (sister) is born.
1820	Frederick Dickens (brother) is born.
1821	Dickens begins studying at the Rev. William Giles School. He remains at this school even after his family moves back to London in 1822.
1822	Dickens composes his first tragedy, *Misnar, the Sultan of India*. Alfred Lamert Dickens (brother) is born.
1824	John Dickens is arrested for debt and imprisoned at the Marshalsea prison. Charles begins working at Warren's Blacking Warehouse and moves into a poor neighborhood. His father is released three months later.
1824-1826	Dickens attends Wellington House Academy in London but is forced to leave when his father is evicted from his home.
1827	Dickens studies at Mr. Dawson's school and works as a law clerk and spends time reading in the British Museum. Augustus Dickens (brother) is born.

1830	Dickens meets Maria Beadnell, the daughter of George Beadnell, a prosperous banker.
1831	Dickens becomes a reporter for the *Mirror of Parliament*.
1832	Dickens works as a staff writer for the *True Sun*.
1833	Dickens publishes his first piece, "A Dinner at Poplar Walk," in *Monthly Magazine* under the pen name "Boz." Maria Beadnell ends her relationship with Dickens.
1834	Dickens works as a staff writer on the *Morning Chronicle*. His "street sketches" begin to appear in the *Evening Chronicle*. Dickens meets Catherine Hogarth. John Dickens is arrested for debt.
1836	*Sketches by Boz*, illustrated by George Cruikshank, is published. Dickens and Catherine Hogarth marry in April. Two plays are produced, *The Strange Gentleman* and *The Village Coquettes*, both at the St. James's Theatre. Dickens starts work as the editor of *Bentley's Miscellany*. He meets John Forster.
1836-1837	*Pickwick Papers* is published in monthly installments.
1837	*Pickwick Papers* is published in book form; *Oliver Twist* begins to appear in *Bentley's Miscellany*. Dickens moves to 48 Doughty Street in Bloomsbury (now home of the Charles Dickens Museum). *Is She His Wife?*, a play, is produced at the St. James's Theatre. Dickens's first child, Charles Culliford Boz Dickens, is born. Catherine's sister Mary dies.
1838	*Nicholas Nickleby* is published in installments and is completed in October of 1839. Dickens's first daughter, Mary, is born.
1839	The Dickenses move to Devonshire Terrace. Daughter Kate Macready Dickens is born. *Nicholas Nickleby* appears in book form.
1840	Dickens edits *Master Humphrey's Clock. The Old Curiosity Shop* is published.
1841	*Barnaby Rudge* is published in *Master Humphrey's Clock*. Son Walter Landor Dickens is born.

1842	Dickens and his wife travel to the United States. *American Notes* is published, and Dickens begins work on *Martin Chuzzlewit*.
1843	*Martin Chuzzlewit* appears in monthly installments. *A Christmas Carol* is published.
1844	Dickens travels to Italy. *The Chimes* is completed. Son Francis Jeffrey Dickens is born.
1845	Dickens produces and acts in Ben Jonson's *Every Man in His Humour*. *The Cricket on the Hearth* is written, and Dickens begins work on *Pictures from Italy*. A fourth son, Alfred D'Orsay Tennyson Dickens, is born.
1846	Dickens creates and edits the *Daily News* but resigns shortly afterward. He begins work on *Dombey and Son*. He travels to Switzerland. *The Battle of Life* is published.
1847	Another son, Sydney Smith Haldimand Dickens, is born. Dickens begins managing a theatrical company.
1848	Dickens's older sister Frances (Fanny) dies. His theatrical company performs for Queen Victoria. Dickens publishes his last Christmas book, *The Haunted Man*.
1849	Dickens begins work on *David Copperfield*. A sixth son, Henry Fielding Dickens, is born.
1850	Dickens begins publishing *Household Words*, a weekly journal. Daughter Dora Annie Dickens is born and dies.
1851	Dickens's father dies.
1852	*Bleak House* begins appearing in monthly installments. The first bound volume of *A Child's History of England* appears. Dickens's last child, Edward Bulwer Lytton Dickens, is born.
1854	*Hard Times* is published in *Household Words* and later appears in book form.

1855	*Little Dorrit* appears in monthly installments. The Dickens family travels to Paris.
1856	Dickens purchases Gad's Hill Place. He rehearses Wilkie Collins's *The Frozen Deep*.
1857	Dickens performs in *The Frozen Deep*. He meets Ellen Ternan. Hans Christian Andersen visits Gad's Hill.
1858	Dickens begins a series of paid public readings. He and Catherine separate, and Dickens tries to dispel rumors of an affair with Ellen Ternan.
1859	Dickens begins a new weekly, *All the Year Round. A Tale of Two Cities* is published.
1860	Dickens begins writing the series *The Uncommercial Traveller. Great Expectations* appears in weekly installments.
1861	First installment of *Great Expectations* is published in *Harper's Weekly*, New York, in November.
1863	Dickens continues his readings in Paris and London. His daughter Elizabeth dies and his own health is in serious decline.
1864	*Our Mutual Friend* appears in installments.
1865	Dickens and Ellen Ternan survive a train crash in Kent. *Our Mutual Friend* appears in book form. The second collection of *The Uncommercial Traveller* is published.
1866	Despite poor health, Dickens continues to give readings in the English provinces.
1867	Dickens travels to the United States and gives readings in Boston and New York. He meets President Andrew Johnson.
1869	Dickens begins work on *The Mystery of Edwin Drood*.
1870	On June 9, Charles Dickens dies at age fifty-eight.

Long Fiction

Pickwick Papers, 1836-1837
Oliver Twist, 1837-1839
Nicholas Nickleby, 1838-1839
The Old Curiosity Shop, 1840-1841
Barnaby Rudge, 1841
Martin Chuzzlewit, 1843-1844
Dombey and Son, 1846-1848
David Copperfield, 1849-1850
Bleak House, 1852-1853
Hard Times, 1854
Little Dorrit, 1855-1857
A Tale of Two Cities, 1859
Great Expectations, 1860-1861
Our Mutual Friend, 1864-1865
The Mystery of Edwin Drood, 1870

Short Fiction

"A Dinner at Poplar Walk," 1833
Sketches by Boz, 1836
A Christmas Carol, 1843
The Chimes, 1844
The Cricket on the Hearth, 1845
The Battle of Life, 1846
The Haunted Man, 1848
Reprinted Pieces, 1858
The Uncommercial Traveller, 1860
George Silverman's Explanation, 1868
Christmas Stories, 1871

Drama

The Strange Gentleman, 1836
The Village Coquettes, 1836
Mr. Nightingale's Diary, 1851 (with Mark Lemon)
No Thoroughfare, 1867 (with Wilkie Collins)

Children's Literature

A Child's History of England, 1852-1854

Nonfiction

American Notes, 1842
Pictures from Italy, 1846

Bibliography

Ackroyd, Peter. *Dickens*. London: Sinclair-Stevenson, 1990.

_____. *Dickens' London: An Imaginative Vision*. London: Headline Book Publishing, 1987.

Alexander, Doris. *Creating Characters with Charles Dickens*. University Park: Pennsylvania State University Press, 1991.

Ayres, Brenda. *Dissenting Women in Dickens's Novels: The Subversion of Domestic Ideology*. Westport, CT: Greenwood, 1998.

Barickman, Richard, Susan MacDonald, and Myra Stark. *Corrupt Relations: Dickens, Thackeray, Trollope, Collins, and the Victorian Sexual System*. New York: Columbia University Press, 1982.

Bloom, Harold, ed. *Charles Dickens's Great Expectations*. Philadelphia: Chelsea House, 2000.

Bolton, Philip H. *Dickens Dramatized*. London: Mansel, 1987.

Bowen, John. *Other Dickens: Pickwick to Chuzzlewit*. New York: Oxford University Press, 2000.

Brinton, Ian. *Dickens's "Great Expectations."* New York: Continuum, 2007.

Brown, Ivor. *Dickens in His Time*. London: Nelson, 1963.

Cain, Lynn. *Dickens, Family, Authorship: Psychoanalytical Perspectives on Kinship and Creativity*. Burlington, VT: Ashgate, 2008.

Campbell, Elizabeth. *Fortune's Wheel: Dickens and the Iconography of Women's Time*. Athens: Ohio University Press, 2003.

Carey, John. *The Violent Effigy: A Study of Dickens' Imagination*. London: Faber and Faber, 1979.

Carlisle, Janice. *The Sense of an Audience: Dickens, Thackeray, and George Eliot at Mid-Century*. Athens: University of Georgia Press, 1981.

Chancellor, E. Beresford. *Dickens and His Times*. London: Richards Press, 1976.

Chesterton, G. K. *Charles Dickens*. London: Methuen, 1906.

Clayton, Jay. *Charles Dickens in Cyberspace: The Afterlife of the Nineteenth Century in Postmodern Culture*. New York: Oxford University Press, 2003.

Collins, Philip, ed. *Dickens and Crime*. London: Macmillan, 1962.

_____, ed. *Dickens: The Critical Heritage*. London: Routledge, 1971.

Connor, Steven. *Charles Dickens*. Oxford: Blackwell, 1985.

_____, ed. *Charles Dickens*. London: Longman, 1996.

Cotsell, Michael, ed. *Critical Essays on Charles Dickens's "Great Expectations."* Boston: G. K. Hall, 1990.

Dabney, Ross. *Love and Property in the Novels of Charles Dickens*. Berkeley: University of California Press, 1967.

Daldry, Graham. *Charles Dickens and the Form of the Novel*. Totowa, NJ: Barnes & Noble, 1987.

Davies, James A. "*Great Expectations*: The Ghost of a Man's Own Father." *PMLA* 91.3 (1976): 436-49.

_____. *The Textual Life of Dickens's Characters*. London: Macmillan, 1989.

Davis, Paul B. *Charles Dickens A to Z: The Essential Reference to His Life and Work*. New York: Facts On File, 1998.

Drew, John M. L. *Dickens the Journalist*. London: Palgrave Macmillan, 2003.

Eagleton, Terry. *Criticism and Ideology: A Study in Marxist Literary Theory*. New ed. London: Verso, 2006.

Eliot, T. S. "Wilkie Collins and Dickens." *Times Literary Supplement* 4 Aug. 1927: 525-26.

Epstein, Norrie. *The Friendly Dickens: Being a Good-Natured Guide to the Art and Adventures of the Man Who Invented Scrooge*. New York: Viking Press, 1998.

Flint, Kate. *Dickens*. Brighton, England: Harvester Press, 1986.

Ford, George. *Dickens and His Readers: Aspects of Novel-Criticism Since 1836*. Princeton, NJ: Princeton University Press, 1955.

Ford, George H., and Lauriat Lane, Jr., eds. *The Dickens Critics*. Ithaca, NY: Cornell University Press, 1961.

Forster, John. *The Life of Charles Dickens*. 2 vols. 1872-1874. New York: Dutton, 1966.

Frank, Lawrence. *Victorian Detective Fiction and the Nature of Evidence: The Scientific Investigations of Poe, Dickens, and Doyle*. New York: Palgrave Macmillan, 2003.

Gager, Valerie. *Shakespeare and Dickens: The Dynamics of Influence*. New York: Cambridge University Press, 1996.

Garis, Robert. *The Dickens Theatre: A Reassessment of the Novels*. Oxford: Clarendon Press, 1965.

Gilooly, Eileen, and Deirdre David, eds. *Contemporary Dickens*. Columbus: Ohio State University Press, 2009.

Gissing, George. *Charles Dickens: A Critical Study*. New York: Dodd, Mead, 1904.

Hardy, Barbara. *The Moral Art of Charles Dickens*. London: Athlone Press, 1970.

Hawes, Donald. *Who's Who in Dickens*. New York: Routledge, 1998.

Herst, Beth F. *The Dickens Hero: Selfhood and Alienation in the Dickens World*. New York: St. Martin's Press, 1990.

Hobsbaum, Philip. *A Reader's Guide to Charles Dickens*. Syracuse, NY: Syracuse University Press, 1998.

Hopkins, Sandra. "'Wooman, Lovely Wooman': Four Dickens Heroines and the Critics." In *Problems in Feminist Criticism*. Ed. Sally Minogue. London: Routledge, 1990. 199-244.

Hori, Masahiro. *Investigating Dickens's Style*. New York: Palgrave Macmillan, 2004.

Hornback, Bert G. *Great Expectations: A Novel of Friendship*. Boston: Twayne, 1987.

House, Humphry. *The Dickens World*. New York: Oxford University Press, 1941.

Huxley, Aldous. "The Vulgarity of Little Nell." In *Vulgarity in Literature*. London: Chatto & Windus, 1930. 54-59.

Jacobson, Wendy S., ed. *Dickens and the Children of Empire*. New York: Palgrave, 2000.

James, Henry. "*Our Mutual Friend.*" *Nation* 1 (Dec. 1865): 786-87; Rpt. as "The Limitations of Dickens" in *Views and Reviews*. Boston: Ball, 1908. 153-61.

Johnson, Edgar. *Charles Dickens: His Tragedy and Triumph*. 2 vols. New York: Simon & Schuster, 1952.

Jordan, John O., ed. *The Cambridge Companion to Charles Dickens*. New York: Cambridge University Press, 2001.

Kaplan, Fred. *Dickens: A Biography*. Baltimore: Johns Hopkins University Press, 1998.

_____. *Dickens and Mesmerism: The "Hidden Springs of Fiction."* Princeton, NJ: Princeton University Press, 1975.

Kincaid, James R. *Dickens and the Rhetoric of Laughter*. Oxford: Clarendon Press, 1971.

Kingsmill, Hugh. *The Sentimental Journey: A Life of Charles Dickens*. London: Wishart, 1934.

Larson, Janet. *Dickens and the Broken Scripture*. Athens: U of Georgia Press, 1985.

Leavis, F. R. *The Great Tradition*. London: Chatto & Windus, 1948.

Leavis, F. R., and Q. D. Leavis. *Dickens: The Novelist*. London: Chatto & Windus, 1970.

Lerner, Laurence. *Angels and Absences: Child Deaths in the Nineteenth Century*. Nashville: Vanderbilt University Press, 1997.

Loutitt, Chris. *Dickens's Secular Gospel: Work, Gender, and Personality*. New York: Routledge, 2009.

Lucas, John. *The Melancholy Man: A Study of Dickens's Novels*. London: Methuen, 1970.

McKnight, Natalie. *Idiots, Madmen, and Other Prisoners in Dickens*. New York: St. Martin's Press, 1993.

Marcus, Steven. *Dickens: From Pickwick to Dombey*. New York: Basic Books, 1965.

Mazzeno, Laurence W. *The Dickens Industry: Critical Perspectives 1836-2005*. Rochester, NY: Camden House, 2008.

Meckier, Jerome. *Hidden Rivalries in Victorian Fiction: Dickens, Realism, and Revaluation*. Lexington: University Press of Kentucky, 1987.

Miller, J. Hillis. *Charles Dickens: The World of His Novels*. Cambridge, MA: Harvard University Press, 1958.

Mitchell, Sally. *Daily Life in Victorian England*. Westport, CT: Greenwood Press, 1996.

Moore, Grace. *Dickens and Empire: Discourses of Class, Race, and Colonialism in the Works of Charles Dickens*. Burlington, VT: Ashgate, 2004.

Newlin, George, ed. and comp. *Every Thing in Dickens: Ideas and Subjects Discussed by Charles Dickens in His Complete Works—A Topicon*. Westport, CT: Greenwood Press, 1996.

Newsom, Robert. *Charles Dickens Revisited*. New York: Twayne, 2000.

Newton, Ruth, and Naomi Lebowitz. *The Impossible Romance: Dickens, Manzoni, Zola, and James*. Columbia: University of Missouri Press, 1990.

Orwell, George. *Dickens, Dali, and Others*. New York: Mariner Books, 1970.

Paroissien, David. *A Companion to Charles Dickens*. Oxford: Blackwell, 2008.

Patten, Robert. *Charles Dickens and His Publishers*. Oxford: Clarendon Press, 1978.

Pope-Hennessy, Una. *Charles Dickens*. London: Chatto & Windus, 1945.

Pykett, Lyn. *Charles Dickens*. Critical Issues. Basingstoke: Palgrave, 2002.

Rosenberg, Edgar, ed. *Great Expectations: Authoritative Texts, Backgrounds, Contexts, Criticism*. New York: Norton, 1999.

Sadrin, Anny. *Great Expectations*. London: Unwin Hyman, 1988.

Sanders, Andrew. *Authors in Context: Charles Dickens*. New York: Oxford University Press, 2003.

Schad, John. *The Reader in the Dickensian Mirror: Some New Language*. New York: St. Martin's Press, 1992.

Schlicke, Paul. *Dickens and Popular Entertainment*. London: Allen & Unwin, 1985.

Scott, P. J. M. *Reality and Comic Confidence in Charles Dickens*. London: Macmillan, 1979.

Shaw, George Bernard. *Shaw on Dickens*. Ed. Dan H. Laurence and Martin Quinn. New York: Frederick Ungar, 1985.

Slater, Michael. *Charles Dickens*. New Haven, CT: Yale University Press, 2009.

_____. *Dickens and Women*. London: Dent, 1983.

Smiley, Jane. *Charles Dickens*. New York: Viking Press, 2002.

Smith, Grahame. *Charles Dickens: A Literary Life*. New York: St. Martin's Press, 1996.

_____. *Dickens and the Dream of Cinema*. Manchester, England: Manchester University Press, 2003.

_____. *Dickens, Money, and Society*. Berkeley: University of California Press, 1968.

Spilka, Mark. *Dickens and Kafka: A Mutual Interpretation*. Bloomington: Indiana University Press, 1963.

Stewart, Garrett. *Dickens and the Trials of Imagination*. Cambridge, MA: Harvard University Press, 1974.

Stoehr, Taylor. *Dickens: The Dreamer's Stance*. Ithaca, NY: Cornell University Press, 1965.

Stone, Harry. *Dickens and the Invisible World: Fairy Tales, Fantasy, and Novel-Making*. London: Macmillan, 1980.

_____. *The Night Side of Dickens: Cannibalism, Passion, Necessity*. Columbus: Ohio State University Press, 1994.

Tambling, Jeremy. *Dickens, Violence, and the Modern State*. London: Macmillan, 1995.

Traill, Nancy H. *Possible Worlds of the Fantastic: The Rise of the Paranormal in Fiction*. Toronto: University of Toronto Press, 1996.

Trudgill, Eric. *Madonnas and Magdalenes: The Origins and Development of Victorian Sexual Attitudes*. New York: Holms & Meier, 1976.

Van Ghent, Dorothy. "The Dickens World: A View from Todgers's." *Sewanee Review* 58.3 (1950): 419-38. Rpt. in *The English Novel: Form and Function*. New York: Holt, 1953.

Vogel, Jane. *Allegory in Dickens*. Tuscaloosa: University of Alabama Press, 1977.

Waters, Catherine. *Dickens and the Politics of the Family*. New York: Cambridge University Press, 1997.

Welsh, Alexander. *The City of Dickens*. Cambridge, MA: Harvard University Press, 1986.

Westburg, Barry. *The Confessional Fictions of Charles Dickens*. De Kalb: Northern Illinois University Press, 1977.

Williams, Raymond. *The English Novel: From Dickens to Lawrence*. New York: Oxford University Press, 1970.

Wilson, Angus. *The World of Charles Dickens*. New York: Viking Press, 1970.

Wilson, Edmund. "Dickens: The Two Scrooges." *The Wound and the Bow*. Boston: Houghton Mifflin, 1941.

CRITICAL
INSIGHTS

About the Editor

Eugene Goodheart is Edytha Macy Professor of Humanities Emeritus at Brandeis University. He has written extensively on nineteenth- and twentieth-century literature and modern literary and cultural theory. He is the author of eleven books, including *The Skeptic Disposition: Deconstruction, Ideology, and Other Matters* (1984, 1991), *The Reign of Ideology* (1997), *Does Literary Studies Have a Future?* (1999), *Darwinian Misadventures in the Humanities* (2007), and a memoir, *Confessions of a Secular Jew* (2001). His many articles and reviews have appeared in, among other journals, *Partisan Review, The Sewanee Review, New Literary History, Critical Inquiry*, and *Daedalus*.

About *The Paris Review*

The Paris Review is America's preeminent literary quarterly, dedicated to discovering and publishing the best new voices in fiction, nonfiction, and poetry. The magazine was founded in Paris in 1953 by the young American writers Peter Matthiessen and Doc Humes, and edited there and in New York for its first fifty years by George Plimpton. Over the decades, the *Review* has introduced readers to the earliest writings of Jack Kerouac, Philip Roth, T. C. Boyle, V. S. Naipaul, Ha Jin, Ann Patchett, Jay McInerney, Mona Simpson, and Edward P. Jones, and published numerous now classic works, including Roth's *Goodbye, Columbus*, Donald Barthelme's *Alice*, Jim Carroll's *Basketball Diaries*, and selections from Samuel Beckett's *Molloy* (his first publication in English). The first chapter of Jeffrey Eugenides's *The Virgin Suicides* appeared in the *Review*'s pages, as well as stories by Rick Moody, David Foster Wallace, Denis Johnson, Jim Crace, Lorrie Moore, and Jeanette Winterson.

The Paris Review's renowned Writers at Work series of interviews, whose early installments include legendary conversations with E. M. Forster, William Faulkner, and Ernest Hemingway, is one of the landmarks of world literature. The interviews received a George Polk Award and were nominated for a Pulitzer Prize. Among the more than three hundred interviewees are Robert Frost, Marianne Moore, W. H. Auden, Elizabeth Bishop, Susan Sontag, and Toni Morrison. Recent issues feature conversations with Salman Rushdie, Joan Didion, Norman Mailer, Kazuo Ishiguro, Marilynne Robinson, Umberto Eco, Annie Proulx, and Gay Talese. In November 2009, Picador published the final volume of a four-volume series of anthologies of *Paris Review* interviews. *The New York Times* called the Writers at Work series "the most remarkable and extensive interviewing project we possess."

The Paris Review is edited by Philip Gourevitch, who was named to the post in

2005, following the death of George Plimpton two years earlier. A new editorial team has published fiction by André Aciman, Colum McCann, Damon Galgut, Mohsin Hamid, Uzodinma Iweala, Gish Jen, Stephen King, James Lasdun, Padgett Powell, Richard Price, and Sam Shepard. Poetry editors Charles Simic, Meghan O'Rourke, and Dan Chiasson have selected works by John Ashbery, Kay Ryan, Billy Collins, Tomaž Šalamun, Mary Jo Bang, Sharon Olds, Charles Wright, and Mary Karr. Writing published in the magazine has been anthologized in *Best American Short Stories* (2006, 2007, and 2008), *Best American Poetry, Best Creative Non-Fiction*, the Pushcart Prize anthology, and *O. Henry Prize Stories*.

The magazine presents two annual awards. The Hadada Award for lifelong contribution to literature has recently been given to Joan Didion, Norman Mailer, Peter Matthiessen, and, in 2009, John Ashbery. The Plimpton Prize for Fiction, awarded to a debut or emerging writer brought to national attention in the pages of *The Paris Review*, was presented in 2007 to Benjamin Percy, to Jesse Ball in 2008, and to Alistair Morgan in 2009.

The Paris Review was a finalist for the 2008 and 2009 National Magazine Awards in fiction, and it won the 2007 National Magazine Award in photojournalism. The *Los Angeles Times* recently called *The Paris Review* "an American treasure with true international reach."

Since 1999 *The Paris Review* has been published by The Paris Review Foundation, Inc., a not-for-profit 501(c)(3) organization.

The Paris Review is available in digital form to libraries worldwide in selected academic databases exclusively from EBSCO Publishing. Libraries can contact EBSCO at 1-800-653-2726 for details. For more information on *The Paris Review* or to subscribe, please visit: www.theparisreview.org.

Eugene Goodheart is Edytha Macy Professor of Humanities Emeritus at Brandeis University. He is the author of eleven books of literary and cultural criticism as well as the memoir *Confessions of a Secular Jew* (2004).

Patricia Marks was Regents' Distinguished Professor of English at Valdosta State University.

Elizabeth Gumport is an MFA candidate at Johns Hopkins University. Her writing has appeared or is forthcoming in *Canteen, The New York Observer, n+1*, and *The Believer.*

Shanyn Fiske is Assistant Professor of English and Director of the Classical Studies Minor at Rutgers University in Camden, New Jersey. She is the author of *Heretical Hellenism: Women Writers, Ancient Greece, and the Victorian Popular Imagination* (2008). She has published articles on Charles Dickens, Charlotte Brontë, Alicia Little, and other nineteenth-century writers.

Laurence W. Mazzeno is President Emeritus of Alvernia University in Reading, Pennsylvania. He is the author of nine books, including *The Dickens Industry, Tennyson: The Critical Legacy*, and the forthcoming *Jane Austen: Two Centuries of Criticism*. He is a former editor and current member of the editorial board for *Nineteenth-Century Prose*. A frequent contributor to reference books and encyclopedias, he has also written extensively for popular periodicals and online journals.

Nancy M. West is Associate Professor of English and Associate Chair of the Department of English at the University of Missouri at Columbia. Her lectures focus on Victorian literature and media, nineteenth-century novels, photography, and the works of Charles Dickens. She has numerous publications to her name, including *Kodak and the Lens of Nostalgia* (2000), and her essays have appeared in *The Centennial Review, Modern Language Quarterly*, and *The Writery.*

Joseph M. Duffy, Jr., was Professor of English at the University of Notre Dame between 1954 and 1988. He was a Fulbright scholar and in 1971 was the recipient of the Danforth Foundation's E. Harris Harbison Gifted Teaching Award. He was a book reviewer for *Commonweal* and published articles on Jane Austen and Charles Dickens in such journals as *Nineteenth-Century Fiction* and *ELH.*

Alan P. Barr is Professor of English and Chair of the Department of English at Indiana University Northwest, where he has taught since 1968. His articles and essays have been published by such literary journals as *Victorian Literature and Culture*, the *Massachusetts Review, Dickens Quarterly*, and the *Shaw Review*. He is the editor of *Modern Anglophone Drama by Women* (2007) and *Modern Women Playwrights of Europe* (2001) and author of *Victorian Stage Pulpiteer: Bernard Shaw's Crusade* (1973).

Julia F. Saville is Associate Professor of English at the University of Illinois at Urbana-Champaign. Her research interests are Victorian poetry, women's studies, and British literature. She has written one book, *A Queer Chivalry: The Homoerotic Asceti-*

cism of Gerard Manley Hopkins (2000), and several essays and book contributions. Her current work in progress is a book manuscript on the contribution of British poets to popular democratic movements worldwide.

G. Robert Stange was Professor of English Literature at Tufts University from 1967 to 1985 and Chair of the English Department for five years. Specializing in British literature and culture, he wrote several articles, essays, and books on the works of Tennyson, Browning, Coleridge, and Yeats. His anthology *Victorian Poetry and Poetics* (1968) chronicled his own passion for Victorian literature and is considered one of his finest publications.

Monroe Engel is a novelist and was Professor of English at Harvard University. He has published several books of literary criticism, including *Uses of Literature* (1973), *The Maturity of Dickens* (1959), and *The Politics of Dickens' Novels* (1956).

Robert A. Donovan is Emeritus Professor of English at the State University of New York, Albany. He has taught at Cornell University and is the author of *The Shaping Vision: Imagination in the English Novel from Defoe to Dickens* (1966).

Michele S. Ware is Associate Professor of English at North Carolina Central University. She teaches courses in English composition, American literature, the twentieth-century novel, and African American literature. She has published several reviews and articles, such as "The Architecture of the Short Story: Edith Wharton's Modernist Practice" (2004), "'Just a Lady': Gender and Power in *To Kill a Mockingbird*" (2003), and "Making Fun of the Critics: Edith Wharton's Anticipation of the Postmodern Academic Romance" (1998).

Patricia E. Johnson is Associate Professor of literature and humanities at the Pennsylvania State University-Capital College at Harrisburg. Her articles on such British authors as Charlotte Brontë, George Eliot, and Charles Dickens have been published in *Studies in the Novel, Victorians Institute Journal,* and *Mosaic.* She is the author of *Hidden Hands: Working-Class Women and Victorian Social-Problem Fiction* (2001).

Lionel Trilling was Professor of English at Columbia University and a renowned American literary writer and critic. As a member of the New York Intellectuals and frequent contributor to the *Partisan Review,* he published many collections of literary essays, including *Speaking of Literature and Society* (1980), *A Gathering of Fugitives* (1956), *The Opposing Self: Nine Essays in Criticism* (1955), and *E. M. Forster: A Study* (1943).

Matthew J. Bolton is Professor of English at Loyola School in New York City, where he also serves as Dean of Students. He received his doctor of philosophy degree in English from the Graduate Center of the City University of New York (CUNY) in 2005. His dissertation at the university was titled "Transcending the Self in Robert Browning and T. S. Eliot." Prior to attaining his Ph.D. at CUNY, he also earned a master of philosophy degree in English (2004) and a master of science degree in English education (2001). His undergraduate work was done at the State University of New York at Binghamton, where he studied English literature.

Acknowledgments

"Charles Dickens" by Patricia Marks. From *Magill's Choice: Notable British Novelists*. Copyright © 2001 by Salem Press, Inc. Reprinted with permission of Salem Press.

"The *Paris Review* Perspective" by Elizabeth Gumport. Copyright © 2011 by Elizabeth Gumport. Special appreciation goes to Christopher Cox, Nathaniel Rich, and David Wallace-Wells, editors at *The Paris Review*.

"Order in Disorder: Surrealism and *Oliver Twist*" by Nancy M. West. From *South Atlantic Review* 54, no. 2 (May 1989): 41-58. Copyright © 1989 by the South Atlantic Modern Language Association. Reprinted by permission of the South Atlantic Modern Language Association.

"Another Version of Pastoral: *Oliver Twist*" by Joseph M. Duffy, Jr. From *ELH* 35, no. 3 (1969): 403-421. Copyright © 1968 by The Johns Hopkins University Press. Reprinted with permission of The Johns Hopkins University Press.

"Mourning Becomes David: Loss and the Victorian Restoration of Young Copperfield" by Alan P. Barr. From *Dickens Quarterly* 24, no. 2 (June 2007): 63-77. Copyright © 2007 by *Dickens Quarterly*. Reprinted by permission of *Dickens Quarterly*.

"Eccentricity as Englishness in *David Copperfield*" by Julia F. Saville. From *SEL: Studies in English Literature 1500-1900* 4 (Autumn 2002): 781-797. Copyright © 2002 by *SEL: Studies in English Literature 1500-1900*. Reprinted by permission of *SEL: Studies in English Literature 1500-1900*.

"Expectations Well Lost: Dickens' Fable for His Time" by G. Robert Stange. From *College English* 16 (1954): 9-17. Originally published by the National Council of Teachers of English.

"The Sense of Self" by Monroe Engel. From *The Maturity of Dickens* by Monroe Engel, pp. 146-168. Cambridge, Mass.: Harvard University Press. Copyright © 1959 by Monroe Engel. Copyright © renewed 1987 by Monroe Engel. Reprinted by permission of the publisher.

"Structure and Idea in *Bleak House*" by Robert A. Donovan. From *ELH* 29, no. 2 (1962): 175-201. Copyright © 1962 by The Johns Hopkins University Press. Reprinted with permission of The Johns Hopkins University Press.

"'True Legitimacy': The Myth of the Foundling in *Bleak House*" by Michele S. Ware. From *Studies in the Novel* 22 (1990): 1-9. Copyright © 1990 by University of North Texas Press. Reprinted with permission of University of North Texas Press.

"*Hard Times* and the Structure of Industrialism: The Novel as Factory" by Patricia E. Johnson. From *Studies in the Novel* 21 (1989): 128-137. Copyright © 1989 by University of North Texas Press. Reprinted with permission of University of North Texas Press.

"*Little Dorrit*" by Lionel Trilling. From *The Kenyon Review* 15 (Autumn 1953): 577-590. Copyright © 1953 by Lionel Trilling. Reprinted with permission of The Wylie Agency LLC.

Ablow, Rachel, 120
Ackroyd, Peter, 22, 26-27, 31, 34, 38, 49
All the Year Round, 11, 34, 53
American Notes (Dickens), 10, 42
Amy Dorrit. *See* Dorrit, Amy
Arthur Clennam. *See* Clennam, Arthur
Ayres, Brenda, 52

Balakian, Anna, 70
Balzac, Honoré de, 7, 146, 156, 158
Barickman, Richard, 51
Barnaby Rudge (Dickens), 10, 27, 42
Basch, Françoise, 51
Beadnell, Maria, 9, 243-244
Bentley's Miscellany, 9
Bernard, Catherine A., 66
Biblical allusions, 148, 215
Bill for Protection of Females (1848), 32
Blackpool, Stephen (*Hard Times*), 6, 223, 225-226
Blake, William, 85, 101, 106, 241
Blanchard, E. L., 42
Bleak House (Dickens), 5, 7, 9-10, 28, 35, 43, 45, 66, 72, 74, 86, 134, 136, 166, 178, 208, 222, 245
Boege, Fred W., 202
Bowen, John, 53
Brothels Suppression Bill (1840), 32
Brown, E. K., 191
Brownlow, Mr. (*Oliver Twist*), 61, 73, 77, 85-86, 96-97, 99-100
Bulwer-Lytton, Edward, 136
Burgess, Anthony, 260

Cain, Lynn, 54
Campbell, Joseph, 208, 217

Carey, John, 49
Carlyle, Thomas, 6, 107, 131, 134
Cecil, David, 45
Chartist movement, 25-27
Chesterton, G. K., 15-16, 44, 241
Child labor, 29
Chirico, Giorgio de, 63
Clayton, Jay, 53
Clennam, Arthur (*Little Dorrit*), 4, 7, 237, 239, 243-245, 254-257
Coketown, 5, 223-224, 227-228
Coleridge, Samuel Taylor, 93, 112, 260
Colley, Linda, 126
Collins, Philip A. W., 35
Collins, Wilkie, 11, 34
Connor, Steven, 52
Contagious Diseases Acts (1864, 1866, 1869), 32
Convicts. *See* Criminals
Copperfield, David (*David Copperfield*), 17, 105, 128, 131, 133, 135-136, 139-140, 142, 160, 202
Criminals, 32, 34-36, 148, 154, 157, 169, 175, 199, 238

David Copperfield. *See* Copperfield, David
David Copperfield (Dickens), 5, 9-10, 16, 33, 42, 105, 128
David, Deirdre, 54
Debtor's prisons, 5, 8, 234
Dedalus, Stephen (*Ulysses*), 258
Dickens, Catherine Hogarth (wife), 9
Dickens, Charles; compared to Charles Baudelaire, 250; childhood and early life, 5, 8-9, 16, 22, 27, 165; courtship and marriage, 9-11; and crime, 34;

early career, 9, 26, 34, 53; feminist interpretations of, 50-52; compared to William Shakespeare, 3, 42, 49, 234, 251, 253; and Ellen Ternan, 11, 45, 171; and the theater, 3, 8-10, 47; in United States, 10-11; view of wealth, 8, 153

Dickens, Elizabeth Barrow (mother), 8

Dickens, John (father), 8, 140

Dickens Fellowship, 44

Dickens Quarterly, 48, 53

Dickens Studies, 48

Dickens Studies Annual, 48

Dickensian, The, 48

Dolge Orlick. *See* Orlick, Dolge

Dombey and Son (Dickens), 8, 10, 24, 28, 33, 42, 51, 136, 141, 180

Dorrit, Amy (*Little Dorrit*), 30, 242, 259

Dostoevski, Fyodor, 158, 239

Dreams and nightmares, 16, 48, 59-60, 67, 70, 75, 89, 227, 237

Drew, John M. L., 53

Eagleton, Terry, 52, 222

Edwin Drood. See Mystery of Edwin Drood, The

Eliot, T. S., 45, 103, 248

Engels, Friedrich, 221, 223

Estella. *See* Havisham, Estella

Esther Summerson. *See* Summerson, Esther

Eugene Wrayburn. *See* Wrayburn, Eugene

Factory Act (1833), 25, 29

Fagin (*Oliver Twist*), 5, 61, 70, 72, 76, 84, 86-87, 91, 96, 98, 101

Fielding, Henry, 41, 127-128, 210-211

Finching, Flora (*Little Dorrit*), 175, 244-245, 260-261

First Reform Act (1832), 25

Flora Finching. *See* Finching, Flora

Ford, Ford Madox, 45

Forster, E. M., 200

Forster, John, 9, 23, 27, 39, 43, 128, 131, 140, 159, 163

Freudian theory, 48, 60-61, 66, 68, 107, 111, 114, 122, 238

Gager, Valerie, 49

Gallagher, Catherine, 222, 233

Garis, Robert, 47

Garnett, Robert, 120

Garrett, Peter K., 53

Ghosts, 75, 258

Gilooly, Eileen, 54

Gissing, George, 44

Gothic novels. *See* Novels, gothic

Gradgrind, Louisa (*Hard Times*), 7, 223, 225, 229

Great Expectations (Dickens), 5, 7, 11, 16, 34, 37, 43, 69, 145, 178, 180, 193

Hard Times (Dickens), 5-6, 11, 16, 43, 45, 86, 134, 180, 221

Hardy, Barbara, 49, 219

Haunted Man, The (Dickens), 86

Havisham, Estella (*Great Expectations*), 150, 152, 156, 160, 170

Havisham, Miss (*Great Expectations*), 7, 150-151, 158-159, 169, 172

Heep, Uriah (*David Copperfield*), 6, 108, 115, 117, 134-135, 138, 166

Higbie, Robert, 50

Hogarth, Catherine. *See* Dickens, Catherine Hogarth

Homback, Bert, 105

Home for Homeless Women. *See* Urania Cottage

Homer, 257, 259-260

Hopkins, Sandra, 51

House, Humphrey, 46
Household Words, 10-11, 26, 53
Humor, 44, 48, 105, 119, 137, 166
Huxley, Aldous, 45

Imagery, 50; darkness and light, 65, 72-73, 76, 88, 152, 209; factories, 5, 134, 166, 222-223, 225, 227, 229; fire, 86, 152, 223-224, 226, 229-230, 232; ghosts, 75, 258; seeds, 16; spitting, 3; stars, 76, 109, 152, 172, 251; streets, 7, 23, 74-76, 87, 97; water, 8, 92, 167-168, 259
Industrialization, 5, 21, 37, 221, 230, 233

Jacobson, Wendy S., 52
James, Henry, 43, 234
Jean, Marcel, 68, 70
Johnson, Edgar, 47, 207, 217, 247
Joyce, James, 248, 250, 254

Kaplan, Fred, 49, 260
Kincaid, James R., 29, 31
Kingsmill, Hugh, 45
Kreilkamp, Ivan, 249

Larson, Janet, 50
Leavis, F. R., 46, 49, 221
Leavis, Q. D., 49, 213
Lewes, George Henry, 44, 59
Little Dorrit (Dickens), 5, 11, 43, 45-46, 134, 178, 180, 222, 234, 250-251, 254, 257, 260
Little Nell. *See* Trent, Nell
London, 7, 21-24, 31, 36, 38, 47, 62, 64, 153
Louisa Gradgrind. *See* Gradgrind, Louisa
Loutitt, Chris, 54
Lucas, John, 120, 126, 232

McKnight, Natalie, 50
McMaster, Juliet, 117
Magwitch (*Great Expectations*), 37, 148, 153, 169, 172, 175
Marcus, Steven, 47, 53, 62
Marshalsea prison, 8, 27, 178, 234-235, 242, 245, 257, 259
Martin Chuzzlewit (Dickens), 3, 10, 42, 63-64, 69, 74, 131, 146, 262
Marxist literary theory, 52, 179
Master Humphrey's Clock (Dickens), 9
Matthews, J. H., 65
Mezei, Arpad, 68, 70
Micawber, Wilkins (*David Copperfield*), 5, 8, 117, 131, 135, 137-141
Michie, Helena, 51
Milbank, Alison, 52
Miller, D. A., 50
Miller, J. Hillis, 47, 69, 191, 216
Millett, Kate, 51
Miss Havisham. *See* Havisham, Miss
Mitchell, Sally, 29, 34, 37
Mitford, Mary Russell, 22
Modernist literature, 208, 248
Moore, Grace, 38
Mr. Brownlow. *See* Brownlow, Mr.
Mr. Micawber. *See* Micawber, Wilkins
Murder, 34, 73, 75, 99, 172, 194-195
Mystery of Edwin Drood, The (Dickens), 11, 35, 37, 67-68, 74

Names and naming, 6, 17, 67, 86, 115-116, 119, 121, 133, 152, 170-171, 187, 215, 218, 224, 242, 246
Narration and narrators, 11, 59, 91, 106, 116, 129, 159, 163, 199, 201, 203, 207, 209, 217, 250, 254-255, 257, 260-261
Nead, Lynda, 21, 24

Nell Trent. *See* Trent, Nell

New Historicism, 52

New Poor Law Amendment Act (1834), 25

Nicholas Nickleby (Dickens), 9, 27, 42, 85, 93, 134, 262

Nightmares. *See* Dreams and nightmares

Novels; gothic, 66, 75; Victorian, 202, 249, 253, 255, 260-262

Odyssey (Homer), 257

Old Curiosity Shop, The (Dickens), 10, 21, 42, 44

Oliver Twist. *See* Twist, Oliver

Oliver Twist (Dickens), 5, 9, 11, 26, 33, 35, 42, 60, 84, 210-212

Orlick, Dolge (*Great Expectations*), 5, 66, 158, 172

Orphans, 9, 28, 64, 110, 147, 184, 211, 241

Orwell, George, 16, 45, 129, 165

Our Mutual Friend (Dickens), 8, 11, 16, 28, 35, 43, 86, 92, 103, 129, 146, 178, 180, 234, 245, 250-251

Parker, David, 53

Paroissien, David, 53

Patten, Robert, 49

Pickwick Papers (Dickens), 9, 22, 41, 127, 261

Pip (*Great Expectations*), 5, 7, 16, 37, 69, 146-147, 151, 154, 168, 171, 176

Poovey, Mary, 31, 51

Pope-Hennessy, Una, 47

Portrait of the Artist as a Young Man, A (Joyce), 252

Prostitution, 31-34

Pykett, Lyn, 41

Ruskin, John, 6, 107, 179

Sanders, Andrew, 27

Seymour, Robert, 9

Shaw, George Bernard, 44, 178, 235

Sketches by Boz (Dickens), 41, 127

Slater, Michael, 51, 54

Smiley, Jane, 41

Smith, Grahame, 48, 54

Smollett, Tobias, 42, 127-128, 210-211

Social commentary, 5, 27, 31, 44, 46, 50, 87, 134, 137, 149, 151, 153, 156, 178, 180, 186, 197, 221, 233, 235, 240, 242

Spector, Stephen J., 222, 233

Spilka, Mark, 48

Stephen Blackpool. *See* Blackpool, Stephen

Stephen Dedalus. *See* Dedalus, Stephen

Stephen, Leslie, 41

Stevenson, Lionel, 46

Stewart, Garrett, 50

Stoehr, Taylor, 48, 59, 62

Stone, Harry, 70

Summerson, Esther (*Bleak House*), 7-8, 66, 68, 202, 206, 210, 212, 215, 241

Surrealism, 59-60

Tale of Two Cities, A (Dickens), 11, 15, 27, 43

Tambling, Jeremy, 50

Thackeray, William Makepeace, 42

Themes; abandonment, 9, 190; childhood, 16, 27, 29, 64, 84; death and dying, 66, 68, 78, 89, 91, 97, 109-111, 115, 145, 166, 254; dreams and nightmares, 16, 59, 65, 68, 70, 77, 89, 227; hope and redemption, 7, 37, 44, 91, 96, 190, 231; loss of innocence, 61, 105, 161; love, 5, 98, 105, 109-110, 119, 148, 151, 157, 159, 161,

171, 176, 213, 241; poverty, 5, 7, 21, 23, 30, 85, 136, 166, 173; responsibility, 180; revenge and retribution, 7, 48, 151

To the Lighthouse (Woolf), 248

Tom Jones (Fielding), 210-211

Trent, Nell (*The Old Curiosity Shop*), 39, 44, 254

Trilling, Lionel, 46

Twist, Oliver (*Oliver Twist*), 8, 28, 33, 64, 66, 68, 71, 77, 85-86, 92, 96, 210-211

Ulysses (Joyce), 248, 250, 252, 255, 258, 260, 262

Urania Cottage, 32-33, 37

Uriah Heep. *See* Heep, Uriah

Van Ghent, Dorothy, 46

Victorian literature. *See* Novels, Victorian

Victorianism, 5, 21, 29, 32, 34, 38, 43, 46, 48, 51, 66, 105, 107, 123, 125, 127, 132, 138, 146, 153, 164, 249

Walkowitz, Judith R., 31

Waste Land, The (Eliot), 248

Williams, Raymond, 52, 233

Wilson, Angus, 210

Wilson, Edmund, 45, 191, 206

Wolfreys, Julian, 53

Woodcourt, Allan (*Bleak House*), viii, 86, 186, 193, 196, 218

Woolf, Virginia, 248

Wordsworth, William, 84, 89, 106, 111, 236

Wrayburn, Eugene (*Our Mutual Friend*), 4, 83, 251, 255

Wright, Thomas, 45

Yeats, William Butler, 156